CORN FLAKES WITH JOHN LENNON

AND OTHER TALES FROM A ROCK 'N' ROLL LIFE

ROBERT HILBURN

RODALE

Rodale books may be purchased for business or promotional use or for special sales.
For information, please write to: Special Markets Department, Rodale Inc., 733
Third Avenue, New York, NY 10017

Printed in the United States of America
Rodale Inc. makes every effort to use acid-free ♾, recycled paper ♻.

Book design by Drew Frantzen

Library of Congress Cataloging-in-Publication Data

Hilburn, Robert.
    Corn flakes with John Lennon : and other tales from a rock 'n' roll life / Robert
Hilburn.
        p.   cm.
    Includes index.
    ISBN-13 978–1–59486–921–1   hardcover
    ISBN-10 1–59486–921–9   hardcover
    1. Hilburn, Robert.   2. Music journalists—United States.   3. Rock musicians—
Anecdotes.   I. Title.
ML423.H5876A5 2009
781.66092—dc22
    [B]   2009026604

Distributed to the trade by Macmillan

2   4   6   8   10   9   7   5   3   hardcover

LIVE YOUR WHOLE LIFE™

We inspire and enable people to improve their lives and the world around them

For more of our products visit **rodalestore.com** or call 800-848-4735

Permissions

Photos

All photos in the book are copyrighted by the *Los Angeles Times* and used with permission—except one of John Lennon and Robert Hilburn (© Bob Gruen and used with permission) and the ones of Johnny Cash and Janis Joplin (both © Jim Marshall and used with permission).

All caption quotes are from personal interviews with the artists, except for Elvis Presley's stage remarks at the Sahara Tahoe in 1974.

Song Lyrics

"Baby, Let's Play House"
Words and Music by Arthur Gunter
Copyright © 1954 (Renewed) by Embassy Music Corporation (BMI) International Copyright Secured. All Rights Reserved. Reprinted by Permission.

"Bad"
Words by Bono and The Edge
Music by U2
Copyright © 1985 UNIVERSAL MUSIC PUBLISHING INTERNATIONAL B.V.
All Rights in the US and Canada Controlled and Administered by UNIVERSAL-POLYGRAM INTERNATIONAL PUBLISHING, INC.
All Rights Reserved. Used by Permission.

"City of Blinding Lights"
Music by U2
Lyrics by Bono
Copyright © 2004 UNIVERSAL MUSIC PUBLISHING INTERNATIONAL B.V.
All Rights in the US and Canada Controlled and Administered by UNIVERSAL-POLYGRAM INTERNATIONAL PUBLISHING, INC.
All Rights Reserved. Used by Permission.

"God"
Copyright ©1978 Lennon Music. All Rights Administered by Sony/ATV Publishing LLC, 8 Music Square West, Nashville, TN. 37203. All Rights Reserved. Used by Permission.

"I Am the Walrus"
Copyright © 1967 Sony/ATV Music Publishing LLC. All Rights Administered by Sony/ATV Music Publishing LLC, 8 Music Square West, Nashville, TN 37203. All Rights Reserved. Used by Permission.

"Living Proof"
By Bruce Springsteen
Copyright © 1992 Bruce Springsteen (ASCAP)
Reprinted by Permission. International copyright secured. All Rights Reserved.

Me And Bobby McGee
Words and Music by Kris Kristofferson and Fred Foster
(c) 1969 (Renewed 1997) TEMI COMBINE INC.
All Rights Controlled by COMBINE MUSIC CORP. and Administered by EMI BLACKWOOD MUSIC INC.
All Rights Reserved. International Copyright Secured. Used by Permission.

"Mother"
Copyright 1970 Lennon Music. All rights administered by Sony/ATV Music Publishing LLC, 8 Music Square West, Nashville, TN 37203. All Rights Rreserved. Used by Permission.

"Sam Stone"
Words and Music by John Prine
© 1972 WALDEN MUSIC and SOUR GRAPES MUSIC (ASCAP)
All Rights Reserved. Used by Permission

"Your Song"
Words and Music by Elton John and Bernie Taupin
Copyright © 1969 UNIVERSAL/DICK JAMES MUSIC LTD.
Copyright Renewed
All Rights in the U.S. and Canada Controlled and Administered by UNIVERSAL-POLYGRAM INTERNATIONAL PUBLISHING, INC. All Rights Reserved. Used by Permission.

INTRODUCTION
BY BONO

'm not sure Robert Hilburn exists. I know he is not human. He might be a ministering angel or some kind of specter . . . he is certainly an enigma. Bob doesn't drink or smoke, and his quiet conversation is the antithesis of the noisy, messy rock 'n' roll music he loves. He is the silent man on the other side of the "wall of sound." His is the clarity that the chaos of creativity is always attracted to.

His column in the *Los Angeles Times* put the fear of God into rebels of the lowest common denominator, but encouraged faith from wild iconoclasts. High priests of schlock 'n' roll withered rather than weathered the quietest storm that ever blew into town. Without ever being pious or elitist, he has the Levitical/Jesuitical energy of a keeper of the flame. So many of the artists he loved and detailed were consumed by the fire. It reinforced in Bob a reverence for the life force in rock—its truth-telling vitality rather than its corny mythologies, death-cult shtick, or tragic hipness.

This book documents his love of performers in country, rock, and pop and early hustles of Elvis and the Colonel; his love of words, with writings about Leonard Cohen, Hank Williams, Kris Kristofferson, and Bob Dylan; and his love of the chemistry set that is band member-ship, from the Beatles to U2 to Nirvana. All documented by his gra-cious person and unforgiving prose.

As a writer, his words have an economical sense and frugality that put him across the street from other great commentators and critics of the rock era, like Greil Marcus with his prosaic and profes-sorial tone and the late Lester Bangs's beat-up poetry. For three decades at the *Times,* Bob steadily deciphered the shouts and hollers, whispers and miasma of a music business that rose and fell over the period he sat at his desk.

Success loves simplicity. Simplicity in our business, or indeed any business (particularly writing), is having an ear for the top-line melody . . . harmony is critical . . . counterpoint, rhythm, etc., but having an ear for the top-line melody is knowing the real event that's taking place in a room, the real point that's being made—the "what's actually going down" as opposed to the melodrama of media. That means that if you didn't have time to fully immerse yourself in the convulsive, controversial world of Public Enemy or N.W.A in the late '80s, Bob Hilburn could be trusted with dispatches from the front line. If you wanted to know what domestic life was like for Mr. and Mrs. Cobain, Bob would not be distracted from good housekeeping.

Intellectually and intuitively rigorous, Bob will let himself go—but to a sound, not to a "scene." The sound has to be articulate, even if the words are not, which might explain his early support for our not-so-humble combo from the north side of Dublin. He was always looking for subject matter that was fresh and patiently observed what Van Morrison described as "inarticulate speech of the heart." U2 was shambolic and erratic, but he seemed to see the "what might be" in the "what was."

Bob's role as critic was to encourage suspension of disbelief not just in the audience, but in the artist as well. That is an environment in which music grows. He made us better.

Many critics do bands the favor of contextualizing their work, and Bob certainly did that. But there was always the sense from him that too much reverence for the past can shut the future up. Though twice the age of some of his discoveries, he was a diviner of new talent, watchful for a through-line with what had come before, but scouting for surprises, whether it was Chuck D or John Lydon, John Prine or Axl Rose. He made the present porous, he argued the case for what was about to happen. I think the biggest kick for Bob was sitting on Planet Rock and watching the new wave breaking. He figured every generation had a resonant frequency and that his job was to be a tuning fork. Not remotely interested in passing trends, it was the purity of each pitch he was listening for—i.e., would it last? That ear again. Was it worth the fuss? We were not, at that time, but his words made us readier.

U2 arrived on the cover of the calendar section of the *LA Times* in March 1981, and it changed our fate. We have never played a concert in Los Angeles that did not sell out since then. The first time we met, Bob bought me an ice cream and kept his smile to himself as I tried so hard to explain U2's flavor-of-the-month status as a taste that would endure. When we hit a peak at the Los Angeles Coliseum, he explained our appeal in one easy sentence: "At a Rolling Stones concert," he said, "you feel good about who you are despite where you've been. At a Bruce Springsteen or a U2 show, you feel good about the person next to you."

All three artists would love that sentence to be true.

His admonishments were just as deft. On one occasion, high on the possibilities of U2's success and owning up to an array of nonmusical ambitions, I was chastened by his swift reminder of the many Beatles or Cole Porter songs I knew, followed by the question, how many of our songs did I think would be remembered after our scene had died down?

Bob Hilburn is too modest to talk much about himself. Not suffering from that problem, I got as close as you can get to a glimpse of him by forcing him to answer some of my questions in exchange for answering his. I was hungry to know what he knew and thought about luminous beings like Bob Dylan and characters like John Lennon, who had survived inhuman talent with their humanity. He would open up about his favorites, but as soon as I asked about his own life, he would head back to his office. When I asked repeatedly about his family, he rarely offered up any contradiction to the thought that they too might not exist. He was probably teaching me Modesty. I might have missed it.

What's remarkable about the book you hold in your hand is that for the first time he reveals himself as well as his subjects . . . well, a little. Unlocking the puzzle of his own beginnings in music, he tells the story of his uncle Bill who was made an outsider by epilepsy and how tightly he held on to the recordings of Hank Williams. He reveals how he managed to hustle Elvis Presley into not calling him sir, and how Bruce Springsteen's honesty raised the standard for him and everyone. He sees the story of rock through the lens of his years and wonders a few times if he, and it, has peaked. He returns again and again to the same characters, hoping the answer will be no in both cases.

He is strangely, for a man who lives in the epicenter of it, almost immune to fame.

He can't help but laugh at a rendezvous of Michael Jackson and Prince.

With Bob Dylan, he treasures the moments that are unmasked, like Bob Dylan talking him through his conversion to Christianity or going for a coffee completely unrecognized at a truck stop in Chicago; and discovering John Lennon hiding chocolate from Yoko, who John constantly refers to as "Mother."

Maybe Bob Hilburn is a figment of our imagination, but the book exists. When John Lennon, in "I Am the Walrus," sings about "sitting on a corn flake waiting for the van to come," most folks picture a drug dealer or overlord. No one thinks of Robert Hilburn as the driver of the van. John didn't know Bob Hilburn when he wrote the song. After reading this book, you will think of no one else.

March 2009

CHAPTER ONE

John Lennon raced into Yoko Ono's home office in the mammoth old Dakota building with a copy of Donna Summer's new single, "The Wanderer." "Listen!" he shouted as he put the 45 on the record player. "She's doing Elvis!" I didn't know what he was talking about at first. The arrangement felt more like rock than the singer's usual electro-disco approach, but the opening vocal sure sounded like Donna Summer to me. Midway through the song, however, her voice shifted into the playful, hiccuping style Elvis had used on so many of his early recordings.

"See! See!" John said, pointing at the speakers.

The record was John's way of saying hello again after five years. I had spent time with him in Los Angeles in the mid-1970s, during the period he later referred to as his "lost weekend"—months when he was estranged from Yoko and spent many a night in notorious drinking bouts with his buddies Harry Nilsson and Ringo Starr. John got so boisterous one night that he was thrown out of the Troubadour, one of the city's landmark music clubs. He invited me to dinner a few times, and I later found out it was when he had an important business meeting the next morning and didn't want to wake up with a hangover. I got the nod over Harry and Ringo because I didn't drink anything stronger than Diet Coke. We would eat at a chic Chinese restaurant and then return to his suite at the Beverly Wilshire Hotel. Those hours would race by because we loved talking about our favorite rock hero, Elvis, which brings us back to "The Wanderer."

I've experienced hundreds of memorable concert and interview moments, so it's hard to rank them in any favorite order, but my final hours with John in New York are certainly on the short list. It was just weeks before his death in December of 1980, and his playing the Summer record was an endearing greeting—and one that was typical of John. Of the hundreds of musicians I've met, John was among the most down-to-earth.

I was in New York to spend three days with John and Yoko while they finished *Double Fantasy,* John's first collection of new material since the mostly forgettable *Walls and Bridges* six years earlier. He returned to New York after the "lost weekend" period and spent the next five years rebuilding his life with Yoko and helping to raise their son, Sean. On this day, he looked nice and trim in jeans, a jean jacket, and a white T-shirt. He was maybe twenty-five pounds slimmer than the last time I'd seen him. "It's Mother's macrobiotic diet," he said later, and employing his nickname for Yoko. "She makes sure I stay on it."

By the time we headed to the recording studio, it was nearly dark. As the limo pulled up to the studio's dimly lit entrance, I could see the outlines of a couple dozen fans in the shadows. They raced toward the car as soon as the driver opened John's door. Flashbulbs went off with blinding speed. Without a bodyguard, John was helpless, and I later asked if he didn't worry about his safety. "They don't mean any harm," he replied. "Besides, what can you do? You can't spend all your life hiding from people. You've got to get out and live some, don't you?"

Inside the studio, I heard several tracks from *Double Fantasy,* which was John's most revealing album since *Imagine.* Some critics branded the gentle, relaxed tone of the collection too soft. They missed the old Lennon bite. To me, however, the collection was a marvelous reflection of John's mood, and Grammy voters were right when they named it album of the year.

I spent hours at the apartment and the studio talking to John about the changes since Los Angeles. He felt at peace for one of the few times in his life. He was deeply in love with Yoko and thrilled to be a father again. He also spoke with affection about the Beatles days and how much he still looked forward to seeing Paul. That surprised me because of the sarcastic barbs he'd launched in interviews and the biting lyrics he'd written about Paul since the breakup of the band. "Aw, don't believe all that," he said, smiling. "Paul is like a brother. We've gotten way past all that." He also spoke fondly of Ringo, but more distantly about George. He felt slighted by some things in George's autobiography, *I, Me, Mine,* especially George's failure to give John credit for helping him learn guitar techniques.

Mostly, we talked about the "house husband" period that was just ending, a time of emotional drying out, a chance to reset priorities. He may have declared "I don't believe in Beatles" in "God" on his 1970 album, *Plastic Ono Band,* but it took the five-year sabbatical that followed the "lost weekend" for him to break away from the suffocating pressures of being an ex-Beatle, including the need to mirror in his music and in his life the image of the witty, sarcastic John. During his time away, he learned that there was personal joy and fulfillment away from the rock 'n' roll merry-go-round. For *Double Fantasy,* he even wrote a tender song about his newfound outlook and freedom, "Watching the Wheels."

On that November night, the studio atmosphere was so relaxed that John invited me to contribute to the album's sound effects. Yoko and I took turns dropping coins in a tin bowl to duplicate the sound of someone giving change to a beggar. We had to do it several times before the noise level was just right. For most of the evening, I just watched John and Yoko at work—and took advantage of breaks to ask them questions. The studio tape must have been running much of the time, because years later a bootleg of that interview surfaced in Japan.

One thing troubled me during the all-night recording sessions: the way John would slip from time to time into an adjoining lounge. The first thing that came to mind was drugs, because I was so used to seeing musicians pass around bowls of cocaine with the casualness of M&Ms. John had had drug problems earlier in his life, and I feared he had relapsed—despite all his talk about feeling healthier than ever. Maybe the pressure of being back in the studio was greater than he was letting on. At one point, I happened into the lounge and saw John at the far end of the narrow room. He was reaching for something on a cabinet shelf, and my first instinct was to go back into the studio so I wouldn't violate his privacy. But he spotted me and called me over, putting his finger up to his lips in a signal to be quiet. When I was next to him, he reached into the cabinet again and pulled out something wrapped in a towel.

"Want some?" he asked. "Just don't tell Mother," he said with a conspiratorial look. "She doesn't want me doing this anymore."

As he opened the towel, I had to laugh.

John Lennon's private stash turned out to be a giant-size Hershey bar. He broke off a chunk for me and one for himself. Holding his piece in a toast, John smiled and said, "Good to see you again."

· ·

Years later, I told the chocolate-bar story to Bono, and he loved it—the idea of a Beatle, someone who had been exposed to every possible temptation, delighting in something as simple as a candy bar. It was a little after midnight and Bono and I were the last customers in a restaurant in the Clarence Hotel in Dublin. Much had changed since early in the band's career, when I had sat with Bono on the steps of the same grand old hotel as he told me about his dreams for U2. Now, he and the Edge, his bandmate, owned the Clarence. I'd been interviewing him for a couple of hours about U2's latest album, but now the tape recorder was off and Bono was asking the questions. He liked hearing stories about some of his favorite rock stars, especially John, Elvis, and Bob Dylan.

I've known Bono ever since U2 first came to America in the early 1980s, and I always looked forward to these postinterview chats. I was impressed early on by his belief in the power of rock 'n' roll to elevate, which I felt was the music's greatest quality. But I also came to appreciate his hunger for stories about the personal sides of his rock 'n' roll heroes. Originally, I thought it was just the fan in him asking the questions, but as U2 became more successful, I realized that it was reassuring for Bono to hear about the human qualities of his heroes.

So many great artists have told me how hard it is to balance all the acclaim and attention against their private doubts, insecurities, and needs.

Over time, I began to see in Bono many of the qualities of his heroes, especially John. He and Bono would have been great mates. John would have been delighted by Bono's love of Elvis, but, more importantly, by his ability to campaign for his social beliefs. Like John, Bono absolutely believes that social change is possible, not just a utopian dream. While John chiefly believed in singing about it, Bono feels a responsibility to use his fame to take his case directly to world leaders in commerce and politics. In turn, Bono is inspired as a songwriter by observing firsthand the impact that rock 'n' roll has in motivating those world figures. "I see it in everyone I meet, whether it's Bill Clinton or Bill Gates," he told me. "Music . . . the music of rock 'n' roll has shaped their social values. This music is a guidepost for the modern world."

Bono and I kept at it for another two hours—talking about the time I made out a set list for Dylan in Israel; when I visited Leonard Cohen, another of his favorites, at a Zen colony near Los Angeles; and all the times I saw Elvis in Las Vegas. I had told him some of these stories before, but he delighted in listening to them again. Finally, I begged off. I had to be up at 7:00 the next morning to catch a plane for London. On the flight home, I thought about what Bono had said about music changing people's attitudes and values, and I realized how much I, too, had been affected by all the years of listening to this revolutionary sound.

. . . .

I've always felt that one of the main challenges for a rock critic is to focus on those musicians who contribute to expanding that art form. In searching for those artists, I frequently ended up writing about false promises: artists who ran out of ideas, self-destructed, or compromised their music in hopes of wider sales. But I was also fortunate enough to connect with the most important artists of the rock era.

I came to appreciate the tremendous toll that rock can take on an artist's personal life, how there is often far more drama offstage than on. In the end, all it takes to be a star is luck and a commercial sound, which explains why we have so many mediocre hit makers. To be a true artist, you need enormous talent, fierce ambition, an original vision, and an unyielding toughness. I saw some artists triumph because they were tough and others die because they weren't tough enough.

I've also spoken to thousands of fans about what they want from music. Some are just after entertainment, others respond to unchecked anger and rebellion, still others like a band because their friends do, and there are those who value artists with the insight and craft to uplift and inspire us. No single rock 'n' roll diet works for everyone. We all have different musical DNA, and we all follow different musical paths. Yet there is a unifying quality about rock 'n' roll that helps instill confidence and hope in millions of fans at times in their lives when little else makes sense.

What linked Elvis Presley and Chuck Berry, Johnny Cash and Ray Charles, the Beatles and Bob Dylan was the old-fashioned American notion that each individual can make a difference, whether you are a truck driver from Memphis or a blind piano player from southwest Georgia. Rock 'n' roll is the promise of a better day, and the best artists spread that message with an almost missionary zeal. I've always believed in that liberating message, which is probably why I respond most to artists who fight to keep the promise alive.

CHAPTER TWO

Most youngsters in the 1950s got their early rock 'n' roll education from late-night radio shows hosted by disc jockeys with colorful names like the Moondog and Huggy Boy, but my musical classroom was an upstairs bedroom in my grandparents' house on the family plantation in central Louisiana. While mainstream pop records by Bing Crosby and Glenn Miller were played in the large downstairs living room, I listened to country and blues records in Uncle Bill's room. I was only six or seven when he started sharing his records with me, but even at that age I felt there was something immediate and exciting about them. Downstairs, my family played records as background music while they talked. When Uncle Bill played Hank Snow or Jimmie Rodgers, he gave the music his complete attention, as if the singers were speaking directly to him, maybe even telling his story. I was fascinated by the power all those records had on him.

Music was just one reason I enjoyed being around my uncle. He was in his mid-twenties and strong enough, at about five-ten and two-hundred-plus pounds, that he could lift one side of his blue Ford coupe to change a tire. He also listened to baseball games on the radio with me and joked around with the black field hands on the plantation, which made a big impression on me because I noticed how stiff and withdrawn the field-workers were around other white people. Though New Orleans had long been at the forefront of racial tolerance in the South, much of rural Louisiana had a strong redneck streak.

Campti, the closest town to the plantation, had only about a thousand residents, and its main street consisted of just a half-dozen retail stores, including a bank, a pharmacy, and a run-down movie theater. The only time you saw blacks downtown was when they were running errands for white property owners or waiting in line on the stairs to go into the "colored" balcony at the theater. On Saturday nights, Uncle Bill moved freely between the white honky-tonk and the black roadhouse. The closest I got to either place was waiting in the car while he went inside to pick up bottles of moonshine whiskey at the roadhouse. I'd listen through the open car window to the records on the jukebox, and they sounded just like the blues my uncle played at home.

By the time I was in elementary school, my parents were divorced. They had married soon after high school, and their union marked the big-deal coming together of the region's two prominent families—the Nelmses (my father, Charles) and the Taylors (my mother, Alice Marie). My dad's family owned massive acres of timberland, while my mom's family operated one of the largest cotton plantations in the area. As a result, both of my parents were pampered and, however much they were in love, they clashed constantly once they moved out on their own. The divorce papers were filed after just a couple of years. A few years later, my mom married my stepfather, John Hilburn, a California native who was a lieutenant at an air force base in the area. After the war, he worked as an electronics engineer in the aerospace industry, which meant we moved a lot, spending a few years in Dallas and then in various places in Southern California.

I spent a few weeks of most summers in Campti, which was in the fabled Red River Valley that was settled by the French in the eighteenth century. I would wait in the evenings for Uncle Bill to come home so I could sneak upstairs and listen to music with him, and it really did feel like sneaking sometimes. I was never forbidden to see him, but my grandmother and aunts encouraged me to stay downstairs with the rest of the family. Gradually, I got the sense that Uncle Bill was some kind of black sheep in the family, but I had no idea why. I noticed that even neighbors often spoke of him in hushed or sympathetic tones when they came to spend time with my grandmother in the house's breezeway.

One summer when I was about ten, my uncle found a new favorite named Hank Williams, a skinny, young country singer from Alabama who sang with such conviction and character that he made most of the other country singers seem as anonymous as the pop singers of the time. Without a word of introduction, my uncle put the record on the phonograph and watched for my reaction. The song was "Lovesick Blues," and I loved the energy and personality in Williams's voice.

Williams hit country music with such compelling force that when he sang "Lovesick Blues" during his Grand Ole Opry debut in 1949, the audience called him back to sing the song again for an unprecedented six encores. My uncle played the record that night in Campti with the same overpowering fascination, picking up the needle on the phonograph and putting it back down time and again on the 78 with the shiny black and yellow MGM Records label.

The record made me more eager than ever to go upstairs and listen to music. But one night after I headed up the darkened stairs, I learned about the mystery surrounding my uncle. The sound of moaning was coming from his room, and I heard the crash of a lamp hitting the floor. When I opened the door, Uncle Bill was on the ground in his khaki work clothes, twisting and turning as he gasped for air, his tongue sticking out of the side of his mouth. I ran downstairs for help and my aunt Nan raced to Uncle Bill's room. Creeping back up the stairs, I saw her on the floor, cuddling her brother in her arms, wiping his wet forehead with a cloth until the doctor arrived with his black satchel. I sat trembling on the stairs until Aunt Nan finally opened the door and sat down beside me. She said softly, "Bobby, your Uncle Bill is sick."

That night was the first time I heard the word "epilepsy," and I was so shaken by seeing my uncle helpless on the floor that it was a long time before I felt comfortable around him again. Looking back, I can see how my family and my uncle both were ashamed about something that we now know is merely a disease of the nervous system. He certainly sensed the unease around him, which is why he must have felt more comfortable on the "wrong" side of town, in the honky-tonks and roadhouses. As a second-class citizen, he found refuge in the sad tales and hard times outlined in his country and blues records.

When I got back to Dallas, I listened to the country music station for hours, hoping to hear "Lovesick Blues" and then, as time went on, other Hank Williams songs such as "Cold, Cold Heart" and "I Can't Help It (If I'm Still in Love with You)." I found myself pulling for Hank Williams because it felt like a victory for Uncle Bill, who didn't have a lot of victories in his life. Plus, it was hard not to identify with country music if you grew up in a small town listening to the lonesome train whistles in the night.

That summer was the last one I saw much of my uncle. My family moved to California in the early 1950s, and it was years before we went back down South. By that time, Uncle Bill was married and living at his own place. He may have stopped by my grandfather's house during my visits, but it was only briefly and I never met his wife and son. He died before I returned to Louisiana on my own.

. . . .

Once I got to Southern California, my listening habits shifted to rhythm and blues because I found more of it on the radio. This wasn't the minimalist blues I had heard down South, but a more upbeat, youthful sound that felt sexy, mysterious, and forbidding. What more could a thirteen-year-old ask of a record? We lived for three years in Del Mar, a small, upscale beach town just north of San Diego. There weren't many kids who were into country or R&B, so music was a private search for me.

That changed dramatically when my family moved to Los Angeles's San Fernando Valley in 1954. It was my first year of high school, and a few of the kids were even deeper into R&B than I was. We'd listen at night to R&B stations until we fell asleep and then rush to school the next morning to talk about what we'd heard. One early debate was over what the "work" in Hank Ballard and the Midnighters' smash hit "Work with Me Annie" was all about. We got the answer a few months later, when the sequel was released: "Annie Had a Baby." We also talked endlessly about records like the Crows' "Gee" and the Chords' "Sh-Boom" that didn't make any sense at all, but whose vocal and instrumental vitality made you feel part of something fresh and even a bit wild.

We went in packs to one of the many drugstores in the valley and Hollywood where, instead of paying nearly a dollar for a new single, we could buy a used record for a nickel (if it was slightly scratched) or a dime (if it was in good condition). We were so eager for new sounds that we took a chance on anything with a promising title or an intriguing group name on an R&B label. I also spent hours on Saturdays at Wallichs Music City, a store at Sunset and Vine in Hollywood where you could listen to records for as long as you wanted in private booths. Country music, by this time, was a more private passion because any mention of it at school would draw either blank stares or a wisecrack about that "hillbilly" music.

People were starting to use the term "rock 'n' roll" to describe this new R&B sound, but even as late as February 1955, traditional pop records like the Four Aces' "Three Coins in the Fountain" and Nat "King" Cole's "Mona Lisa" still topped the charts. Two films played as important a role in breaking that stranglehold as any single record. The first was *The Wild One,* the 1953 film in which Marlon Brando's performance as the leather-clad leader of a motorcycle gang popularized the notion of the contemporary rebel. When asked what he was rebelling against, Brando responded with a sneer, "What you got?" The rebel image was dramatized even more strikingly two years later in *Blackboard Jungle,* the gritty story about a new wave of rebellion that was sweeping through urban high schools.

There was enormous anticipation for *Blackboard Jungle* after parents' groups warned the movie could encourage students to riot. I saw it during its opening weekend at the Pantages Theater in Holly-wood, a grand old movie palace that had once hosted Academy Awards ceremonies. The transforming moment came when we heard Bill Haley and His Comets' "Rock Around the Clock" over the opening credits. When the song thundered through the massive speakers, kids around me climbed over the seats and each other to get into the aisles to dance to the impossibly loud beat. Part of the excitement was in listening to this new music in a crowd through monstrous speakers. Until then, we had mostly listened alone, through tiny speakers in our rooms.

Despite its importance at the time, "Rock Around the Clock" isn't much remembered today by anyone under the age of fifty. Haley was a country music bandleader who saw the commercial benefits of blending country and R&B, and "Rock Around the Clock" was his masterpiece with its wailing sax, driving guitar, and fierce percussion. But he was old by teen standards (about thirty), and he looked even older with a lame spit curl hanging down his forehead. "Rock Around the Clock" may have been the clarion call for the rock 'n' roll generation, but that generation still needed a leader—someone who was everything that Haley wasn't: young, handsome, sexy, and rebellious.

. . . .

As I was getting ready for school a few weeks later, I was switching radio stations in my usual search for new tunes when I came upon a record that was unlike anything I had ever heard. I couldn't even tell whether I was listening to a country or an R&B station; the record felt so unique that the station could have been from Mars. I just knew it was great. The singer had the emotional punch of Hank Williams and the sensual edge I knew from blues and country honky-tonk. He was throwing out the words so fast that it was hard to keep up. His nervous, hiccuping delivery made the music and words seem especially frantic and sensual:

> Oh, baby, baby, baby, baby, baby
> Baby, baby, baby, b-b-b-b-b-b-baby, baby,
> Come back, baby, I wanna play house with you.

That alone was enough to jolt me. There may have been some question about what "Work with Me Annie" was about, but I knew what "playing house" with a girl meant. If that wasn't enough to make the record seem racy and exotic, the singer declared in the final verse that he'd rather see his girl dead than with another man.

Dead?

I couldn't wait to get the record, though I wasn't sure what my folks would think of it. They were tolerant of my rock 'n' roll tastes, but this might be pushing it. I waited for the announcer to identify the singer, but the name sounded so strange that I wasn't sure I'd heard it right. It was something Presley. Ellis? I did, however, pick up the call letters of the station, XERB. No one at school had heard of "Baby, Let's Play House" or XERB, which turned out to be a powerhouse station just across the border in Mexico that played country music between evangelical sermons and horse racing results. I kept listening after school that day, but didn't hear the song again. I went that night to the local record shop, Anita's, and asked the owner if she knew who I was talking about.

She didn't recognize the title or the name, either, but she looked in a catalog and found a reference to "Baby, Let's Play House" on Sun Records, a small, Southern label. I still couldn't make out the first name when she said it, so she turned the catalog toward me so I could see it: E-L-V-I-S. I asked if he had any more records out and she found three more in another catalog. She ordered them for me, but I only had enough allowance to buy one record a week—and the wait probably made the records all the more enticing.

I played them over and over, trying to picture what the singer looked like. I watched Dick Clark's *American Bandstand* in vain and went to the newsstand to look through magazines like *Song Hits* that printed lyrics and the artist's photo, but saw nothing of Elvis. I finally turned to *Billboard,* a record industry trade publication, and there he was. Just seeing him was another rush. Elvis was twenty, but he looked young enough to be in high school, and the sideburns were certainly cooler than Haley's spit curl.

None of the LA stations played his records, so it wasn't until the following January that Elvis began catching on at school. That's when RCA Records, which bought his contract from Sun, released "Heartbreak Hotel." I felt the record lacked the raw edge of the Sun singles, but I was such an Elvis fan that I didn't care. His voice, sideburns, magnetic smile, infectious music, and raw defiance helped me navigate the confusions and insecurities of my teen years. What made him the most influential figure ever in rock was that he helped bring a liberating sense of self-identity to an entire generation—even to a bunch of teenagers in Liverpool, England. When John Lennon said "Before Elvis, there was nothing," I knew exactly what he meant.

I went around singing like Elvis in my head and even bought a used acoustic guitar for ten dollars so I could stand in front of the mirror and pretend to be him. But two things stopped me cold: I couldn't play the guitar, and when I sang one of his songs into a tape recorder, I was shocked by the result. Instead of his smooth, appealing voice, mine was high pitched and thin. I not only gave up thinking about being a singer, I also avoided speaking up in class for weeks.

Eventually, I realized that there was something I could do with music: I could write about it. I reviewed Elvis's first movie, *Love Me Tender,* for the high school paper in 1956. It was a rave, and kids came up to me in class to say how much they liked the review. It was such a thrill that I still have a copy of that issue of the Reseda High School *Regent's Review.*

Ever since Campti, I had been attracted to newspapers because they—like radio, records, and movies—represented the glamour of the larger world. A dozen or so copies of the *Shreveport Times* were delivered every morning to the town's general store, and I would ride into town with one of my uncles to pick up the family copy. Sometimes we'd get to the store before the papers arrived and I would stand out on the wooden front steps watching for the deliveryman. My favorite parts of the paper were the movie pages, where I would look at the ads, and the sports section, where I could follow the major league and Texas League baseball scores. One of my aunts lived in Shreveport, and the paper had a daily column devoted to social news around town. I didn't realize it at the time, but all a subscriber had to do was phone the columnist about some personal item and chances were it would be printed. One morning when I was seven, Aunt Nan rushed in with the paper and pointed to a paragraph that read, "Little Bobby Hilburn from Dallas was in town visiting his aunt."

That was as exciting as hearing a record on the radio, and I took the paper back to Dallas and showed the kids in the neighborhood. I'd also sit in my room and stare at the column, which was called something like "Talk of the Town."

One day something dawned on me.

My name could only be in the column once, but the name of the guy who wrote the column was in the paper every day. I started daydreaming about writing for a newspaper, though I had no idea what I'd want to write about.

· ·

My sixth-grade teacher in Dallas asked my class to write about our summer vacations. I wanted to do something novel and ended up describing how a friend and I had spent several afternoons pretending to be FBI agents by following people from store to store downtown, making sure they didn't see us. All the while, we were making up elaborate tales about the evil deeds these "commie spies" had done. The stimulus for this was a movie called *I Was a Communist for the FBI,* whose ads proclaimed, "I learned every dirty rule in their book—and had to use them—because I was a communist—but I was a communist for the FBI!"

The teacher asked me to read the story to her other sixth-grade classes and it was such a hit that several kids asked if they could play the game with us. I enjoyed the attention and wanted to write more stories. Later, I was editor of the student paper at Reseda High School. The faculty advisor, Sol Kaufler, felt the *Regent's Review* should only report about campus affairs, but I argued that we could make the paper more relevant to students by writing about off-campus subjects. I'm not sure I convinced him, but he let me experiment by reviewing Elvis's first movie and doing a campus poll each week to discover the most popular records.

At California State University, Northridge, I was editor of the college paper, the *Sundial,* for three years and student body president for one. As editor, I again argued that coverage shouldn't be limited by the campus's boundaries, and Erling Erlandson, the journalism department head, was supportive.

Like young people across the country, I idolized John F. Kennedy and wanted to interview him when he came to Los Angeles in 1958 to address a group of Young Democrats. After getting into the hotel ballroom with my press pass, I asked the program chairman if I could speak to the senator. He said he couldn't help me with that, but told me that Kennedy was meeting with the organization's leaders in a nearby room. I went to the room, where I saw Kennedy going down a long line of well-wishers, shaking hands and sharing a few words with each. I stepped to the end of the line and surprised him when I said I was from the college paper and would like to ask him a few questions. One of his aides started to push me aside, but Kennedy said he'd have time for a short interview.

Afterward, I was more hooked than ever on writing for a newspaper. I wanted a job that was fun, and I began to see a press pass as a passport to all kinds of exotic worlds, from politics to sports to show business. I was struck by how many adults, including my stepfather and my friends' parents, had so little passion for their work. This was after World War II when suburbs were springing up across the country, offering veterans a slice of the American Dream. But the new homes and new cars didn't necessarily bring happiness. Watching adults around me sleepwalking their way through life made me desperate to find a job I enjoyed. I wasn't sure journalism was the answer, but it seemed like a good starting place.

Following graduation in 1961, I was hired by the *Valley Times* and got a variety of assignments, from covering city government to writing personality profiles. I did interviews with film people (director Otto Preminger and actress Ann-Margret), music people (Jackie DeShannon), and sports figures (LA Dodgers outfielder Wally Moon).

But there was also a downside to the job. When someone died accidently, I had to go to the family's residence to ask for a photo of the deceased to run with the story. Even more unsettling was seeing dead bodies at crime scenes. The worst was when I was sent to a home in the hills of Tarzana where a woman in her thirties was lying nude on the kitchen floor with giant boning shears stuck in her chest. I could barely stay in the room long enough to ask the detectives for the information I needed for the story. When I got back to the office, the editor said I looked green.

In time, the tragedies and emergency calls in the middle of the night were enough to make me leave the paper. I took a public relations job for the Los Angeles Unified School District in 1963.

By this time, I was married and had two children, and my interest in rock had waned because most of my early rock heroes had faded from the radio. Every other pop style, including swing, had lost its commercial force after a few years, so I figured the same thing was happening to rock. I'd still go see Elvis movies for old times' sake, but when it came to records, the few I bought were usually along the lines of Frank Sinatra, Johnny Cash, or Ray Charles, whose two *Modern Sounds in Country and Western Music* albums, both released in 1962, brought together my two early musical loves—country and R&B— with breathtaking elegance and dimension.

It wasn't until the Beatles' debut on the *Ed Sullivan Show* in 1964 that I paid attention again. I heard echoes of Elvis, Carl Perkins, and Chuck Berry in this young English band's music. While I didn't think of the Beatles as a breakthrough, they sounded a lot better on the radio than Bobby Vinton or Neil Sedaka. I began looking forward to hearing them, along with the music of some other British groups, especially the Rolling Stones, who seemed even closer to the rawness and adventure of 1950s rock. Meanwhile, I was turning out press releases about school bond measures and reminders to parents about the need for vaccinations. After a couple of years, I realized that I was missing the self-expression and recognition that journalism offered.

The idea of writing about music struck me in the early months of 1965, when a friend at the school board gave me a copy of an album that proved to be as electrifying as the early Elvis singles: Bob Dylan's *The Times They Are a-Changin'*. This protest-minded folk music spoke to my interest in politics. Rock's urgency and defiance in the 1950s was in the explosive beat and the attitudes of the performers, not in the mostly disposable words. It was the reverse with Dylan. The music itself was relatively calm, but his words were urgent and liberating to young people who felt helpless in a country that seemed increasingly to violate its ideals, whether it was in the segregated South or the jungles of Vietnam. Dylan's songs addressed those issues as forcefully as a battle cry. When he warned the older generation to stand aside or face the consequences, the images struck like a bullwhip.

I wasn't sure if I was ready to follow Dylan's call to action. I admired what he said, but I had been raised to respect authority and to believe that our government told the truth. This new world sounded radical and a bit frightening. I didn't know if things were as black and white as Dylan presented them. Still, there was no denying the album's power. Maybe, I thought, Dylan's folk music would be the new rock 'n' roll. It wasn't until I heard the blistering guitar lines and percussive drive behind Dylan's voice on the song "Subterranean Homesick Blues" that I realized Dylan wasn't going to convert rock fans into folk fans. He was going to turn rock 'n' roll on its head. In doing so, he could give the music new life by making it appeal to adults as well as teenagers. I could see a future for this music I had once loved.

Dylan was inviting his audience to think and dream and act, and I wanted more. Through him and other socially conscious songwriters, I began to recognize that patriotism didn't mean accepting everything the government told us; it was important to question authority. I wasn't a hippie, but I fell hard for the questioning spirit of the times.

Dylan made me want to write about music. Plus, I must confess, there was a second lure: All those free records and concert tickets! My first thought was the *Los Angeles Times*. It was the summer of 1966, and the paper had one of the largest circulations in the country. Best of all, a friend knew Charles Champlin, the *Times*'s entertainment editor. Once I got in Chuck's office, I was so eager to sell myself that I went on for twenty minutes nonstop about the excitement I felt was brewing in rock 'n' roll and why it was time for the paper to hire a rock writer. In those days, most newspapers still thought of pop music as an interest limited to teenagers. But Chuck was sympathetic to what I was saying. He had even introduced Dylan at a press conference in Los Angeles a few months earlier. The only problem, he said, was that the paper already had someone assigned to rock: a copy editor who covered rock music on the side, and his two stories a week were all the paper could handle.

Then I brought up country music and R&B. Chuck said the rock writer was also covering R&B, and he didn't think there was that much interest in country music in Los Angeles. In a panic, I went into a lengthy speech about how the music was getting more and more popular, thanks to great artists like Johnny Cash, and how Southern California was one of country's biggest markets. "Who would you like to write about?" he asked, showing me a list of upcoming concerts. One name stood out: Hank Williams Jr., who had been a baby when Hank Sr. died in 1953. I thought it would make a good feature story— the teenage son of the greatest country music songwriter singing his father's songs. How did he feel about it? How did the audience feel about him?

"Good idea," Chuck said. "Give me five hundred words."

. . . .

I didn't know what the next step was, so I phoned the promoter of the concert, who said he'd leave my name at the box office, but that I was on my own in getting the interview. As it turned out, Hank Jr. was in the lobby signing autographs when I arrived at the auditorium in Long Beach, so I just got in line with the fans. When I reached the young singer, I introduced myself. His mother, Audrey, who was with him, just about jumped up and down with excitement. She knew the promotional value of an article in a paper as big as the *Times*. Even though there were still a couple dozen fans in line, she grabbed Hank Jr. and led us to the dressing room. Hank Jr. was just seventeen, but he had been doing his father's songs for nine years. Everywhere he went, he said, his daddy's fans came out to tell him how much the old songs meant to them.

The moment seemed too good to be true—being paid to go to concerts, meeting the stars, and then looking forward to seeing my story in the paper. But my strongest memory of that night was after I left the dressing room and walked to the side of the stage to see who else was performing. As I approached the wings, I heard a dynamic voice that blended some of the country authority of Johnny Cash with the rebelliousness of a young rock 'n' roller. I couldn't believe someone this good was only third on the bill. To top it off, he was singing the Beatles'

"Norwegian Wood"—something I never expected to hear at a country music show.

The handsome young singer was so high on drugs that he seemed to be floating above the ground when he headed past me toward the dressing room. I must have looked out of place with my blue business suit and notepad because he stopped and stared at me. Maybe he thought I was a narcotics agent. Instead of just telling him I had enjoyed his music, I blurted out, "I'm Bob Hilburn from the *Los Angeles Times*." He nodded and declared, "I'm Mickey Mouse from Nashville."

That was my introduction to Waylon Jennings, and it wasn't long before I was writing about him. I thought Waylon—with his rugged good looks, seductive voice, and feel for great songs—was what Elvis might have become if he had turned to country music rather than wasting all those years on movies.

It was fun to write about Hank Jr., but it was even more satisfying to share my enthusiasm for a talented newcomer like Waylon. I was as sure he was going to be a star as I had once been sure Elvis was going to be huge.

Chuck said my story had generated some mail and that he'd welcome more stories. I knew there was a lot more happening in the rock world than in the country field, and I was sometimes frustrated that I wasn't able to write about those artists, too. But the time I spent covering country music was a valuable apprenticeship. After work, I spent nights and weekends listening to every new country album that came out, hoping to spot new talent. I felt a sense of mission, and I was lucky because no one was second-guessing me at the paper.

By this time, *Rolling Stone* magazine was just getting started in San Francisco and I could find occasional stories on rock musicians in national magazines. But there was a virtual blackout on country music. The style was so unfashionable that even country music DJs joked about how their listeners rolled up their car windows when they stopped at an intersection. To millions of Americans, country music was synonymous with "hillbilly" or "backwoods." But those nights with my uncle in Louisiana enabled me to look past the corny humor and rhinestone suits to hear the marvelous artistry, and I wanted to use the power of the paper to help bring it respect and a larger audience.

After all those years of thinking about how much country songs meant to my uncle Bill, I could see that those records were so powerful because they were made by people who were battling their own problems—people who were often telling their own stories.

I made enough progress at the paper that I got more ambitious with my story suggestions. In the fall of 1968, I came up with what I thought was an irresistible pitch: covering Johnny Cash doing a live concert at Folsom State Prison. I was dumbfounded when it was rejected in a note from one of the assistant editors that said simply, "We don't want to give any space to that drug addict."

THREE

argued my case for covering the Folsom Prison show with Charles Champlin. The paper wouldn't turn down stories on Bob Dylan, the Beatles, or the Rolling Stones even though they, too, had drug histories, I said; they were too important artistically and culturally to ignore. Cash, likewise, was an artist whose music went far beyond the normal country music terrain to make some of the same social commentary that Dylan did. Cash wrote about the common man with an uncommon grace, and here was a chance to hear him perform one of his signature songs, "Folsom Prison Blues," in front of two thousand inmates. The show was being recorded for a live album and I would be the only music writer on hand. Champlin listened, nodded, and—bless him—agreed.

I flew to Sacramento—the prison is about twenty miles from there—a few days later with Hugh Cherry, a local country music disc jockey who was going to emcee the concert. Cherry had been a DJ for years and he knew all the country stars, from Hank Williams to Hank Snow. He, too, felt Cash was special. "He's one person who doesn't just think about hit singles," Cherry said during our flight. "He thinks about songs that make a difference in people's lives."

True enough. I was first attracted to Cash because I loved his jukebox hits, like "Folsom Prison Blues" and "Guess Things Happen That Way," but I came to recognize at Folsom, and in the many, many days I spent with him over the years, that he was one of America's true artists. He talked for hours about his concept albums—the ones about the railroads, Native Americans, and church music—and I marveled at the depth of his commitment. I could see that artists like Lennon and Dylan had developed an artistic conscience because they operated in musical traditions that encouraged comment. But Cash was in a field where none of his contemporaries aimed for anything more than another hit for the jukebox.

It was evening when Hugh and I got to the El Rancho Inn, where Cash had turned one of the banquet rooms into a rehearsal hall. He and his three-piece band made so much noise that quite a few hotel guests—many of them on their way to a five-hundred-dollar-a-plate dinner for Governor Ronald Reagan that was also being held there—peered in to see what was going on. After learning that Cash was in the room, Reagan stopped by to say hello. They spoke for a few minutes and then Cash returned to the rehearsal. John wasn't a great singer technically, but he was a superb communicator whose conversational style captured life's everyday search for comfort and salvation. Even in the most joyous tunes, however, his instrumental backing tended to be stark, as if reminding us of life's accompanying hardships. The *chicka-boom-chicka* guitar approach was as steady and true as an amplified heartbeat.

During a rehearsal break, Hugh introduced me to John (as he preferred to be called), and he seemed flattered that I had come all the way from Los Angeles to write about the show. When he asked where I was from, I said, "Campti, Louisiana, which is near Natchitoches." His face brightened. "I know Natchitoches," he responded. "I used to be on the *Louisiana Hayride* in Shreveport. That's cotton country." I knew John was from cotton country in rural Arkansas, which made me feel at ease.

The next morning, Folsom Prison looked as still as a cemetery.

Its massive gray walls seemed to insulate all sound from escaping to the outside world. A prison official ushered us through several gates and into a large courtyard where long lines of inmates, dressed in blue denim shirts and pants, were waiting. Several nodded and waved as John walked by. I had assumed the show would be in an auditorium, but we were eventually taken to the cafeteria, where the inmates had been seated.

As John sang about lost souls and redemption, he struck such a nerve with the convicts that many believed he had actually spent time behind bars himself. In the movie *Walk the Line,* the 2005 Cash biography starring Joaquin Phoenix, the inmates become so excited that they rush to the edge of the stage. That scene was a filmmaker's liberty. Some inmates had held a guard at knifepoint just two weeks before, and the warden had warned that he would stop the concert if anyone left his chair. As John sang about killing a man just to watch him die, the red-letter line from "Folsom Prison Blues," guards with rifles prowled an overhead ramp, keeping an eye out for trouble.

The album came out that summer and was a huge hit on both the country and pop charts. Columbia Records used part of my *Times* story as the liner notes on the sleeve of the "Folsom Prison Blues" single. John was in great spirits when we met for dinner at a Hollywood restaurant; he was proud of how the collection validated his creative impulses. He said he had signed with Columbia in 1958 after spending a few years on Sun Records because the larger label had promised him full artistic freedom. Columbia's president, Goddard Lieberson, had even given him recordings of classic African American folk and spiritual songs of the South. John carried the set with him for years, frequently playing it for inspiration. As John's sales had slipped in the mid-1960s, however, he had started encountering resistance to some of his ideas. The executives who ran the country music division had fought the idea of recording a live prison album. Smiling, John quoted his label bosses, "'No one wants to listen to someone singing for a bunch of convicts.'" But Bob Johnston, a maverick Columbia staff producer who had earlier worked with Dylan, took John's side and helped get the green light for the project.

John confessed that there was another reason for Columbia's opposition to the prison album. "I think they had pretty much given up on me," he said—too many pills, too many missed shows, too many troubled recording sessions. He even said he had given up on himself at times, but he had straightened himself out with the help of singing partner and future wife, June Carter, and his faith. He claimed to have been pretty much off pills for a couple of years, but admitted that he worried every day about relapsing. He felt blessed and unworthy as a Christian, and he often rubbed dirt under his fingernails as a reminder of his humble roots. He also vowed to use his fame to inspire others.

I told Chuck Champlin in 1969 that I would love to do an occasional rock or R&B feature if an assignment was ever available. That led to my writing about Roger Miller, the country writer and singer who had cracked the pop market with his clever wordplay in such songs as "King of the Road."

When I got to Roger's home in the San Fernando Valley, he introduced me to a couple of young songwriters. I had heard of one of them—Mickey Newbury, who had written a few country hits—but I hadn't heard of the other guy. After the interview, Roger gave me an advance copy of his next single. I played it as soon as I got home and I was floored. With its lonesome, bittersweet feel, the song had an instant appeal, and I just loved the line where Roger sang, "Freedom's just another word for nothing left to lose." I raced to the phone and called Roger's number. When he answered, I said, "I just love the new single. What a great song." He paused for a second, then said he liked "Me and Bobby McGee," too, but he hadn't written it. "It was written by the guy who is here with me and Mickey. You met him—Kris Kristofferson." I later got together with Kris and wrote a glowing review of his LA club debut.

Around this time, Chuck told me that Pete Johnson, who had been writing about rock, was leaving the paper, and he wondered if I'd like to take over the beat. It was a part-time job, but I'd be doing a story a week instead of one a month and I'd have the entire spectrum of pop music as my subject. I told Chuck I'd love to take the post and I started listening to rock albums, hoping to find someone who excited me as much as Cash. Finally, I saw that Janis Joplin was coming to the Hollywood Bowl. She was the biggest female in rock. I had seen her in *Monterey Pop,* and she looked like a woman possessed as she clutched the microphone, stomped her feet on the stage, and stretched her vocal cords to alarming limits. I read everything I could find on her, including Paul Nelson's story in *Rolling Stone* that called her the Judy Garland of rock—someone who was overpoweringly talented, yet emotionally fragile.

After getting approval from the paper, I called Columbia Records to try to set up an interview. The publicist chuckled, explaining that Janis wasn't always easy to deal with. He gave me the number of the hotel where she'd be staying and wished me luck. Between committee meetings that day at the school board, I kept trying to reach her, but there was no answer until late that evening. She picked up the receiver and I was taken aback by the sound of her voice. There was so little life in her voice that it was eerie. I didn't know if Janis was high or simply depressed. Either way, she didn't want to do an interview—it had been a bad day, something about rotten business matters and rotten boyfriends, "Hell, rotten everything." Just when I thought all was lost, she suggested that I stop by the rehearsal the next day. Maybe we could talk then, she said. I felt like I was going on an audition for the paper: If I could only step inside her world and get a good story, maybe the *Times* would hire me full time. Janis Joplin—drug reputation or not—was big news in 1969.

. . . .

Far more than they are today, rock stars in the late 1960s were seen as pop culture gods. I had no idea then how hard adjusting to that icon status was on many of them, especially someone like Janis, whose art was driven by a deeply rooted lack of self-esteem. As we'd learn years later with the suicide of Kurt Cobain, no generation is immune from the pressures and temptations of fame. But the role was particularly difficult for many in the 1960s because that generation prided itself on stepping into the unknown. Janis was at the front end of that exploration. At the time, all the talk was about how she was opening a door for women in a rock world that had been almost exclusively male. In retrospect, the most memorable quality in her music and performances was a raw intensity that let you see clearly her vulnerability and fears.

Janis stood on the Hollywood Bowl stage during the afternoon rehearsal, increasingly impatient over not being able to hear herself in the monitors. She was wearing all sorts of hippie-gypsy garb—scarves, boas, dark oversize glasses, and numerous rings. When a technician kept explaining that the system was already at the maximum decibel level allowed at the Bowl, she erupted, "I don't give a fuck about the dB's, man, I just want to be able to hear myself." With that, she knocked over the microphone and marched backstage.

I followed her to her dressing room and stood outside for a few seconds, fearful of another eruption if I knocked. I was hoping someone from her crew would come by and run interference for me. But apparently no one else wanted to take the chance of crossing her, either. After about ten minutes, I knocked on the door *g-e-n-t-l-y*. No response. After another minute or so, I tapped my knuckles on the door. I wondered if she could even hear me. I took a deep breath and knocked a little harder. "Fuck off!" she screamed. This time I did wait until a member of her crew came my way. When I mentioned the interview, he looked skeptical. He told me to wait while he went inside.

Eventually, the door opened and I saw Janis leaning back on a sofa, appearing as drained and lifeless as she had sounded on the phone. Nothing about her suggested "star." This powerhouse of a woman seemed ordinary, almost anonymous. I had read how she had been called the "ugly duckling" from Port Arthur, a refinery town near the Gulf of Mexico, and, sure enough, she probably didn't get second glances on the street. As I watched her on the sofa, all the flamboyant attire and jewelry she wore on stage seemed like her way of compensating for the beauty and personality that nature had failed to provide. Minus that camouflage or an audience to energize her, she seemed small and weak. Janis reached slowly for a pack of cigarettes. She dropped her glasses on a cushion next to her and rubbed her eyes for a good thirty seconds. She was tired, she said, repeating the frustrations she'd outlined in the phone call—tired of fighting with businessmen and musicians, and of the writers who all kept asking the same questions about where all the pain in her voice came from and whether she shouldn't cut down on the partying.

When the crew member closed the door on his way out, I felt like I was in a cell. Janis's music was about yearning for freedom—indeed she seemed trapped. I thought about a quote of hers I had read, something about how hard it was to make love to twenty-five thousand people on stage and then sleep alone. I suddenly felt like an intruder. I didn't want to be just one more guy asking about the pain and self-destructiveness. But I also knew I had to write a story.

Trying to be sensitive, I asked, "Is there anything you'd like to talk about?"

Janis stared across the room at me, then lowered her head and twisted her rings, one finger at a time.

"Man, don't you even have your own questions?"

I laugh now, but my heart sank at the time. I sat with my head down, not knowing what to do. Instead of shutting down, however, Janis slowly opened up. Maybe it helped that I was new on the job, someone apart from the industry machine that she hated. She sort of apologized and I sensed my chance. I remembered the dinner with Johnny Cash and tried to talk just as frankly to her. I asked her if she felt like the Judy Garland of rock.

She stared at me so intently that I feared I had gone too far, that she was starting to feel chewed up again. But her eyes softened.

"People seem to have a high sense of drama about me," she said softly. "Maybe they can enjoy my music more if they think I'm destroying myself. Sure, I could take better care of myself, I suppose. I could eat nothing but organic food, get eight hours of sleep every night, stop smoking. Maybe it would add a couple of years to my life. But what the hell? I got into this because of something inside me. I'm not one of those people with a learned skill. I can't just get out on stage and fake it. I've got to let loose with what's inside. I started singing so I could get into dances free. It just flowed and flowed. I don't have any idea what I'm going to be doing three years from now. You do what you have to do today and you do what you have to do three years from now."

For the next hour, Janis spoke in detail about her music and her lifestyle, especially the one constant in her world: loneliness. I took notes as fast as I could.

"Somehow you lose all the old friends," she said, now lying on the sofa, her head flat against the cushion. "The travel circumstances pull them away. It is hard to make new ones. When we're not on stage, we rehearse, lie around in bed, check in and out of motels, watch television. I live for that hour on stage. It's more excitement than you'd expect in a lifetime. It's a rush."

For the first time, she smiled. Leaning forward, she asked me for a favor.

"Use that, will you, honey? That line about 'It's a rush.' That's a dope term. My friends would get a kick out of seeing it in print."

On stage that night, the star reemerged. Sporting the gypsy clothing, Janis removed the microphone from its stand with supreme confidence and raced to the edge of the stage, wanting to be as close as possible to the audience. She reached out and just about handed her heart to the screaming fans.

My profile was a big hit. Jim Bellows, the paper's celebrated associate editor, sent me a complimentary note and hinted about a full-time job. I was doubly excited because Bellows was known for having encouraged such promising young writers as Tom Wolfe and Jimmy Breslin. I also got word that Janis had seen the story and wanted to say thanks for using the "rush" line. She left word for me at the paper a couple of times, but we didn't connect for almost a year. When I did speak to her, she said she was coming to town to record an album. She'd found some new songs by a new writer named Kris Kristofferson.

Kristofferson?

I told her I loved Kris's songs, and that ignited a competition between the two of us over who could get the most excited about him.

I told her about meeting Kris at Roger Miller's house and championing his music. After listening to me go on and on, she couldn't resist some one-upmanship: "He's not bad in bed, either." Really? I asked. Was she going with Kris? "No," she said with a chuckle. "That was a while ago."

Then, she started raving again about his songs. She didn't know how her fans would react to her singing a tune as gently philosophical as "Me and Bobby McGee" after all of her fireball hits, but she said she was going to record the song anyway. She wanted to change her image; she didn't want to be known just as a screamer. She also talked about "Help Me Make It Through the Night" and sang a line from "Sunday Mornin' Comin' Down." I got the impression she might do a whole album of Kris's songs.

Janis did come to town to record that album and I planned to see her when the record was finished, but ultimately those lonely hours between shows were too much for her. Less than a year after that Hollywood Bowl concert, Janis was found dead in a hotel room within walking distance of the Bowl stage where I had first seen her. She had apparently accidentally injected herself with a lethal dose of heroin. Released posthumously, "Me and Bobby McGee" turned out to be her only No. 1 single. When she sang the song's key line, "Freedom's just another word for nothing left to lose," she sang with such longing that millions of fans probably thought Kris wrote it just for her.

The experience with Janis reinforced something I had learned in country music—the best music doesn't just fill a void in the listener, as it had for my uncle, it can also fill a need in the artist. Janis's story also showed how an artist's music can be an illuminating reflection of the artist's life. That link seems obvious today. Before Elvis and the Beatles, however, mainstream pop music rarely felt real or vital. Perry Como, Patti Page, and the others were like actors playing roles. And that tradition remains. Much of what we call popular music, whatever the specific genre, results from hollow professionalism—the sound of musicians and record producers pretty much working within the conventional boundaries of the day, recycling whatever ideas and styles are most likely to sell records. The most extreme pretend pop is the whole *American Idol* phenomenon.

The memorable artists help us explore our emotions, either through their intense originality or by looking bravely at their own deepest fears and grandest dreams. To reach that far inside themselves, these artists need to be driven, almost obsessed, and, I repeat, they have to be tough. Janis was all those things as an artist. It was as a person that she fell short. She wasn't tough enough.

CHAPTER
FOUR

he first time I saw Elvis live was when he was a guest on *The Milton Berle Show* in Burbank in 1956. The owner of my neighborhood record store gave me a ticket to the broadcast because she knew 1 had been into Elvis long before the other kids. The audience was stacked with fans, mostly shrieking girls hoping to get a glimpse. Unfortunately, we were so far from the stage we could barely see him through all the equipment.

But in Las Vegas in 1970, I got to watch the show from a front-row table. Elvis was the most charismatic performer I had ever seen—far more confident and in command than I remembered from his TV appearances in the 1950s. Elvis's early moves—for all the excitement they created—were often clumsy, as he would swing his hips during one part of a song, then just sort of jump up and down at another.

In Vegas, his moves were graceful and the frenzied moments were far more effective because he tempered them with calm, tension-building ones. Rather than shouting his vocals as before, Elvis also sang with control and character. While it was fun to hear the old hits, he was the most dynamic on newer material, such as the scorching

"Suspicious Minds," that allowed him to show a larger emotional range. His five-piece band and the backing orchestra also provided more energy and snap than his old three-piece group had. In my review, I called his performance flawless and, unlike the high school review of *Love Me Tender,* it wasn't just the fan in me talking.

My goal was to interview him, and that was going to be hard because of Elvis's flamboyant manager, Colonel Tom Parker. The former carnival show barker recognized the value of publicity, which is why he plastered Elvis's photo on billboards all over town. He even arranged for hundreds of Welcome Elvis posters to be placed throughout the hotel. But this thinking didn't extend to interviews, and Parker made himself almost as hard for the press to reach as Elvis. I saw him that first night in Las Vegas minutes before Elvis walked on stage. Parker strolled into the showroom through a side door and took his seat in a center booth with his celebrity guests. When Elvis went into his final song an hour later, Parker quickly walked out that same side door—not to be seen again until Elvis's midnight show. After watching the Colonel's routine at the early show, I joined the fans by his booth just before the midnight performance and caught him by surprise when I identified myself and said I would love to talk to him for a few minutes. "Well, I'm kinda busy right now," he said sarcastically. "Besides, I don't do interviews. Enjoy the show." I took my seat at a table a few rows away and watched the concert. As he made his exit after the show, he paused at my seat, leaned down, and said, "Be sure to give the boy a good review."

I went back to Las Vegas three times during Elvis's engagement and made it a point each time to pay my respects to Parker, but he didn't show any sign of budging. I then started lobbying Grelun Landon, an RCA publicist who had helped me when I was writing about country music. I asked Grelun, who had been hired on Parker's recommendation, to speak to the Colonel on my behalf. "I already have, and the Colonel said he likes what you have been writing about Elvis, but I don't think he's ever going to change his policy about interviews." When I stressed that I was just trying to interview Parker, Grelun gave me a tip. He said to stop asking and to just show up at Parker's office at the hotel. I followed his advice and told the Colonel that I'd given up on trying to interview him, but I would love to stop by his office sometime for a visit. To my surprise, he replied, "Tomorrow around two would be a good time."

Parker's office was a two-room suite whose walls, too, were covered with Elvis posters. The Colonel sat behind a desk, puffing on a cigar, surrounded by four or five members of his staff. Without leaving his chair, he introduced me to his aides like I was some big deal. "I want you all to meet Mr. Robert Hilburn. He's the one who wrote that nice article on the boy for the *Los Angeles Times*."

I knew he was putting me on, but I went along with it. Looking at all the posters, I said I understood why he put billboards all over town, but why plaster them throughout the hotel? Anyone staying there already knew Elvis was appearing there.

"Well, Robert, I'll tell you," he said as if sitting me on his knee. "You put posters all over the hotel because you want people to feel like they are part of the show as soon as they step into the hotel. We want people to feel the excitement every minute they're in the hotel. We'd have Elvis sheets on the bed if we could."

The Colonel's staff laughed even though I'm sure they'd heard the joke hundreds of times. Parker then started telling other stories, each drawing more laughter. I realized that it wasn't just Elvis who had an entourage. Most of the stories involved the ways Parker used his power to gain a few extra bucks in some business deal. This was strange. Here was a man with a multimillion-dollar property and he was boasting about pocket change. At one point he reached into his desk and pulled out a handful of calendars the size of playing cards with Elvis's photo on the back. Parker said the RCA promotion department had come up with the idea and presented it to him for approval. "I told them it was such a good idea that I'd give them a discount on the use of the boy's photo." Yes, he chuckled, he made RCA pay a few cents per card even though the whole idea was to promote Elvis. As his cronies again roared, Parker gave me the handful of calendars.

I sat through many of the same stories when I visited the Colonel again that summer, and I sensed he was getting more comfortable. He began phoning me with Elvis information, closing each call with "Remember, it was the Colonel who tipped you off." The "tips" were nothing more than press releases—the date of a new Elvis album's release or some sales milestone. But I thanked him and said I was looking forward to seeing him again in Vegas. I expected more of the same chitchat the night Parker stopped by my seat in the showroom. But he had something special to tell me. "Would you like to meet the boy?" he asked. The boy? Did he mean Elvis? I tried to downplay my emotions. "Sure," I replied calmly, and Parker told me to wait at the table after the show and he'd come get me. I don't remember much about the show that night. I was so busy thinking about what I could possibly say to Elvis to connect with him and get a real interview.

At the end of the set, Parker led me to the backstage area where Elvis was waiting. Just as we got to the dressing room, Parker said, "By the way, this isn't an interview. Just a chance to say hello." Still, I was hoping for a miracle. I took a deep breath before stepping into the room, but I could feel my knees actually shaking when I saw Elvis joking with the guys in his Memphis Mafia entourage. When he saw Parker and me, he walked our way. With his tailored shirt and slacks and his finely chiseled features, he looked even better than he did on stage. There wasn't an ounce of fat on him and his smile was magnetic. Even though he had another show to do that night, he seemed as if he didn't have a care in the world—and he probably didn't. He had reclaimed his crown as the King of Rock 'n' Roll.

Elvis reached out and shook my hand. "I wanted to thank you, sir, for what you wrote about me." He was referring to a story from months earlier that had praised him and spoken of the importance of rock 'n' roll in pop culture. He said it meant a lot to him.

After a few moments, Elvis took me to a corner of the room where we could be by ourselves. As we moved away, Parker whispered to me, "Remember, no interview." Then he left us alone. "I hope you understand, sir," Elvis said about the no-interview policy. "It's just something the Colonel thinks is best." Elvis seemed down-to-earth enough, except the "sir" business felt strange since I was four years younger. Elvis mentioned how badly he had done the first time he'd played Vegas in the 1950s and how nervous he had been about coming back, but he said he loved doing live shows again after those "stupid" movies.

Desperately wanting to keep Elvis talking, I asked some questions about his early days on Sun. What style did he like best growing up: country, blues, or gospel? He said he had liked all three, plus he liked pop singers, especially Bing Crosby and Dean Martin. I asked him who had chosen the songs he had recorded for Sun—old blues tunes like "That's All Right" and vintage country ones like "Just Because." Had he, or Sun Records owner Sam Phillips? "Oh, that was me, sir." Each time he said "sir," I felt rebuffed. That Southern politeness was for strangers, not friends. Finally, I just forgot about my questions and I told him how much I loved "Baby, Let's Play House," but that my favorite moment in the show was when he sang a gospel number.

I hit a nerve. He said it was his favorite part, too. He told me about going as a teenager to gospel concerts that lasted all night, and how he got to know lots of the gospel singers. I asked him why he didn't do more gospel numbers, and he said the Colonel told him people don't want to hear church music. I noticed that Elvis was talking more naturally; he had dropped the "sir." I tried to take advantage of his enthusiasm to suggest we do an interview just about his gospel favorites, telling him it might encourage people to listen to more gospel music. "That's a really good idea," he said.

Then Parker returned and said I needed to give Elvis time to prepare for the second show. In Parker's presence, Elvis went back to using "sir." I later told Grelun Landon about the visit, and he smiled when I said Elvis might even do an interview about gospel. "Not as long as the Colonel's alive," he responded, explaining that he had often heard Elvis talk about going against the Colonel's wishes and then back down at the last minute. "I think Elvis is afraid he'd lose everything if the Colonel wasn't there to guide him."

But what about the Colonel trusting me enough to let me meet Elvis? Grelun smiled again. Between us, Grelun said, it wasn't the Colonel's idea. Elvis mentioned the story I had written to the Colonel and the Colonel implied that he was responsible for the article, that he had been buttering me up. The Colonel said he'd pass on Elvis's best wishes, but Elvis said he'd like to thank me himself. The Colonel wasn't too sure, but he finally relented.

After Elvis was established in Vegas, the Colonel put him on tour and Elvis loved it—at least in the beginning. He was so playful in the matinee concert at the Inglewood Forum in California a few months later that he introduced himself to the eighteen thousand fans by saying, "Hello, I'm Johnny Cash." He also changed the lines in some of the songs and seemed even more animated than ever in his Apache-style jumpsuit with a red rope around his waist. The electricity from the thousands of flashbulbs popping in the opening moments of the show supercharged the atmosphere. He looked invincible. There was no reason to think that Elvis wouldn't be thrilling audiences for a long time. As Willie Nelson wrote, though, it's funny how time slips away.

CHAPTER

FIVE

I didn't know at first what to think of the young Englishman who headlined the Troubadour club in West Hollywood on August 25, 1970, even though my review of the performance would change both of our lives. Rather than coming on stage with the power and personality of a hot new rock act, Elton John sat businesslike at the piano, singing "Your Song," a gentle, beautifully crafted number about the way falling in love can leave you tongue-tied:

> *Anyway, the thing is, what I really mean*
> *Yours are the sweetest eyes, I've ever seen.*

The tone felt wonderfully soothing after the emotional turbulence of the 1960s. Elton's approach, it turned out, was one of the first signs that the creative center of pop music was changing direction in the new decade. There would still be lots of energy and aggression on the scene, but the yearning for a softer tone was also apparent when James Taylor's folk-pop hybrid "Fire and Rain" became an immense hit around the same time as "Your Song."

The remarkable thing about the two records was that neither

had much in common with rock 'n' roll, but they were so embraced by rock fans that the recordings expanded the boundaries of rock. Taken literally, "Fire and Rain" was about loss. But it was also easy to read the opening lines of the second verse—which have Taylor asking Jesus to help him make a stand—as the prayer of a generation seeking to regain its balance and optimism after a decade in which three of the nation's most revered leaders had been assassinated and thousands of other lives had been lost to drugs and the escalating Vietnam War.

Taylor would also grace the Troubadour stage, but Elton was first up, and the engagement proved to be the most celebrated in the club's history.

Owner Doug Weston, who opened the intimate room on Santa Monica Boulevard in the 1960s to take advantage of the folk music boom, had a superb ear for singer-songwriters. A tall, charismatic figure with long, flowing blond hair, Doug delighted in saying that people would often make reservations without even knowing who was playing, and it was no exaggeration. The club's honor roll of artists already included Joni Mitchell, Laura Nyro, and Tim Hardin. Because of Weston's track record, performers were, in many ways, auditioning for the entire record industry when they stepped onto that small wooden stage. Every Tuesday night, industry insiders, including radio station programmers, critics, and concert bookers, showed up to pass judgment. It was an innocent, exciting time when underground FM radio DJs played music they loved rather than first testing it on focus groups or waiting until they saw the record doing well in other cities. There were many times when you could tune in some of the local stations the day after a Troubadour opening and not only hear the act's record, but also the DJ going on at length about what a great show it had been. And the acts didn't just play one night—they played two shows a night for six nights, which meant an entire week of buzz.

Elton's US record company, Uni, was so excited about his prospects that it lobbied Weston for weeks to book the unknown even though the pay was just five hundred dollars for the week. One of Elton's impressive calling cards was that his music publisher was Dick James, who also represented John Lennon and Paul McCartney. The label worked hard to get Elton's music played on key FM stations during the week before the show and enlisted one of its hottest acts, Neil Diamond, to introduce Elton.

After all the buildup, Elton looked like he was in a little over his head as he sat at the piano with a slight, scrubby beard and wearing a long-sleeved T-shirt with "Rock 'n' Roll" written on the front. Backed by Dee Murray on bass and Nigel Olsson on drums, Elton appeared extremely shy and nervous. He kept his eyes on the piano and the microphone in front of him. Someone next to me whispered that Elton had better be a good songwriter, because he certainly wasn't a very compelling performer. After a while, I closed my eyes and just listened to the music. His songs and arrangements touched on the various strains of pop in a way that both summarized what had gone before him and yet was strikingly original. The term "pop-rock" wasn't used much in those days, but Elton's music, greatly aided by Bernie Taupin's lyrics, represented a balance between the accessibility of pop and the energy of rock.

In "Your Song," for instance, Bernie—just twenty years old—wrote the hesitant, unresolved lyrics that most writers would call unfinished. When Elton sang them that night, I wrote some of the words in my notebook. I also was encouraged that another John–Taupin song, "Sixty Years On," showed a willingness to engage a subject rarely touched upon in mainstream pop—aging.

As the show progressed, Elton's nervousness vanished and he put more and more of himself into the vocals and piano playing. Just when the hushed audience seemed in his spell, Elton surprised everyone by plunging into "Burn Down the Mission" with the kind of fury that reminded you of Jerry Lee Lewis or Little Richard. He stood up, kicked away the piano bench, and fell to his knees while pounding on the keys. Suddenly, the Troubadour audience was on its feet. The guy next to me wasn't whispering any longer. He joined in the thunderous applause.

"Rejoice," my *Times* review began. "Rock music, which has been going through a rather uneventful period lately, has a new star. He's Elton John, a 23-year-old Englishman whose United States debut Tuesday night at the Troubadour was, in almost every way, magnificent."

By the end of the six-day engagement, dozens of the most respected figures in pop, including Quincy Jones and Brian Wilson, had stopped by to see this young sensation. The national news magazines, too, called for interviews, and Ed Sullivan's office sent someone by. I was so impressed that I followed Elton to San Francisco, where he played the Troubadour's sister club. It was the first time I had been out of town on a story since the Folsom Prison show, but I convinced the paper that Elton was going to be huge, and I wanted the first interview.

Sitting with Elton and Bernie the following week at a sound check, I thought about how this was the first time I was more experienced at interviewing than my subjects were. Unlike Janis Joplin, Elton was full of energy and eager to talk. Asked to name some of his favorite artists, he went on for several minutes, mentioning a third of the artists I had in my record collection, starting with the Beatles, Dylan, and everyone on Motown. His enthusiasm was evident when he stepped to the stage for the sound check. Normally, sound checks last fifteen to twenty minutes, but Elton spent more than an hour on this one, running through not just his own songs, but also some favorites from childhood and others that were more contemporary—from "Long Tall Sally" and "In the Midnight Hour" to "The Weight" and "Long Black Veil." He was like a human computer of rock 'n' roll. The response that night was again ecstatic.

I went to dinner afterward with Elton, Bernie, and the rest of their tour party. It was my first taste of Indian food, and Elton convinced me to try it spiced so hot it made my eyes water. The mood was celebratory. "Your Song" was already on its way to becoming a radio smash on both pop and rock stations, and the debut album was headed into the Top Ten, where it would remain for weeks.

Elton and Bernie were still full of enthusiasm three years later when they brought a copy of their latest album, *Goodbye Yellow Brick Road,* to my house before it was released, and we listened to every song. He was so intent that he didn't even notice that my fourteen-year-old daughter, Kathy, was taking advantage of the visit to walk some of her friends through the room to prove that Elton was really at our house. Elton's faith in the album was well founded. It spent 103 weeks on the US sales charts.

When Elton returned to the Troubadour in 1975 to celebrate the fifth anniversary of his American debut there, demand for tickets was so great that they were sold through a mail lottery. After all the stories of self-destruction in rock, Elton's joy was all the more refreshing—until I noticed that he seemed downbeat as he sat in a small trailer behind the club after the show.

Uncharacteristically, he didn't want to say hello to all the well-wishers. Elton pulled me aside and said he wanted to tell me something just as a friend. The man who I thought was the anti-Joplin said his life was spinning out of control and that he had tried to commit suicide. All the joy in him seemed to have vanished.

· ·

After the first Elton review, I started getting credited with helping to create a superstar. Managers and record company executives, thinking I had a magic touch, invited me to lunch to pitch their latest discoveries. It was a heady time and I bought into the myth. I went from being just one of the crowd every Tuesday at the Troubadour to someone who was perceived to have the power to jump-start the star-making machinery. When I got stuck in traffic one night, Weston delayed the start of the show until I arrived. He'd also stop by my seat during intermission to ask me who I thought he should book. I mentioned Waylon one night, and sure enough, Waylon's name was soon on the marquee even though Doug had rarely booked a country act before.

With all the attention, I felt increasing pressure to avoid letting hype influence my judgment. I set such high standards for new acts that I ended up panning Cat Stevens because I thought his work was inconsistent. It was an error that Chris Blackwell, the founder of Island Records, never let me forget. The first time we met, Chris, who also signed U2, looked at me bemusedly and said, "Oh, you're the chap who didn't think Cat Stevens had what it takes."

The answer to my search for the Next Big Thing came in a phone call from Kris Kristofferson in 1971. He said he had seen an ex-postman in Chicago and thought he was just about the best young singer-songwriter since Dylan. That was more than enough for me to pick up a pencil and start taking notes. Kris said the writer's name was John

Prine and he was only twenty-four, but that he wrote with the wisdom of someone three times his age. Kris went on to describe every song on Prine's debut album, which was coming out on Atlantic Records. He had already asked Jerry Wexler at Atlantic to send me a copy.

The LP arrived at the house the next day and I put it on around 10:00 p.m., after the kids were in bed, and warned myself not to let Kris's enthusiasm influence me. I didn't stop listening to it until about 3:00 a.m. I had put hundreds of new releases on my turntable during the past year and had been lucky to find even one good song on an album, and here were twelve of them and they were all different: character sketches of lonely young people and lonely old people and Vietnam vets who came home with heroin habits. Against a siren-esque guitar line, Prine sang the chorus to "Sam Stone":

> *There's a hole in Daddy's arm*
> *Where all the money goes*
> *And Jesus Christ died for nothin'*
> *I suppose*

The song ends with Stone's descent.

> *And there's nothing to be done*
> *But trade his house that he bought*
> *On the GI bill*
> *For a flag-draped casket*
> *On a local heroes' hill.*

I phoned Atlantic Records the next day and set up a phone interview with Prine, who had grown up listening to Dylan, Hank Williams, and Woody Guthrie and had been playing clubs for only a few months before Kris came across him. I listened to the album every night for a week before finally writing a two-thousand-word review that ran on the front page of the *Times*'s Sunday entertainment section, an unprecedented spot for a debut album review. I knew that some people might call Prine's voice too ragged, his arrangements too country, and his themes too down. But my guess was a lot of people were just going to call him great.

The piece ran two days before Prine opened at the Troubadour and the engagement was sensational. When I arrived on the first night, Weston was standing outside the club on Santa Monica Boulevard, eager to tell me about all the calls he'd gotten for tickets after my article came out. I could feel the Elton buzz already. On stage, Prine had an inviting, self-effacing manner that went over well with the crowd, and he introduced his songs with winning bits of humor.

There was, however, no repeat of the Elton fireworks.

While John's debut album, *John Prine,* was hailed by critics across the country, radio airplay was minimal and the album only reached No. 154 on the national sales chart. I was still such a believer that I called Asylum Records founder David Geffen and suggested he might want to manage him. David tried to buy John's management contract, but the manager would only sell 50 percent of it. David didn't want to pick up any new partners, so he passed. David did later sign John to Asylum, but it was too late. Radio stations, always the key to mass acceptance, had already made up their minds on John. He was a cult artist, and therefore not for them. John went on to have a respectable career and win Grammys in the folk category.

I learned my lesson. I didn't have a magic wand. I couldn't predict, much less ordain, stardom. I now knew that I should concentrate on looking for great new artists, regardless of their commercial potential.

CHAPTER
SIX

thought the John Prine experience would tip off record companies that I couldn't "make" a star, but the courting continued because they respected Prine's talent and were impressed that I would write so much about someone who was a commercial long shot. Meanwhile, Elton's success continued to spread and just about every story written about him mentioned the impact of my review. I felt myself closing the gap between writers at the other publications that I saw as rivals. I beat *Rolling Stone,* the *New York Times,* and the *Washington Post* to Elton and to Prine, and I kept searching for new acts, going out to clubs four or five times a week and then listening to new albums when I got home.

In my search, I heard about a festival that reminded me that I was ignoring one of the great talent pools. In March 1972, Willie Nelson was hosting a three-day event outside of Austin, Texas, that also featured Waylon Jennings, Charlie Rich, and Kris Kristofferson. Until then, I had thought of Willie and Waylon as simply country acts, but the more I thought about the lineup, the more I began to see how these artists might appeal to pop and rock fans as well. That was

Willie's goal. He had gotten tired of fighting the establishment in Nashville and returned to Texas, where he found his music appealed to both country music fans and young rock fans—a sort of redneck–longhair coalition. The festival promoters were hoping for sixty thousand people each day. My problem was getting the paper to send me to Texas. Travel budgets were tight.

Just as I had often turned to David Geffen for suggestions, I also found Bill Graham, the imaginative San Francisco concert promoter, to be a great sounding board. Whenever I went to one of his shows, I ended up backstage talking to him. During one visit, we reminisced about a mutual favorite, Janis Joplin, and I mentioned that it was my profile of Janis that had convinced the *Times* to hire me as the paper's first full-time rock critic. Bill smiled. "The Janis story may have contributed, but the reason they wanted a full-time rock critic was Woodstock. Once businessmen around the country started seeing photos of three hundred thousand rock fans huddled together in the rain, they wanted to reach that market."

When I put together a memo on the Austin festival, I remembered Bill's words. I ended the note with the words, "It might just be the country music Woodstock." Approval was granted.

After all my talk about Willie and Waylon and a cultural revolution, my heart sank when I got to the 240-acre Dripping Springs site on the first day of the festival and found not sixty thousand, but about six hundred people. That was four people per acre. So much for the Woodstock of country music that I had promised the paper. But then I remembered an old lesson from journalism school about the reporter whose first assignment was covering the wedding of the mayor's daughter. He comes back to the newsroom about an hour later and says he's going to lunch. When the editor asks him about the story, the reporter says, "Oh, the wedding was cancelled at the last minute, so there is no story." Sometimes "no story" is the best story, and that was the case at Dripping Springs. Besides, I was convinced by the third day of the festival—when the crowd had "swelled" to about 7,500—that something significant was happening in the Texas hill country.

During Willie's and Kris's sets especially, I could feel an unlikely bonding taking place between country and rock fans over songs that spoke about yearning for individuality in a society that was encouraging greater and greater conformity. And sure enough, the Dripping Springs experiment was just ahead of its time. In future years, Willie's annual Reunion festival would attract nearly a hundred thousand fans.

I got more insight into the music scene at a private party hosted on the final night by University of Texas football coach Darrell Royal, a huge fan of Nelson and country music. I was invited by Kris and soon found myself listening as he, Willie, Waylon, and Charlie took turns singing one of their songs and then passing the guitar to the next writer, who would then sing one of his. Kris was the biggest star in the room that night, but within three years, Charlie would have the No. 1 country song in the nation, "Behind Closed Doors," and Waylon and Willie would be well on their way to Country Music Hall of Fame careers.

Late in the evening, Waylon's wife, Jessi Colter, a singer and songwriter herself, took me into the kitchen so she could talk to me about Waylon. She said he needed some help. My first thought was drugs. Waylon had given me some pills earlier, after I had joked about how hard it was to keep up with everything going on during the weekend. I figured a couple of the pills wouldn't hurt, so I took them and threw the rest down the toilet. But Jessi had other problems on her mind. "Bob, he's so beat down by Nashville that I think he's going to quit," she said. "He just can't take it anymore."

From my vantage point, everything was going fine with Waylon's career. He was making great records; he had won a Grammy for his version of "MacArthur Park," and his recording of "Good Hearted Woman" was a country smash. But Jessi said he was constantly fighting with the people at his label, RCA, about what songs to record and what musicians to use on the records. He also felt that RCA was putting less and less into promoting his records as a way of punishing him.

On my way to the car, I ran into Waylon and, trying to appear casual, asked him how things were going. He said everything was going fine except with the record company. He went through some grievances and I sympathized. I urged him to call me if I could ever help. Then I headed for the hotel, where I stared at the ceiling for hours. Around dawn, the pills must have finally worn off. For the first time in three days, I fell asleep—and slept right through my wake-up call, missing my flight home. I vowed to take no more uppers.

Waylon called a few weeks later to say he was working on a new album titled *Ladies Love Outlaws.* He asked if I would do the liner notes. The *Times*'s editors didn't want its critics doing liner notes because they thought it was a conflict of interest and I agreed, but I also wanted to do anything that might help Waylon, so I said yes. I doubted that anyone there would see the album anyway.

Things were looking better for Waylon a couple of years later when I ran into him in Las Vegas. He was just coming off two straight No. 1 country singles and he was having a hard time figuring out which song should be his next single. He asked if I'd listen to the album with him and pick a track. The tune that caught my ear was a country-rock exercise called "Rainy Day Woman." Waylon liked it, but thought it might be a little too raucous for the country audience. I said, "Waylon, we're both country fans, aren't we? If we like it, why shouldn't other country fans?" RCA later took his suggestion and released the song, and I was excited to see it go all the way to No. 2 on the country charts. For years, he got a kick out of asking me when I was going to pick his next hit.

· ·

Besides watching country, I also kept up with what was happening in R&B and soul music. Two of my favorites, Otis Redding and Sam Cooke, were both gone before I started writing at the *Times,* and I felt that Ray Charles and James Brown—both essential artists—were beyond their creative peaks. Curtis Mayfield was another great R&B star who did much of his most important work with the Impressions in the 1960s, but he continued to move forward as a solo artist in the 1970s, and I spent considerable time with him around the time of the *Superfly* success in 1972. Curtis was near James Brown's status culturally, though his vocals were mere whispers compared to James's screams. As an African American growing up in Chicago in the 1940s and 1950s, Curtis knew about the dehumanizing sting of discrimination, but he chose to deliver a consistently positive message—as if he had personally seen the promised land of the Reverend Martin Luther King Jr.'s sermons and wanted to share the vision in his songs.

I sensed a lot of Curtis in another young artist whom I saw for the first time in 1972, when he opened for Joe Cocker at the eighteen-thousand-seat Inglewood Forum: Stevie Wonder. I had enjoyed Stevie's early Motown hits, but I didn't think of him as an important artist until that concert, when his music showed far more funky and progressive touches than the early records had. Some fans sitting near me weren't happy with Stevie's new direction, but I thought it was a major breakthrough and arranged to meet him a few days later at a Hollywood coffee shop. Of course, he was late. Stevie was always late for interviews.

The plan was to meet at 3:00, but there was no sign of him by 3:45. Just when I was about to give up, a young man in a suit walked into the nearly empty restaurant and headed to my table. He said Stevie was just wrapping up a few things in the studio and would be on his way soon. It was almost 6:00 when a large sedan pulled into the parking lot and I watched Stevie get out, assisted by a couple of men. They proceeded through the front door and headed down the aisle toward me. Stevie's head was turning from side to side the way it frequently does when he's on stage, but there was no expression until he sat down opposite me. Then, he gave me this big, disarming smile and said, "Hello, I'm Johnny Cash." I didn't know how he knew I was a Cash fan, but the smile washed away my frustration. Stevie exuded warmth, much like Cash. His aides took a table near us and Stevie's face lit up again when I gave the waitress my order. He asked me to say something else, and I didn't know what to make of it, so I just started reading things from the menu.

"Milton!" Stevie finally said, again smiling. "You sound like my brother." He called his assistants over to hear my voice. "See if Robert's voice doesn't sound like Milton's." The aides broke out laughing. "You're right, Stevie."

Stevie, just twenty-one, had recently released *The Music of My Mind,* an album for which he handled the writing, production, and even most of the instrumental chores himself, but he said I should expect even more of his next album, *Talking Book.* He again turned his head toward his aides and asked them to bring him a test pressing of the album. "I'm not supposed to be giving these out, but I'd like your opinion." Then he wrote his phone number on a piece of paper and said to call any time, day or night, because he was often in the studio until the wee hours. When I got home, I played the album and was immediately impressed by the range and craft as Stevie moved from the lushly romantic "You Are the Sunshine of My Life" to the ridiculously funky "Superstition," both of which would be No. 1 singles. I phoned the number and was surprised by the voice that answered. It didn't sound like Stevie at all; it sounded like me. It was Milton, and he said he'd give my message to Stevie. I didn't know if Milton had answered Stevie's phone or if Stevie, as a gag, had given me Milton's number so I'd be surprised by hearing my "own" voice when he answered.

When *Talking Book* was released, it earned Stevie enormous respect. On a roll, he topped that album nine months later with *Innervisions,* a collection featuring the socially charged "Higher Ground" and "Living for the City." The LP won a Grammy for album of the year, and Stevie returned in the summer of 1974 with another album, *Fulfillingness' First Finale,* that would also win him the Grammy for album of the year.

I was spending a lot of time with Stevie by this point and enjoyed him immensely. He was open and playful. He loved to walk into rooms and make a big fuss about switching on the light—or sometimes switching it off—as if it made a difference in his sightless world. There was a quiet, almost spiritual aura about him as he spoke passionately about social ideals and the inherent goodness of people. When *Songs in the Key of Life* was finally finished in 1976, it consisted of two full-length LPs and a four-track bonus record. I was worried that he had lost his perspective. Usually, double albums were signs of egos out of control.

My first surprise when I got to the studio to listen to the album was that Stevie was already there. I kidded him about being prompt and he said he hoped I didn't think he was being rude when he was late for interviews. "When I don't make it somewhere on time, it's not that I'm trying to be late," he said. "It's just that I'm usually in the studio trying to get what's in my head onto tape and I never know how long that is going to take. But the music has to come first."

The record was the culmination of everything Stevie had done, combining the fluid, appealing textures of the early Motown sound and the social concerns and inventive tones of his adult years. He would never again reach the heights he did on that album, but he was at that moment the consummate musician in all of pop. In the press-room after he won his third album-of-the-year Grammy, I went up to Stevie and congratulated him. He smiled, put his arm around me, and said, "Milton!"

CHAPTER
SEVEN

N obody leaves here until Smith & Wesson says so," Phil Spector declared on one of the late nights I spent with him in his Spanish-style, forty-room mansion just off Sunset Boulevard. The mansion and his lifestyle invited comparisons, much to his chagrin, to the character Norma Desmond in the film Sunset Boulevard. Desmond, a star of silent films who was discarded by Hollywood when talkies arrived, spent decades behind the walls of her mansion fantasizing about making a grand comeback. No one hanging out at Spector's thought that he would actually use the gun he waved in the air, but I never saw anyone leave until he gave the okay, which sometimes meant waiting until 6:00 a.m.

I had met Phil at a party that Doug Weston held at his house in early 1972, and Phil had given me a hug. He had read my review of John Lennon's *Plastic Ono Band,* which he produced, and that was apparently enough to allow me temporary access to his world. He was fiercely loyal to John, campaigning tirelessly against a move by the federal government to deport him for alleged anti-American leanings.

A few days after the party, Phil's secretary called to invite me to Phil's house so we could get to know each other.

Phil was the oddball genius who created a series of records in the 1960s, including "Be My Baby" and "He's a Rebel," that expressed the exuberance, rebelliousness, and loneliness of youth with an unprecedented vitality and sense of spectacle. Tom Wolfe dubbed him the First Tycoon of Teen in a 1960s profile and also told of how Phil once demanded a jet be stopped during takeoff because he had a sudden premonition it was going to crash. The thing that made Spector's story especially compelling was that he was a rebel himself—he made all his hits while thumbing his nose at the recording industry. This cocky, five-foot-seven producer intimidated people and no one liked that, so the industry was gleeful when the hits suddenly stopped for Spector's label, Philles, in the mid-1960s. He eventually reentered the pop scene, producing hits for Lennon and George Harrison, but he was no longer the star. He was now merely a hired hand.

There wasn't a lot known about Spector's world in the early 1970s except that he was reclusive, drank too much, and—like Norma Desmond—kept talking about the big hit that would return him to the top. He lived with his wife, Ronnie, the former lead singer of the Ronettes, one of his most successful groups, and George Brand, a bodyguard with the uncanny ability to sense Phil's moods and step in before trouble erupted. During the many nights I spent with Phil at the house or in the studio, the only time I saw Ronnie was when we all went to the local premiere of *The Concert for Bangladesh* film in 1972 in Westwood. Otherwise, she stayed upstairs, out of sight, which was a bit eerie. She would later describe her life with Phil as akin to being a prisoner in her own house. Though Phil never mentioned it, Ronnie filed divorce papers just a few months after the film premiere.

Phil would sometimes disappear for half an hour without any explanation during my visits to the house. In those moments, George would usually stop by the living room to see if I wanted to watch television or read some magazines. The house, surrounded by a high electric fence, was immaculate. Except for the steady bubbling of the large, dome-shaped aquarium, it was silent in the big room. Souvenirs were everywhere. The long entry hall was lined with old newspaper clippings about Spector and his heroes: Lenny Bruce,

Muhammad Ali, the Kennedys, and the Reverend Martin Luther King Jr. On the table near one couch was a book containing the *New York Herald Tribune* article by Wolfe that had helped to shape Spector's eccentric image. Phil had a good sense of humor about his bizarre role. When I asked once if the Howard Hughes of Rock title he'd been saddled with for his reclusive and sometimes bizarre behavior was accurate, he responded with a smile, "Yeah, I'd have to say it was pretty perceptive."

. . . .

As soon as I started working at the paper, people warned me not to get too close to artists because it could make it difficult to review their work and you can never really tell if the "friendship" is genuine. Even so, I felt there was much value in getting to know some of the most important artists beyond what you can glean in the hour or so you have to interview them. Spector and, later, Lennon were perfect examples. The relationship with Lennon—and it never approached anything like a daily or even weekly tie—came about naturally. I liked him and enjoyed his company. It was different with Spector. I thought he was one of the industry's true geniuses, and that's a powerful attraction. However bruised his psyche, Phil had a bold way of looking at music, employing musicians and songwriters with a fearlessness that enabled him to overcome the insecurities in his head. Once he lost that fearlessness, he lost his magic. Deep inside, I sensed, he knew it.

Phil would be especially edgy when we went out to dinner. He would talk politely for an hour or more, but at some point he often would glance at someone at another table and whisper to me that there might be trouble. On a couple of occasions, he started shouting at patrons. Once he came back from the restroom agitated and asked George for his gun. He wanted to teach some guy a lesson. In these moments, George would gently place his arms around Phil and speak to him in little more than a whisper, slowly calming him down.

At the house, Phil was terrific company some nights, especially when we were alone. He played old records to show how he developed a love of music and how he got some of the ideas behind his wall-of-sound technique. He could have had hits by just using one or two ideas per record, but Phil didn't just want hits. He wanted to be seen as the

Orson Welles of the music business—and he was just that in the 1960s to the biggest bands in the world. The Beatles, the Rolling Stones, and, especially, the Beach Boys' Brian Wilson were in awe of him. Phil would also tell stories about how he had secretly produced some of Elvis's records, but I could never confirm them.

Things would be less fun when he drank, usually wine, and a few times called women on the phone. Even though it was often midnight, he'd tell them he wanted to see them and they'd arrive at the house a few minutes later. At first I assumed the women were prostitutes, but I never saw any money exchanged and nothing sexual happened while I was present. It seemed he had known most of them for years, and some were the daughters of famous actors or film executives. The more he drank, the more insulting he became, making crude remarks about them and women in general.

I wondered why his guests would accept such treatment, but Phil seemed to have some kind of hold on them—maybe they had seen another side of him or maybe, like me, they were fascinated by his celebrity or thought they could help him. I used to dread it when he'd make the midnight calls because I knew the evening would change— that the talk would no longer be about music.

The whole thing felt like a ritual. After a couple of hours, the women would say it was late and they had to go. Then Phil would pour some more wine, and the talk would continue. Eventually, the women would start walking toward the front door, and Phil would often rush between them and the exit, sometimes carrying the gun. Once he opened a rear door and called his snarling guard dogs, delighting when the animals would scare his nervous guests. There would be gentle squabbling before he would finally walk over, gently kiss the women on the cheek, and say goodnight.

Phil talked often about making a comeback and showing everyone how they were wrong to think his career was over. He spoke vaguely about going into the studio with someone like Elvis or Bob Dylan. Some nights, he even seemed to believe it. When we were alone, Phil made it to 3:00 a.m. some mornings and all the way to 6:00 a.m. on others before George would mercifully step in and lead him up the stairs.

Despite the eccentric behavior, no one was ever hurt, so I was shocked when Phil was arrested in 2003 on charges of murdering actress Lana Clarkson in his Alhambra mansion (and later convicted of second-degree murder).

Just when I was getting weary of our meetings, Phil greeted me at the door of the house with good news. John Lennon was coming to town to make an album of old rock 'n' roll hits and Phil was going to produce it. On this night, Phil was warm and witty. He didn't invite any women over and he didn't even bring out the wine. He was already thinking about songs he wanted to use in the session. "You've got to come," he said. "You got to meet John."

· ·

Months before I met John, Yoko headlined a benefit concert in the fall of 1973 at Jack Murphy Stadium in San Diego and I drove down, hoping to talk to her. Most of the ten thousand fans, too, were hoping that John would be a special guest. There was even a rumor that George Harrison would show up, but a concert sponsor told me that neither ex-Beatle would be there. John was still in New York, where he and Yoko lived. I wondered how the fans would react to his absence. Many Beatles fans blamed Yoko for the breakup of the band, and they might use the concert to take out their resentment.

I sent word to Yoko's dressing room that I would like to speak to her, though I didn't think the odds were good that she would respond. She and John rarely did interviews. But she came out of the room to greet me. "That was a wonderful story you wrote about John," she said, referring to an article published nearly a year earlier that criticized the government's attempt to deport Lennon. The immigration service said the issue was John's misdemeanor conviction for possession of marijuana four years earlier in England, but many suspected the matter was related to John's outspoken political views.

"We both appreciated it so much," Yoko said. "Isn't it horrible what the government is trying to do?"

From all I had read, I had expected Yoko to be aggressive and demanding. I was delighted by her open, friendly manner. She even seemed delicate and vulnerable in the minutes before taking the stage. Knowing the audience might be resentful, I felt a bit protective. As we spoke in the hallway, a fan headed toward us. The first question was

"Is John here?" When she said he was still in New York, the fan reached in his pocket and pulled out a cassette tape. "I work with a singer," he said. "Can you give this tape to your *husband*?"

Yoko said she couldn't take the tape for legal reasons, and then gently took my arm. "Come," she said. "Let's go inside where we can visit."

Yoko didn't waste time on small talk. She went straight to the heart of the issue at hand—in this case, her public image: "I know some people still think I'm a joke, but what am I supposed to do? I just have to keep going. It was difficult making the first album because even some of the engineers said, 'She won't be able to do it,' that kind of feeling. Now I think they understand what I'm doing. They don't make silly remarks anymore."

On stage moments later, Yoko was anything but timid. Backed by a band that included an old Spector favorite, Jim Keltner, on drums, she was a warrior. She moved about with a striking intensity, frequently punching her fist into the air to punctuate the song's emotion. Applause was modest, however, and after a few numbers, a noticeable exodus began. I didn't hear anyone yell "Where's John," but there was some scattered booing at the end. She didn't return to the stage for an encore.

Yes, she said backstage, she had heard the booing. "I don't mind it," she said. "I felt sorry for the musicians, though." Then she headed out the door for the long ride to Los Angeles. "Thank you again for what you wrote," she said as she stepped into the car. "John wants to thank you himself some day."

I didn't know then that John and Yoko were having problems in their marriage and that when I would finally meet John a few months later, he would be in Los Angeles on his own.

CHAPTER
EIGHT

John came to town in late 1973 to record the oldies album with Phil and to promote his new solo album, *Mind Games,* which he had produced himself. I interviewed him at the Bel Air home of record producer Lou Adler, a chief force behind the Monterey Pop Festival. May Pang, who introduced herself as John's personal assistant, answered the door and took me to the patio where John was waiting. He was wearing jeans and a sweater-vest over his shirt and he walked toward me enthusiastically. "Well, hello at last," he said with a warm smile.

He made me feel at ease as quickly as that. In interviewing rock stars, I was often surprised by how guarded many of them were. You could see them weighing their answers, trying to imagine how the public might react. But John, like Yoko, spoke so openly and fully that I couldn't imagine him holding much back.

"Phil tells me you're a big Elvis fan," he said.

We ended up spending so much time talking about Elvis and other favorites from the 1950s that I was afraid we weren't going to get to the Beatles and his solo career. I was particularly interested in his thoughts on the *Plastic Ono Band* album; the songs struck me as being so personal.

"I always took the songs personally, whether it was 'In My Life' or 'Help!'" he said. "To me, I always wrote about myself. Very few of the completely Lennon songs weren't in the first person. I'm a first-person journalist. I find it hard, though I occasionally do it, to write about, you know, 'Freddie went up the mountain and Freddie came back.' And even that is really about you."

John said he actually preferred *Plastic Ono Band* to its follow-up, *Imagine,* even though the latter sold more copies and got generally better reviews. "I was a bit surprised by the reaction to *Mother,*" he said, referring to *Plastic Ono Band* by his own title for it. "I thought, 'Can't they see how nice it is?'" So, John said, he went back into the studio and wrote new songs about many of the same themes, only this time he put on some strings and other production touches that made the message more accessible. That's why, he said, he privately called the *Imagine* album *Mother with Chocolate.*

The interview didn't run in the *Times* until the album was actually in the stores several weeks later. In the meantime, Phil invited me to one of the sessions for the oldies project. They had been going on for some weeks and the word was that they were pretty raucous, even drunken affairs. On the night I stopped by the studio, the liquor flowed freely. John, a gob of cake in his hand, chased Phil around the control booth while those around them danced to John's just-recorded version of an early Elvis recording, "Just Because."

Pleased with the way the album was going, Phil proclaimed they had already come up with eight potential No. 1 singles. Overhearing him, John feigned modesty. "Well, maybe five."

But John wasn't all playfulness. He had sharp words for one of the studio employees and insulted a record company guest. This wild John was a lot different from the charming guy I had met at Adler's house, and I hoped the rude, drunken behavior was an aberration. But I kept hearing reports, including one about Phil firing a pistol one night and others about a tipsy John out on the town with his buddies and how he sometimes drank as much as a bottle of vodka a day. The first time I saw him this way away from the studio was at the Troubadour, where I was reviewing the opening of R&B singer Ann Peebles, who had a hit single, "I Can't Stand the Rain."

I didn't know John was in the club until he was in the middle of a big commotion. He was so drunk that he had wrapped a sanitary napkin around his head. When one of the waitresses tried to quiet him, he shouted, "Don't you know who I am?" Her answer was repeated the next day in all the record company offices and later in lots of magazine articles: "To me, you're just some asshole—with a Kotex on his head." A bouncer escorted John and his party out onto Santa Monica Boulevard.

Eventually, John returned to New York with May and spent weeks trying unsuccessfully to get Phil to give him the session's master tapes so he could finish the album himself. By then, I was beginning to hear reports about a strain between John and Yoko and the suggestion that his relationship with May was more than simply professional. In the middle of all this, Spector's production company issued a "news bulletin" that Phil had been involved in a near-fatal auto accident while traveling to Phoenix for a few days of rest. The statement said that extensive surgery had been performed and he was in critical condition. I didn't hear from him for months.

. . . .

John was in a terrific mood when he returned from New York a few months later. I interviewed him at the Beverly Wilshire Hotel, where he was staying with May. I mentioned the drunken night at the Troubadour and he broke out laughing, which was typical of him. He was quick to see the absurdity in situations, especially those involving him. "What's funny about the whole thing," he said with a grin, "is that all these old show-biz writers—not just here, but also in England—are always writing about the good old days when Errol Flynn or somebody used to punch out the press or something. But a couple of rockers get rocky one night and all hell breaks loose. It's all over the papers. We even had some people saying the government was right, they ought to kick us out of the country."

John was only supposed to be in town for a few days, but the trip was extended and May phoned one day to say that John would like me to join him for dinner. When I got to the hotel, I figured he'd have a limo waiting downstairs. But John, wearing blue jeans and a black T-shirt, suggested that I drive, and we were soon off to a nearby Chinese restaurant, where we spent a couple of hours talking about Elvis, naturally.

Back at the hotel, he told a story about how he once sat all morning on an upstairs bed at his country estate in England, consumed with trying to write a song and not being able to come up with any ideas. As invincible as each of the Beatles seemed, John said, he constantly battled the pressures of the expectations surrounding the group. Finally, the story went, he said, "Screw it," and he headed downstairs muttering to himself, "I'm nowhere . . . a real nowhere man." He stopped and returned to the room and wrote the song that bears that title. "You see?" he said. "You just write what you feel even if you don't know where it'll take you."

Around 11:30, John turned on Johnny Carson's TV show and ordered corn flakes and cream from room service. He turned the sound down on the TV and stirred the corn flakes and cream with his spoon in an almost ritualistic fashion before taking a bite.

I didn't think much of it until the same thing happened the next time we returned to the hotel after dinner. This time I asked what was up with the corn flakes.

He smiled.

As a child in Liverpool during World War II, he explained, you could never get cream, so it was a special treat. He took another bite and gave an exaggerated sigh to underscore just how sweet it tasted.

The mention of Liverpool made John nostalgic. I already knew a little about John's early days, but it was fascinating hearing him tell the story. John was born in 1940—a year after me—and he was raised by his aunt Mimi after his parents broke up when he was about five. His mother, Julia, started seeing another man who had children of his own and didn't want another one around. John loved Mimi dearly, but he also longed for his mother, who lived only a few miles away.

I told John I could relate because of my parents' early divorce and staying with my grandparents on the farm. I'd race down to the gravel road in front of the farmhouse every Friday afternoon, squinting into the distance and hoping the next car was my mom's, bringing her home for the weekend from her job as secretary to the commanding officer at an army base in the area. Once she got home, she showered me with so much affection that she seemed to be trying to compensate for having to be away and for the absence of my father. Even after she remarried, she continued to make me the focus of her life. Whatever my problems were at school or on the playground, I always knew I'd have my mother's love to fall back on.

John picked up on my story.

During his teens, he said, just around the time he had formed the Quarrymen skiffle group he had begun seeing more of his mother and had gotten the feeling she was trying to make up for all the years of her absence from his life. She was especially excited about the band, and John treasured their time together. But his mother was hit and killed by a motorist while walking to a bus stop. His mother had been taken from him twice. He was seventeen.

I looked down at the empty bowl of corn flakes and tried to imagine not having my mother—and I was in my thirties.

Like so many of us had in the 1950s, John had thought that rock 'n' roll fame would make everything right in his life, but even after his success he continued to search for someone or something to make his world seem complete. That was the theme of the *Plastic Ono Band* album. The very first song, "Mother," started with him screaming, "Mother, you had me, but I never had you / I wanted you, but you didn't want me." It continued, "Father, you left me, but I never left you / I needed you, but you didn't need me."

He found that missing foundation in Yoko, which is why she became more important to him than even the Beatles. In "God," a later song on the record, he again screams, "I don't believe in Elvis. I don't believe in Zimmerman [meaning Bob Dylan]. I don't believe in Beatles. I just believe in me. Yoko and me. That's reality."

As he spoke, I could understand why John felt so adrift. Until that night, I had assumed he had separated from Yoko and was involved in a new relationship with May, but he said that Yoko had pretty much demanded a break in their relationship. He was clearly still in love with her. Without her, he had no shield against the pressures of the rock 'n' roll world and his own depression. He knew his last two albums, *Some Time in New York City* and *Mind Games,* hadn't been among his best, and he welcomed the chance to work with Spector as "a Ronette," just singing old rock 'n' roll and leaving the rest to Phil. When that ended in disappointment, he produced *Walls and Bridges* on his own, and he thought it was a respectable work. But he still wasn't satisfied.

There was no sign of self-pity in John's remarks, more of a sense of surprise that he couldn't figure out how to help himself. That made it all the more disheartening when he said he thought he had been almost suicidal on some kind of a subconscious level during his earlier time in Los Angeles. He said he was no different from the millions of others who use alcohol to block out depression. He hadn't wanted to feel or see anything.

The one thing that pulled him out of it was getting busy on a new album. Now that it was finished, however, he was afraid of drifting back into bad habits. He acknowledged the dangers of following in the paths of Jimi Hendrix, Brian Jones, Janis Joplin, and other casualties of rock 'n' roll excess. He even mentioned the sadness of the Phil Spector spectacle. "There are danger signs everywhere, but all of us in rock keep acting like we are indestructible," he said. "Dylan had the right idea when he said, 'Fuck it,' and went up to Woodstock." Rock 'n' roll was worth a lot, he said, but it wasn't worth dying for.

John pointed out how Elvis, too, had had to deal with the loss of his mother, who died soon after he joined the army. Elvis became so addicted to, well, being Elvis that he ended up destroying almost everything in his life, including his marriage. Even his daughter, Lisa Marie, whom he adored, wasn't enough to shake him from his dangerous lifestyle. For most of the evening, John had been talking in the past tense, as if the worst of his troubles were behind him. But there was still a longing about him. He was a man in search of a life raft.

. . . .

It was only a few weeks after the corn flakes with John that I met Paul McCartney for the first time. What struck me immediately was that he had his own security blanket in Linda. They were in Los Angeles with their three daughters to attend the Academy Awards ceremony, where "Live and Let Die," the theme for one of the James Bond films, was nominated for best song. They were staying at the Beverly Hills Hotel and were at the pool when I arrived.

Linda was subject to almost as much ridicule as Yoko—not for breaking up the Beatles, but for what was alleged to be ruthless ambition. The daughter of a prominent New York attorney, Linda Eastman had used her ties as a rock photographer to get close to the stars, and Paul was her big catch. At least that's the way the gossip went. Her public image was further damaged by her portrayal by the British pop press as domineering. She went everywhere with Paul and even ended up in his new band, Wings, the buzz continued. I didn't know if any of this was true, but I did notice that she was close by Paul's side during the interview—freely interrupting to add to or to clarify things he said. But I wasn't really concerned with Linda; my focus was on Paul and, to my delight, he greeted me as warmly as John had. "Live and Let Die" had lost to "The Way We Were" in the Oscar competition, but he seemed supremely happy, breaking away from our conversation frequently to point out something to one of his young daughters or to remind Linda that they had to see so-and-so before they left town.

I spent nearly two hours with Paul and I could see that he wanted Linda by his side; he credited her with giving him the confidence to move on with his solo career when he was in a period of extreme self-doubt, and said it was his idea for her to be in Wings. "You've got to remember I've always been on stage with friends, whether it was the Quarry men or the Beatles, and Linda is my best friend and I'm sure the idea of her standing on stage with me was a big reason behind asking her to join the band," he said.

Heading home, I couldn't help but compare John and Paul. In some ways, Paul was more personable. If I had met them together, he might have struck me as the friendlier of the two, but, for all of his outward openness, Paul was much more guarded, more worried about what people thought of him than John was. With John, nothing seemed off-limits. This helped to explain the difference between their songs during their solo years. Paul wrote some catchy tunes and he occasionally touched you emotionally, but he rarely revealed himself.

I could see how they had made a great team: Paul's melodic flair and eagerness to reach out to an audience coupled with John's intensity, wit, and unfailing honesty as a writer. In the same way, you could see how Linda, with her easygoing, free-spirited nature and an eager-to-please quality of her own, and Yoko, the far more intense and artistically driven force, were each the ideal mate for the respective ex-Beatles.

· ·

I was delighted a few months after John's return to New York to hear from his close friend Elliot Mintz that John and Yoko had run into each other at an Elton John concert at Madison Square Garden and were back together. Elton had supplied the backing vocal on John's recording of the "Whatever Gets You Thru the Night" single. Though it was one of the flimsiest songs John ever wrote, the rowdy, upbeat tune was his first No. 1 single in the United States since his Beatles days.

Even John probably saw the dynamics involved: The chief reason the single went to No. 1 was that Elton was so hot that disc jockeys couldn't wait to get their hands on new material by him. Elton sang on the record out of friendship, but he made John promise him that if the record went to No. 1, John would join him on stage at Madison Square Garden to sing it. Hoping to play the role of matchmaker, Elton privately invited Yoko to the show. The meeting backstage led to the "house husband" period, when John would do something as revolutionary as some of the music he had made with the Beatles.

I thought about him often, wondering how he was doing in finding something that came close to the comfort and warmth that those bowls of corn flakes provided. It was easy for me to care about him, not just because of the intimacy and grace of his music, but because of the disarming way he revealed himself. If Janis's music had been shaped by desperation, John's was the product of longing and need. He was a believer, and he was smart enough to know when he was getting too close to the edge.

FAVORITE ROAD TRIPS

There are so many songs about traveling. A central theme of both country music and the blues, the sense of wanderlust came naturally to rock 'n' roll. A song Billie Joe Shaver wrote with Willie Nelson in mind says it all: Travel with freedom. I've traveled enough to earn a million-mile frequent-flyer gold card from American Airlines, and I've never lost that feeling of being free, except, maybe, once when my flight was stuck on the runway for six hours in Chicago.

Travel helped me understand the lure of pop music around the world. In Israel, I met a shop owner who was saving his money in hopes of someday going to Graceland. When I told him I had been there, his eyes opened wide and he said, "Can you touch Elvis's grave?"

Here are some of my favorite journeys.

Creedence Clearwater Revival in Europe, Fall 1971

Creedence was my favorite American band at the start of the 1970s. John Fogerty's songs combined colorful regional mythology with social commentary. "Fortunate Son" was framed in a fiery, blue-collar perspective that influenced generations of musicians, including Bruce Springsteen and the Clash. John liked a profile I did of the band and he invited me to join Creedence on the second half of a brief European tour. I was doubly excited because it was my first time on the road with a band and my first trip to Europe.

I joined John, drummer Doug Clifford, and bass player Stu Cook in Berlin and accompanied them to Hamburg the next morning in their private, six-passenger Learjet. On the flight, I wondered what I was getting myself into in this world of "sex, drugs, and rock 'n' roll." Drugs were out for me, but even though I was married, I told myself that if anything else happened it would be undertaken in the spirit of research. I was so shy, however, that I just smiled haplessly at the groupies prowling the backstage halls in Hamburg. Creedence wasn't nearly as outrageous as lots of bands at the time, but the crew was quick to hook up with the girls. I usually headed right back to the hotel after the shows to work on my tour story. Besides dispatches for the *Times,* I also wrote my first article for *Rolling Stone.*

By the time we got to Copenhagen, the crew was kidding me about spending so much time with my typewriter. Two members of the entourage told me not to be surprised if a stranger knocked on my door that night. And sure enough, around 1:00 a.m., a lovely young woman showed up. I had no idea what was going on. If she wasn't a groupie, I didn't want to insult her. We mostly stared at each other and made small talk about music and life in Copenhagen. After an hour, she said she had to get up early for work, so she'd better head home. I walked her downstairs and watched as she got into a taxi.

Creedence broke up soon after the tour and relations between John and the others were still so bitter two decades later that he refused to let them join him in playing Creedence songs at the Rock and Roll Hall of Fame induction ceremony in 1993. Doug called me to complain that I hadn't chastised John for his snub in my story about the induction. He said that he and Stu were hurt that I always took John's side in stories about Creedence. In one final shot at me, he solved for me the mystery of the Copenhagen date: "We felt so sorry for you on the tour that we arranged for that girl to go to your room," he said. "And she wasn't cheap!"

The Rolling Stones in Texas, Summer 1975

Mick Jagger didn't just excite audiences during the group's 1969 and 1972 tours, he frightened them. Whether Mick was whipping the floor with a belt during the sexual aggression of "Midnight Rambler" or celebrating with the lustful "Honky Tonk Woman," he spoke to a primal side of us that could be alarming. At the Inglewood Forum in 1969, hundreds rushed the stage, stepping over folding chairs with such force they left some crushed in their wake. At Altamont, drugs flowed freely in the crowd and a young fan near the stage was stabbed to death by a member of the motorcycle gang that was handling security. The word from the band's publicist on these tours was that Mick wasn't doing any interviews, and it was almost a relief. The Stones' world seemed so lawless that I couldn't even imagine sitting down with them.

That press blackout changed in 1975 when Paul Wasserman, a former movie publicist, took over the Stones account. Mick was tired of all the "bad boy" press, and he wanted Paul to help him assume a more refined image. But it took awhile for Mick to change his ways. Paul arranged for me to interview Mick after the show in San Antonio, the second stop on the tour, but when we walked into the dressing room, Mick said a business meeting had come up. He said he'd call Paul as soon as he was free.

When the phone still hadn't rung at 2:00 a.m., Paul was suspicious and came up with plan B. He marched me to Mick's hotel room, where he pounded on the door. When there was no answer, Paul decided to wait for him to arrive. About two hours later, a weary Jagger came walking down the hall. "Paul, how are you?" he said gamely. "I was going to call you, but I figured it was too late." Mick said he was exhausted and maybe it would be better to do the interview in the morning. Paul, however, said I needed to get back to Los Angeles and that we should go ahead as planned.

Mick opened the door and invited me into the room. He laid on the bed and tried to keep awake as I asked him about his image, his music, and his future plans. I was surprised by how intelligent and controlled he was. This was not someone like Janis Joplin who was wrestling with demons nightly. No way was this guy going to self-destruct. At the same time, he was even more guarded than Paul McCartney. He was not a good interview.

After thirty minutes, I sensed him drifting away and, sure enough, he finally dozed off. Not knowing what to do, I walked out in the hall, where Paul was still waiting. "Did you get enough for your story?" he asked. When I shook my head no, Paul walked past me and through the suite to Mick's bed. "Mr. Jagger," he said, shaking him slightly. "Mr. Jagger, you've got an interview to do."

It was daylight when I finally left the room.

The Sex Pistols in Texas, January 1978

With the Stones abandoning the "bad boy" role in rock, it made sense that someone would try to take it over. The Pistols weren't the first to apply for the job. In the United States, the Ramones thumbed their noses at the march toward cool professionalism and the "adultification" of rock with short, primitive, buzz-saw-driven numbers and bratty expressions of youthful insolence and rebellion. Even more outrageous, the New York Dolls adopted a teasing, rock 'n' rouge attitude and attire that mocked the macho underpinnings of the music.

But it was the Pistols in England who truly shook up the pop music world. The brainchild of pop culture strategist Malcolm McLaren, who had briefly managed the Dolls, the Pistols celebrated rock 'n' roll anarchy in their songs and in their public behavior. They spit and swore at anyone who crossed their path, whether it was TV talk show hosts or record company executives. Kids in Britain went crazy and the Pistols became overnight stars there. They ran into more resistance in America. I first saw the Pistols in San Antonio, and early in the set a few dozen people began pelting the quartet with paper cups, slices of pizza, and empty beer cans. Lead singer Johnny Rotten was a born showman blessed with an amazing sneer and the ability to roll his eyes in a wonderfully mocking fashion. The more the crowd booed, the more he yelled insults at them, including "cowboy faggots."

Rotten was as surly as he was on stage when I sat down with him the following day. He was compelling when he spoke about the economic hard times facing young people in England, but much of his outrage seemed like pure hokum.

By the time the Pistols got to San Francisco a few days later, the audience was fiercely supportive, but it was too late. Internal friction tore the band apart. In its brief life span, however, the Pistols' punk energy touched thousands of young musicians, having an impact that continued all the way through the new wave, grunge, and punk revival movements.

Rotten joined the surviving Pistols for a reunion tour in the 1990s, but his confrontational approach didn't work. Night after night before adoring crowds, he came across more like a character from the rock documentary spoof *This is Spinal Tap* than a one-time revolutionary. When he was seen as a hero, Johnny Rotten's angry-at-the-world act didn't make any sense.

NINE

T he worst thing to do before interviewing Bob Dylan for the first time is to watch *Don't Look Back,* D. A. Pennebaker's 1967 documentary about Bob's 1965 acoustic tour of Britain. In the film, Bob is playful around fans, but sullen when journalists approach. In one scene, he reacts so sarcastically to a reporter's question that you can feel the guy wanting to disappear.

That image was in my mind as I headed to Durango, Mexico, in 1973, hoping to get an interview with Bob, who had pretty much dropped from sight after having a motorcycle accident in upstate New York in 1966. He was in Mexico to film a supporting role in Sam Peckinpah's *Pat Garrett and Billy the Kid* and the MGM publicist had warned me that he wasn't doing interviews, but I headed south anyway, hoping that Kris Kristofferson, who was playing Billy, might be able to open a few doors.

When the day's shooting ended around sunset, the unit publicist introduced me to Bob. I didn't expect him to open up at that first encounter, but I hoped to lay a foundation for a formal interview later in the week. Bob's manner was distant. He nodded and said, "Enjoy Mexico," before walking away.

Kris tried to come to the rescue that evening. He threw a dinner party for Peckinpah and sat me at the table next to Bob, who stared at me suspiciously. Kris broke the ice by telling Bob I was a real music fan and about how my review of his Troubadour show had helped launch his career. I took it as a hopeful sign when Bob didn't move to the other side of the long table.

"You write about music?" he asked after a few minutes, staring at his salad to avoid eye contact. "What kind?"

Everything except classical and jazz, I said—rock, folk, pop, blues, and country.

"Country," he repeated. "Who do you like in country?" I rattled off a long list, all the way back to the Carter Family and Jimmie Rodgers.

"I like them, too."

Bob's voice was so soft that you had to strain to hear him, but at least he was talking. When he didn't want to answer something, he just smiled shyly or muttered, "I don't know about that."

It was all just small talk. I never got close to asking him anything significant.

The only thing left for me to do on the set was to talk to others about Bob. Aware of his desire for privacy, most people, including Peckinpah, spoke only in general terms. But Rudy Wurlitzer, who wrote the screenplay, wasn't as guarded. This was Wurlitzer's first script since *Two-Lane Blacktop,* a road picture starring another pop star, James Taylor. He was a Dylan fan and had been studying him on the set.

"Dylan is sort of freaked by cameras," he said, sitting in a trailer on the set. "He can't stand to have his picture taken. He can't stand that invasion. So, psychologically and emotionally this was really a heavy move for him. I always thought of Dylan as Billy the Kid. He even looks like Billy the Kid, very young-looking with that combination of coldness and detachment, then sudden warmth. He can have incredible vitality for one minute, yet be removed the next."

The story ran on the front page of the entertainment section with the teasing head "Peckinpah Lures Dylan from Behind Wall of Privacy."

A few weeks later, I was walking through the Troubadour when I heard Bob's raspy voice call out to me from one of the club's VIP booths. I turned and Bob didn't look happy.

"Why did you write that stuff about me?" he asked sternly. "Rudy said he never said any of that."

I decided the only way to get his respect was to be frank with him. He certainly hadn't fallen for flattery in Mexico. I thought he was being overly sensitive and I didn't see any reason to act sorry or apologize. "You may be upset that I used the quotes," I said. "But I swear Rudy said them."

Bob didn't say anything. Our eyes locked briefly and I was wondering who was going to blink. Finally, his look softened. He leaned back in his chair and nodded, accepting my answer.

· ·

My chances of interviewing Bob improved greatly in 1973, when I learned from David Geffen that Bob was switching from Columbia to David's Asylum Records and that Bill Graham would be promoting Bob's first concert tour in nearly a decade. David and Bill both promised they would try to help me get to him—though there were no guarantees. Bob hadn't done a lengthy interview since speaking to Jann Wenner at *Rolling Stone* in 1969. But even if the interview didn't happen, I was excited just to see Bob in concert for the first time. There was so much public demand for tickets for the twenty-one-city tour that six million orders were received for the six hundred thousand available seats.

I was on my feet cheering with the rest of the nineteen thousand people in the old Chicago Stadium arena in January 1974 when Bob walked on stage, wearing an old black suede jacket and jeans. None of us had any idea what to expect. Would Bob play anthems from the early and mid-1960s, or would he focus on material written since his last tour in 1966?

Bob seemed to ignore the ovation as he bent over to look for his harmonica and then strap on his guitar. Without a word, he stepped to the microphone and began singing "Hero's Blues," a composition so obscure I had to later ask someone backstage for its title. The song was written during the 1963 *Freewheelin'* sessions, but it wasn't used on the album. It seemed perfect for the tour, however, because it expressed one of Bob's recurring themes: He didn't want to be limited by anyone's expectations of him. One reason he had stopped doing interviews was because he felt journalists were trying to paint him into a corner as the spokesman or hero of a generation, a role he detested. "Hero's Blues" was Bob's way of saying he wasn't anybody's property.

It was a marvelous concert and the audience remained in the arena discussing the evening's music long after Bob and the Band had left the stage. I made my way backstage, where Geffen said I should go to Bob's hotel room the next afternoon. He wasn't promising an interview, but he would do his best to make it happen. I finished my review around 3:00 a.m. and tried to get some sleep. But it was useless. I was too nervous.

The next day, David opened the door of Bob's seventeenth-floor suite and stepped into the hall. "You've got to play it by ear," he said, almost as anxious as I was. "Bob knows you are coming by and he wants to say hello, but he didn't say he'd do an interview." I followed him into the suite's living room, where we stood for a couple of minutes before a bedroom door swung open and a barefoot Bob emerged. He walked over to us, rubbing the sleep from his eyes. "How ya been?" he asked me, far more relaxed that I would have assumed he'd be on the morning after kicking off his first tour in eight years. I mumbled something about loving the show and how "Forever Young," a song off the upcoming album, *Planet Waves,* had gone over so well.

He asked about the crowd's reaction, and I said I had spoken to lots of fans afterward and they all loved seeing him again, but, I said, it was funny how everyone had a special song of his they had wanted to hear that he didn't play.

"Was there a song you wanted to hear?" he asked.

"'Love Minus Zero/No Limit,'" I said, and he nodded.

David was slowly edging toward one of the suite's other rooms so that Bob and I would be alone, but Bob didn't want any part of that.

"Hey," he said to David. "What time do we go over to the arena?"

After David's reply, he said he wanted to get some more sleep and headed back to the bedroom.

Damn, I thought, *so close.*

At the concert that night, I was touched when Bob added "Love Minus Zero/No Limit" to the set list.

On the flight back to Los Angeles, I thought about what a strange guy he was   he'd rejected my interview requests, but been thoughtful enough to sing my favorite song in his show.

CHAPTER
TEN

ondon was the main launching pad for rock careers in the early 1970s, but I kept hearing about this promising young phenom from New Jersey, of all places, named Bruce Springsteen. His 1973 debut album, *Greetings From Asbury Park, NJ,* arrived to industry whispers of the "new Dylan." I was impressed by the album, but concerned that Bruce leaned too much on early Dylan, especially with his machine-gun barrages of surrealistic lyrics. Still, there was enough youthful zest on the album to make me go see him at a Columbia Records showcase in Los Angeles.

I was impressed. He rocked much harder than John Prine, James Taylor, and most of the other young singer-songwriters of the day. As soon as I heard his second album, I threw out all doubts. *The Wild, the Innocent and the E Street Shuffle* was a dazzling step forward. Without sacrificing the surrealistic lyrics, Bruce's songs—about the innocence, frustrations, and urgency of youth—were more disciplined and his musical backing was bolder. Unlike writers who drew character sketches about people in the world around them, he was reaching inside and chronicling what it felt like to be the character in Dylan's "Like a Rolling Stone": young and on your own, with no direction home.

When I heard he was coming to town in the fall of 1974 on a tour with Dr. John, I called the Columbia Records publicity representative for an interview. I was shocked when she said Bruce wasn't doing them. Neither of his first two albums had even made the Top Two Hundred, and here I was offering him a whole page in the Sunday entertainment section, a rarity at the time for any artist.

At my urging, the publicist contacted Bruce's manager, but the word was still no. She then offered another Columbia artist for the Sunday space, but I said I'd do a piece on Clive Davis's new label, Arista. Davis had been head of Columbia until he was fired the year before. "Do you really have to do him?" the publicist asked. She explained that Columbia was holding a convention in town the Sunday the story would run and that it would be embarrassing to see a big spread on Clive's post-Columbia success. I made her a counteroffer. I said I'd postpone the Davis story for a week if she could get Bruce for me. I assume she called someone high up at Columbia who in turn put pressure on Bruce's camp, because she called back two hours later. The interview was on.

. . . .

The Santa Monica Civic Auditorium was packed, and Bruce got three standing ovations during the forty-five-minute set. Bruce brought a remarkable sense of drama to his performance as he roamed the stage in a white undershirt and black pants that gave him the look of a street-corner kid back in New Jersey. Bruce attacked the microphone with a sudden burst of lyrics, then retreated like someone taunting the audience before suddenly stepping back to the mike. Even then, you could see some of the gestures that would become his trademarks, like pointing his guitar's neck toward the ceiling and twisting it in a circle. He was dazzling, and I felt sorry for Dr. John, or anyone, who had to follow him on stage.

When Bruce returned for the encore, I figured he would follow the usual rock 'n' roll strategy of playing an upbeat number to lift the audience higher. But he played the slow, deliberate "New York Serenade" and then walked off the stage to polite applause. I headed back-stage, where I expected to find him in a great mood, but he seemed vaguely displeased. He said he normally played at least ninety minutes in clubs and that's what he felt it took to show an audience what his music was all about.

I mentioned the encore number. Why hadn't he done something more upbeat?

"Actually, I liked that," he said in his shy, hesitant way. "It completed the set for me. It might get more response to do a *boom-boom* thing and really rock the joint, but when I walked down the steps afterward, I felt complete. Otherwise, I feel messed up. It's just being honest with the audience and with myself, I guess. You can't conform to the formula of always giving the audience what it wants or you're killing yourself and you're killing the audience."

I didn't understand. Why was it killing the audience to give them what they wanted?

"Because they don't really want it either," he responded. "Just because they respond to something doesn't mean they want it. I think it has come to the point where they respond automatically to things they think they should respond to. You've got to give them more than that. Someone has to take the initiative and say, 'Let's step out of the mold. Let's try *this* . . .'"

I was still relying on pen and pad to take notes, and it was hard to keep up with Bruce's words. He was talking as fast as he had spat out some of the verses in his songs. Mainly, what struck me was how seriously Bruce took his music and his shows. There was nothing casual about him.

• •

When Dr. John went on stage, Bruce wanted to watch for a while before going to his hotel for the interview. I figured that meant two or three numbers, but he stayed for nearly an hour. Finally, we headed to the hotel, two blocks from the auditorium. Bruce was mostly silent on the walk and I started to worry.

People often ask if I'm nervous when meeting famous musicians, and the answer is that I'm not nervous when meeting them, but I am anxious about how the interview will turn out. I always want to get a good sense of the artist and good quotes for my story. I was especially anxious with Bruce because I thought he had a chance to be huge and I wanted to make a connection, the way I had with Johnny Cash.

Bruce opened the door to his room, switched on a table lamp, threw his jacket on the chair and then laid on the bed with his back against the headboard. He looked drained.

"You know I didn't want to do this interview, don't you," he said. I could have explained why I wanted to talk to him, how I felt his music was so promising and how part of the joy of being a critic is sharing your enthusiasm with readers. But I didn't want to repeat my opening gaffe with Janis Joplin. I often felt interviews were a little like tennis or chess matches, where everything depends upon sizing up the situation and responding quickly when opportunities arise.

I also felt that interviews could be valuable tools in assessing the potential of an artist. There were some artists who I found had so little idea of what they wanted to do musically that I didn't even write stories about them. There were others who were so passionate about what they were doing that I could look past some flaws in the work to see their larger goal.

In Bruce's case, I couldn't figure out the best way to approach him. So, I waited for him to say something. The problem was that he was silent, too. We sat there awkwardly looking at the cluttered floor for a couple of minutes. Finally, I gave in. I tried to point out how interviews could be valuable for an artist because they reached out to his most devoted fans. I mentioned how I grew up liking Elvis and Johnny Cash and Little Richard and would have given anything to know more about them.

"Well, I guess we all liked those guys," Bruce said, warming slightly. He said he saw Elvis on *The Ed Sullivan Show* when he was about nine and he was hooked by rock 'n' roll. He asked his mother for a guitar and she got him one, but she also made him take lessons, which he hated so much that he stopped playing. I tried to keep him talking about his rock heroes, which seemed like safe territory. I asked what got him back to the guitar and he mentioned seeing the Beatles. This time, he said, he taught himself to play and within six months he had formed his first band.

I had already read about his background, but I was learning

about Bruce because of the way he told it. He didn't try to impress me or sell himself in any way. He said he was signed by Columbia. He didn't add that he was signed by John Hammond, the same executive who had signed Billie Holiday and Bob Dylan. After he finished, he was silent again. This time I tried to point out that I was a genuine fan, not just a journalist carrying out an assignment. I mentioned how much I admired "4th of July, Asbury Park (Sandy)" and "Wild Billy's Circus Story," two songs on his latest record, and the way they compressed enough images and ideas for a dozen songs into one, leaving listeners to piece together the meanings for themselves. I asked what he had had in mind when he wrote the songs.

He rubbed his beard and ruffled his hair anxiously. I could see he was trying to find some way to be both cooperative and not violate his own principles.

"There is a certain understatement that is important to maintain," he eventually answered. "Once anything is black and white, it's no fun. People don't want to see things in black and white. Songs have to have possibilities. You can't say, 'Here it is. This is exactly what I mean,' and give it to them. You've got to let them search.

"That's why interviews are weird. Its like, 'Why do you do that and what for,' and I don't even know sometimes. You have to sit down and answer questions you usually don't consider and chances are maybe the answers are wrong and maybe they're right and maybe it's better not knowing. I'm a believer in that."

For someone who was reluctant to talk, Bruce was on a roll.

"Like, I don't dig going into the songs or why I write them or what I'm trying to do because I want people to find out for themselves. They should search out the songs. That's what I'm doing. I'm searching it out. Interviews are like questions and answers when there is no answer, so why is there a question?"

I closed my notebook and said we should just talk—not for the story, but just so I could better understand him. We went back and forth on the subject of interviews and music for the better part of an hour. When it was time to leave, I asked about the songs for his next album. Did he have them written yet?

"The writing is more difficult now," he said, not seeming to mind that I had picked up the notebook and pen again. "I got a lot of things out in that first album. In the new songs, I started slowly to find out who I am and where I want to be. It was like coming out of the shadow of various influences and trying to be me. You have to let out more of yourself all the time. You strip off the first layer, then the second, then the third. It gets harder because it's more personal."

As I walked back to my car, I thought about the seriousness with which Bruce approached his music. I especially liked the idea about having to strip away layers to let more of yourself out in your music. That was the challenge every artist faced, and I thought that if Bruce could keep doing it, he might end up being one of the most rewarding artists of all.

. . . .

Bruce fulfilled all my expectations with *Born to Run* in 1975, an album that made you believe once again in rock 'n' roll and rock 'n' roll heroes at a time when so many early rock stars had either self-destructed or compromised their art and new rock bands were sterile. In the album, Bruce captured the purity of rock in ways that encompassed the best of what had come before him.

On the album's cover, Bruce was even wearing an Elvis fan club pin on his black leather jacket. I didn't think the material was equal, song for song, to Prine's debut album, but the overall impact—from the fiery, sensual music to the urgency of the vocals—impressed me more than any album had since John's *Plastic Ono Band*. If anyone wanted proof that rock 'n' roll could still be majestic, this was it.

On one level, "Thunder Road" was a classic rock 'n' roll tale of the underdog kid, pinned down by his environment, inviting his girl, who has her own doubts and fears, to escape to a better life. But, in the context of all Bruce had told me about his belief in the liberating power of the music, I also felt the song was dealing with the salvation of rock 'n' roll itself. Rather than borrowing the styles of his heroes, he was coming up with his own captivating vision. The headline on my review reflected my enthusiasm: "Born to Run—Music as Reason to Live."

Two weeks after the review, Bruce and his band came to town to play the Roxy, a club on the Sunset Strip, and I spent the afternoon with him. I went to the sound check and then rode to his hotel with

Bruce, Columbia Records publicist Glen Brunman, and Bruce's girl-friend at the time, Karen, a thin, intense young woman with a model's aura. I thought Bruce would be overjoyed by everything that was happening—the album had broken into the national Top Ten and reviews around the country were uniformly glowing. But he seemed wary. I couldn't tell if he had doubts about his own worth or whether he was worried that saturation coverage might lead to a backlash. I looked back at him from the passenger seat. He was slouched down in the backseat and through the rear window, I saw a huge *Born to Run* billboard behind him.

Bruce and the band had a couple of days off in Los Angeles and I got my first chance to meet Miami Steve Van Zandt, the guitarist who was not only a key member of the E Street Band, but also one of Bruce's best friends. Steve mentioned once having played in Dion's band, and I told him Dion was recording with Phil Spector that night. Bruce turned our way when he heard Spector's name: "Spector? Tonight? Do you think we could go with you?"

I had already been championing Bruce to Phil, even playing *Born to Run* for him, and I could tell Phil was impressed. True to his contrarian nature, however, he pointed to aspects of the recording that he said should have been done differently.

I told Bruce and Steve I'd meet them at 7:30 p.m. on the corner of Western and Sunset, the location of Gold Star, the studio where Phil recorded many of his early classics. Traffic was light that evening and I arrived at Gold Star at about 7:15 p.m., and to my surprise Bruce and Miami Steve were already waiting on the corner. They couldn't wait to meet Phil, whose frenzied "wall of sound" production style had been one of Bruce's models when he was working on *Born to Run*.

Phil walked around the studio in his black suit and dark glasses. He spotted Bruce right away, but he didn't acknowledge him because he liked to keep people waiting, just to remind them that he was the star, he was Phil Spector. Yet I could tell that Phil was nervous. After the chaos of Lennon's rock 'n' roll sessions, he doubted that John would work with him again. He had a minor deal with Warner Bros. Records, but he was working with people who had been a long time between hits, like Dion and Cher. How sweet it would be to tell everyone he was in the studio with Bruce Springsteen. During a break in the session, he finally approached us.

"So, you're Bruce Springsteen," Phil said in his most exaggerated, tough-guy snarl.

Bruce stood, shuffled his feet, and gave a nervous laugh.

"I heard your record," Phil said. "Not bad."

Bruce smiled.

"How many copies you sold of *Born to Run*?" Phil snapped. Bruce was embarrassed, so Phil continued. "What you sold, a million? Two million?" he taunted. "If you made *Born to Run* with me, you'd have sold five million."

Bruce didn't know what to say.

Phil tried to move in for the kill.

"You want me to produce your records?"

Bruce again laughed nervously. It was a desperate gesture by Phil, and Bruce had seen enough that night to know that he couldn't work with him. After a long silence, Phil said, "Well, think about it. If you want to really sell records, come see me. I know how to do it."

A few minutes later, Bruce and Miami Steve said good-bye to Dion and headed out the door. Later, Phil came over to me. "Did he say anything?" Phil asked. "Did he say he wants to work with me?" I told him that Bruce hadn't said anything about it. "Well, he knows how to get ahold of me," Phil said. I left a few minutes later and walked to my car a block away. When I turned on the radio, one of Phil's biggest hits, "You've Lost That Lovin' Feelin'," was playing. It was the oldies station.

The next time I saw Bruce was a year after the Roxy show. He was headlining the Santa Monica Civic Auditorium and *Born to Run* was already a staple of rock radio. The growth in the band's performance was dramatic. The songs were delivered with a passion, energy, and conviction that was as forceful as that of the Rolling Stones and the Who, the standards of rock 'n' roll excitement at the time. More than ever, I saw him as someone who was capable of bringing fresh energy and direction to rock. But I also knew the pitfalls he'd face. I saw him as the test of rock 'n' roll's mettle as the music entered its third decade.

After the concert, I asked him how much work he had done on the new album and he explained that everything was on hold because he was involved in a lawsuit with his manager, Mike Appel. Bruce wanted Jon Landau, who had worked with him and Appel on parts of *Born to Run,* to be the sole producer on the next album, and Mike objected. Bruce also felt his contract with his manager was unfair. There was no doubting Mike's belief in Bruce; he had even mortgaged his house to keep the band on the road. The problem was that Mike believed in Bruce too much. Mike wanted Bruce to play large venues right away. Bruce wanted to move more slowly, concentrating more on the music than the trajectory of the career. The dispute left Bruce's career hanging in the balance for more than a year.

CHAPTER
ELEVEN

Everything appeared to be going great for Elvis in the early 1970s. Behind the flashbulbs, sold-out shows, and continuing acclaim, however, he was slowly falling apart. I was hearing about too many drugs, strains in his marriage, and vague references to various illnesses. These reports didn't just come from inside Elvis's camp, but also from the hard-core fans who had penetrated the Colonel's wall of silence better than anyone. These fans, mostly women, assumed that I had access to Elvis because I wrote about him so often. They wanted reassurance. They wanted to believe he was going to be okay.

In truth, Elvis's instincts were beginning to fail him. I watched with dismay some nights at his choice of songs, among them the Three Dog Night hit "Never Been to Spain," and how he was becoming such an indifferent performer. Elvis was sensational the first few times he sang Tony Joe White's Dixie-fried "Polk Salad Annie," but he was now just going through the motions. The same laziness was noticeable on Elvis's albums.

I didn't know how to express my feelings in print; I still had Elvis on a pedestal. I also wondered if I was judging him too harshly. He was still good when measured against other Las Vegas attractions; he just wasn't as good as I wanted him to be. I spent several days trying to write a column expressing these views, but I wasn't comfortable with the results. I finally came up with a compromise. I received a letter from an Elvis fan named Valarie who wanted to know why I hadn't written about Elvis in a while. I wrote her a long letter—fan to fan—that explained my disappointment and how Elvis seemed to be taking his talent for granted, perhaps having been lulled into complacency by the way the fans would cheer anything he did.

"From all of this, Valarie, you may get the idea that I no longer like Elvis," I wrote in closing. "That's not true. In fact, it is just the opposite. The whole reason I'm writing you this letter is that I do like Elvis so very much and that I think he still is a great talent, if only he'd apply himself. Since I'm basically an optimist, I think he will. And when he does, I'll be sure to write you another letter. And we can help lead the applause."

The letter was exactly what I wanted to say, so I used it as a column in the *Times* on February 6, 1972. If Elvis read it, I never heard about it. Meanwhile, things got worse. The phone calls from fans kept coming: more reports of marital problems and drugs, along with concern that he was starting to gain so much weight. I saw Elvis frequently in concert during the year and he was pale and puffy. A friend who worked at the Las Vegas Hilton (the Hilton chain had bought the International) suggested that Elvis was just eating too much—sometimes a half-dozen fried peanut butter and banana sandwiches at a time. But I couldn't believe it was just food. How could someone like Elvis not have enough pride to lose weight before a tour? There was an epidemic of drug use in the record industry. Why should Elvis be immune?

Somehow Elvis pulled himself together in the studio for a few memorable performances, including the scorching "Burning Love" and the more evocative "Separate Ways" and "Always on My Mind." On stage, however, Elvis continued to crumble. In early 1973, I wrote that he was "only operating at 60 percent." The audiences, however, continued to adore him. I just hoped for the best.

As the months went by, Elvis's shows became roller-coaster rides that sometimes left you encouraged—especially on the nights when he put his all into "How Great Thou Art"—but mostly disheartened. Finally, I'd had enough. I wrote a long piece that ran on the front page of the *Times*'s entertainment section that said Elvis should retire. I didn't want to see him embarrass himself any further. "At 40," I wrote, "Elvis's records are increasingly uneven, his choice of material sometimes ludicrous and his concert appearances often sloppy. Worst of all, there is no purpose or personal vision in his music anymore." The one hope for Elvis was to devote himself to music he cared about. Maybe, I said, he would spring back to life if he did a gospel tour.

Looking back, I'm surprised that it took me more than three years after first noticing his decline to write that column. I didn't have any problem complaining about some other major figures I admired, including Bob Dylan and John Lennon. But they were my contemporaries. Elvis was this heroic figure from my childhood. In the 1950s, his long hair, flashy clothes, and uncompromising stance were like electric shocks. It would be years before eighteen-year-olds would be granted voting rights, but Elvis's rise was the first dramatic sociological expression by a generation that would later express its views in more direct ways. Elvis was, in a real sense, the candidate of young people—the means by which we could challenge adult authority and institutions— and his success was our success. For a while, anything seemed possible. It was part of the energy, drive, and idealism that people would later see in the short-lived "Camelot" era of American politics.

When Elvis had returned to the stage after his movie years with such energy and electricity, it was a testimony to all that Elvis had helped us believe in and a reminder of how far we had come. So, it was hard for us to let go of our affection even as he began to squander that trust.

What finally enabled me to treat Elvis the way I would have treated any other artist was the night in Las Vegas when I sat next to someone who was seeing Elvis for the first time. He was in his fifties and had never been a particular fan of rock 'n' roll, yet he had heard so much about Elvis that he wanted to see for himself. Elvis was pitiful that night. He was forty pounds overweight, which made the karate moves look silly, and he tossed off some of the songs so carelessly that it made me wince. At the end of the evening, the man made some derogatory remarks. I tried to defend Elvis. I told him he hadn't seen the real Elvis, but the guy pulled out his show ticket. He said, "Well, it sure says 'Elvis Presley' on here."

He was right, of course.

I had lunch with my RCA friend Grelun Landon a few weeks after the "retirement" article ran in 1975. He said Elvis had read it and was furious. He even used words like "betrayed." But a few weeks later, Grelun called to say he had heard from the Colonel that Elvis had proposed this goofy idea: He said the Colonel had told him, "Elvis wants to do an all-gospel tour. You ever hear anything crazier than that?"

Would a gospel tour have reinvigorated Elvis? Probably not, his personal demons were too great at that point. But we'll never know. Again, the Colonel said no, and Elvis backed down.

· ·

"Elvis is dead. The words still shock."

That's how I started an appreciation of Elvis just before catching a plane to Memphis to cover the funeral in the summer of 1977. A photographer and I went straight to Graceland, the Colonial Revival-style home that Elvis had bought in the 1950s. We figured there'd be a few fans outside the gates and I wanted to ask them what Elvis meant to them. But we found *thousands* of fans lining the street in front of Graceland's closed gates. Later, as I drove around town, there were Elvis messages on billboards and storefront marquees. Every call that night on a local radio talk show was about Elvis. "Wherever he is, I know he's happy," offered a nine-year-old girl. "There'll never be another like him," sobbed a much older male.

By 10:00 a.m. on the day of the funeral, the mass of fans had shifted four miles down Elvis Presley Boulevard to Forest Hill Cemetery, where the public could view the mausoleum where Presley was entombed. The crypt was about fifty feet from where his mother's remains had been placed. I spotted Colonel Parker outside the funeral home, but couldn't reach him. The plane ride home was doubly sad because I read an Associated Press report of an interview with Sonny West, one of Elvis's former bodyguards. West and two other ex-Presley aides had written a book, *Elvis: What Happened?,* in which West claimed Elvis was addicted to drugs. Like other Elvis fans, I thought it was a sensationalist account. I thought of West as a traitor. But the accusations were later confirmed.

John Lennon's line about how rock 'n' roll was "not worth dying for" resonated with me after Elvis's death. How do you race after something because of the glamour and then realize at just the right moment that you've got to stop chasing fame and stake your career on artistry?

Elvis failed that test himself. By not rebelling more against Colonel Tom Parker, Elvis again and again opted for fame over artistry. He may have spoken in public about wasting all those years in Hollywood, but when he had a second chance in Las Vegas, he again let Colonel Parker smother his artistic impulses in pursuit of bigger box-office grosses. Like Lennon and Dylan, Bruce Springsteen was inspired by Elvis's music, but frightened by Elvis's life. That fear was one of the reasons behind his lawsuit against Mike Appel. Bruce said Mike saw himself as Colonel Parker and Bruce as Elvis. The problem, Bruce told me, was that "Mike wasn't Colonel Parker and I wasn't Elvis." Years later, I heard him refer in concert to Elvis's death: "It was hard to understand how somebody whose music took away so many people's loneliness could have ended up as lonely as he did." Then Bruce began singing "Johnny Bye-Bye," a song he wrote shortly after Elvis's death. The closing line of the mournful tune was "You didn't have to die."

. . . .

When your boyhood hero dies, it's only natural to take inventory. I was thirty-seven and wondering if I wasn't getting too old to write about rock 'n' roll. It didn't help when a teenage girl called to say she liked my stories and asked how old I was. Feeling self-conscious, I told her to guess. She said, "Twenty?" I said no. "Twenty-two?" I said no. "Twenty-five?" she asked incredulously. When I again said no, she hung up. Sigh.

In looking back over the first two-thirds of the 1970s, there were also worried about the future of rock itself. In just eight years, I had seen the breakups of the Beatles, Creedence Clearwater Revival, and the Band, as well as the deaths of Janis Joplin, Jimi Hendrix, Duane Allman, Brian Jones, and Elvis. By 1977, John Lennon was on the sidelines and Paul McCartney's music was horribly uneven. Bob Dylan still had remarkable craft, but his impact had waned. The Rolling Stones could wow everyone live, but the albums were spotty. The Who was on the decline. Who could carry rock 'n' roll forward and inspire a new generation in the tradition of Elvis, the Beatles, and Dylan?

In looking back over the first two-thirds of the 1970s, there were hundreds of acts that turned out hits, from Emerson, Lake & Palmer to Yes, Deep Purple, and Queen. Some tried to dazzle you with technique, others with spectacle, others with seductive grooves, but their importance was minimal.

There were also high-quality bands, including Roxy Music and Steely Dan, but their images were too cold and their music too narrow to lead a generation. Joni Mitchell and Neil Young were among the best talents of the decade, but they were too independent to worry themselves with the burdens of leadership. The same was true of Paul Simon and Tom Waits, both brilliant songwriters. Bob Marley was a musician who did want to inspire young people in the tradition of Dylan and Lennon, and, along with Jimmy Cliff, he established reggae as an important subculture. But the music was too exotic and limited thematically for young mainstream America to embrace.

Four entries in the prepunk 1970s showed enough ambition and talent for me to think of them as possible heirs to Elvis, the Beatles, and Dylan: David Bowie, the Eagles, Patti Smith, and Bruce Springsteen. David gave us some memorable anthems, but he wasn't committed to rock 'n' roll. He wanted to be someone, like Frank Sinatra or Judy Garland, who was bigger than any single entertainment field. The result was that he spread himself too thin. The Eagles wrote insightful tales about how the innocence of the 1960s had given way in the 1970s to lust, ego, and greed. But the group that had warned against false values was ultimately torn apart by its own excesses. I had high hopes for Don Henley's solo career, which extended the Eagles' legacy nicely. With his interest in social issues, I could even picture him running for political office. But Don eventually returned to the safety of the Eagles' nest. The band reunited in 1994 and wowed crowds all over again, but they didn't come up with any meaningful new material. Patti altered the rock landscape by demonstrating that a woman could write songs and perform them with all the passion of a man—and then some. But she put her career on hold for nearly two decades after marrying rock musician Fred "Sonic" Smith and moving to Detroit to raise a family.

That left Bruce as the Great Rock Hope. He wasn't alone in making inspiring, heartfelt music. Tom Petty, Jackson Browne, and Bob Seger also carried on gallantly in the mainstream rock 'n' roll tradition. In addition, a new generation of punk and new wave artists, from the Sex Pistols and the Clash in England to Talking Heads and X in America, would help rock recapture its fury and heart. But *Born to Run* had pushed Bruce to the front of the pack. All he needed to do was follow up that album with another creative bull's-eye.

CHAPTER
TWELVE

wo dangerous career traps face anyone gifted and lucky enough to deliver an album as transformational as *Born to Run*. First, you may want to hold on to the newfound popularity so badly that you end up repeating yourself the next time out. The second danger stems in part from becoming preoccupied with avoiding the first: You are so determined to "grow" that you end up moving too far from your strengths. Bruce Springsteen also faced a third challenge in the three years that passed between albums—a fierce legal battle for control of his career. Even though he won the lawsuit against his former manager, he could have come away from the experience so battered emotionally that he lost touch with the uplifting message that fueled his creative impulses. Creativity is delicate—more the result of someone's emotional makeup than sheer craftsmanship.

I thought about these dangers the day my advance copy of Bruce's new album, *Darkness on the Edge of Town,* finally arrived in the spring of 1978. My teenage son, Rob, loved *Born to Run* as much as I did and he wanted to listen to the new record with me, but I wanted to listen to it alone. I didn't want anything coloring my judgment. Once I closed the door, I waited several minutes before putting the LP on the turntable. I felt that so much was riding on Bruce that I was afraid of being disappointed. I had to go all the way back to Elvis's early singles to remember being so apprehensive about hearing a new record. At that time, I was such a big fan that I wanted every new Elvis record to be exciting enough to go to No. 1—to prove that Elvis was still the King of Rock 'n' Roll. In Bruce's case, I loved the way he lifted the sights and spirits of the rock audience. Selfishly, I wanted Bruce to deliver a great album because it meant I could look forward to several years of writing about someone who mattered. I didn't want to spend that time writing about disco, heavy metal, or the Captain & Tennille, and I'm not joking. Though there seem to be lots of appealing acts in rock at any given time, the gap between the good and the very best is enormous, and no one was spreading the rock 'n' roll gospel with the conviction and punch of Springsteen.

When I finally played the album, I picked up right away on the optimism, a holdover from *Born to Run*. As the album progressed, however, I became more intrigued by the expressions of hardships. This was new, ambitious territory for Bruce. He pointed to what stood between people on the edges of society and their dreams. In the title track, he rejected one of rock's underlying themes by saying the victories of youth may not—probably will not—be permanent. This made Bruce's mythical darkness on the edge of town even more threatening than the backstreets of *Born to Run*.

I listened to the album twice and I had my answer, but I wondered what teenage fans might think. Would they resist moving from the romanticism of *Born to Run* to the somberness of *Darkness on the Edge of Town*? I asked Rob to listen to it, then left him alone so I wouldn't give away my feelings. I paced around until the office door opened. When he appeared, I could see his answer in his face. He, too, was enthralled.

I spoke with Bruce in Minneapolis at the opening of the *Darkness* tour and he was much more secure when talking about himself and his music. Sitting in an arena dressing room minutes after the concert, he said he was grateful for the loyalty of his audience during the three years between albums. "When I was off, I never felt lost about what I was trying to do," he said. "The great thing now is to go out there every night and see those kids and get that kind of response. It's like something special with that crowd. In a way, I like to think I was off three years and they were off three years. It's like they were rooting for you. There's a little extra thing that's there now. It's just a little bit more satisfying." Bruce was no longer glancing around the room or taking long pauses before answering questions. He had a new inner strength.

There were still dozens of fans waiting outside the arena when Bruce later stepped through the backstage door and headed for the tour bus. One kid called out to him. When Bruce turned his way, the boy said he was also from New Jersey, and he asked for Bruce's autograph. "From Jersey, eh?" Bruce said as he signed the young man's concert ticket. "Hey," the fan said, "you talk just like you sing." Bruce looked at him and gave his nervous but disarming laugh. "Well, it is me up there, you know."

That bond was at the heart of Bruce's music and passion; it's what made fans want to follow Bruce from city to city to see the shows, knowing that each night would be different. This wasn't a case of someone figuring out the most effective set list and then repeating the songs in the same order and with the same arrangements night after night. This was a living exchange, highlighted by Bruce's stories between songs. I thought inspiration was rock 'n' roll's greatest quality, and one reason Bruce fascinated me was that he made that inspiration the central theme of his music. He saw himself, his band, and his audience as part of a community, a brotherhood of true believers—and he vowed to hold that community together.

Bruce's popularity mushroomed in the fall of 1980 when he returned with his fifth album, *The River.* Though some songs were in the stark tradition of *Darkness,* most of the new songs were more festive, giving the album the variety and zest of Bruce's live shows. The LP and the tour finally turned Bruce into a superstar. As I headed to Cleveland for the opening, I wondered how long Bruce would be able to maintain his standards. I was reassured by what I found. The concert was a marvelous mix of commentary and energy, a night of great tenderness and comfort.

I was particularly interested in how Bruce was able to inject a touch of idealism into even his darkest songs. The answer, he said that night, was that those were the qualities in rock 'n' roll that meant the most to him as a teenager. "I just know that when I started to play, it was like a gift," he said backstage. "I started to feel alive and sometimes that was the only inspiration I had. It was like some little guy stumbling down the street and finding a key. Rock 'n' roll was the only thing I ever liked about myself."

Just as Bob had served as a spokesman for young people in the 1960s, Bruce was becoming a spokesman for a generation that was moving into its thirties. When I asked him about the advancing age of the characters in his songs, Bruce said, "You write about what you know." He said that people feel great possibilities in their twenties, but the world can be much different when they are in their thirties, or at least it looks different. "You may not have the same expectations. You're not as open to options. You may have a wife and a kid and a job. It's all you can do to keep those things straight. You let the possibilities go. What happens to most people is when their first dreams get killed off, nothing ever takes their place. The important thing is to keep holding out for possibilities, even if no one ever makes it. There was a Norman Mailer article that said the one freedom that people want most is the one they can't have: the freedom from dread. That idea is somewhere at the heart of the new album."

Looking back, I can see that part of the wonder and allure of Bruce's albums and shows was that they served as a test to see how long he could remain true to his own dreams. More than any major American rock figure before him, Bruce invited his audience to get close to him. I don't know if it was because he wasn't afraid of what they would see or if he knew the scrutiny would keep him honest. Either way, it was an advance over what the Beatles and Bob Dylan had represented in rock.

Each time Bruce stepped on stage, I felt him move forward. But, eventually, I'd see even him stumble.

· ·

There was good news on the Dylan front. After all my chasing after him, I finally found myself across the table from Bob in a Santa Monica coffee shop. Bob realized he needed a publicist to promote *Renaldo and Clara,* the 1978 film he had made during the multi-artist ensemble Rolling Thunder Revue tour. His choice was Paul Wasserman, the Los Angeles publicist who had a background in film (Jack Nicholson was a client) and rock (the Rolling Stones). One reason his high-profile clients liked Wasso, as he was known in the industry, was that he was good at getting stories written on artists without them having to do many interviews. Wasso convinced Bob that he needed to do at least a few interviews to promote new albums and tours.

In 1978, when Bob announced his first proper tour since the one with the Band in 1974, there were more than 150 interview requests from around the world. Wasso narrowed it down to ten. As Wasso started explaining why it was essential that he do them, Bob looked at the list, picked up a pen, and crossed out all but three names. I was one of the survivors, and Paul arranged for me to meet Bob at his rehearsal hall in Santa Monica. The plan was for me to watch the rehearsal and then slip in a few questions during a break. It didn't sound like the ideal situation because Bob could easily end the interview by saying he had to get back to work.

I was encouraged to find Bob had pushed back the rehearsal for an hour so our talk could be more leisurely. To further ensure that we weren't interrupted, he suggested we go down the street to the coffee shop. Bob seemed more approachable than before. On the walk, he waved back at a man in a white MG convertible and returned the nod of a young woman who passed us on the street. Still, he didn't go out of his way to make me feel at ease. I sensed he was trying to be friendly, but it wasn't easy for someone who had largely avoided the press for ten years to suddenly drop his defenses. Bob tended to answer questions with one or two sentences, and he wasn't big on small talk. I couldn't tell if he was trying to make me feel uneasy or if I was just intimidated by his reputation.

In first meeting Johnny Cash and John Lennon, I had felt I was on trial as a journalist. Could I come up with a story good enough to please the editors at the paper? With Bob, I thought of myself as being on trial as a person. Was I smart enough or interesting enough to keep him engaged? I was so insecure that I wouldn't have blamed him if he had stood up at any point and said he was bored. If that happened, I worried, I probably wouldn't ever get another chance to interview the most important figure in rock. It might be a sign that I was kidding myself, that I was in over my head. Adding to the anxiety was peer pressure. What could I tell my colleagues at the paper? They were all excited that I was interviewing Bob and made me promise to come straight back to the office to tell them how the meeting went.

It didn't start well. Bob brushed off early questions about the 1960s with a stern "That was years ago" or "What is this, a history course?" I gazed down at the tape recorder and watched the little cartridge wheel slowly turning as I tried to think of a question that might catch his interest. Just when everything felt lost, I asked whether all the acclaim in the 1960s had made it easier on him as a songwriter or more difficult. "Acclaim?" he repeated. "Let me tell you what that really was. In the '60s, *Time, Newsweek*—all those magazines—started calling me the 'father of the revolution,' the 'folk-rock king,' and all that stuff. That's what created this 'mythical Bob Dylan' thing. So now, the magazines must figure they made a mistake back then and they've gotta take it down some. I don't know if they'll be successful, but what they say has nothing to do with me. It didn't in the '60s and it doesn't now."

That answer gave me hope. I asked what that attention was like. He said it was so overwhelming that he finally had had to shut down to let things cool off. I assumed he was talking about the period after his motorcycle accident. I wanted to ask about the accident, but Bob was still talking. He said he had felt out of control again on the tour with the Band. He felt disoriented playing all those "hockey arenas" and having everything planned out months in advance. That's why he had adopted the more informal guerrilla tactics employed for the Rolling Thunder Revue, where shows were sometimes announced only days in advance and they played smaller venues.

If he liked smaller tours, why had he embarked again on an ambitious worldwide tour? I was surprised by how frank he was. He needed the money. "I had a couple of bad years," he said. "I put a lot of money into the movie, built a big house, and there's the divorce. It costs a lot to get divorced in California."

I actually seemed to be connecting with Bob. I was going to have a good story. I didn't know if I'd ever talk to him again, but I knew I'd come through my biggest challenge so far as a pop writer.

Bob, too, must have been okay with the story because Wasso called a few months later to tell me Bob wanted to do another interview. This time he was on the road in Kansas City. I went on the bus with him from the hotel to the concert hall and I started asking a few questions, confident that we would pick up our conversation where we had left off. To my surprise, Bob was unresponsive. In a desperate attempt to get things back on track, I asked what I thought was a safe question about his latest album, *Street-Legal*. It did catch his attention, but not in the way I expected.

"I hope you don't make this look like some carny trying to hawk his records," he said, looking me straight in the eye. I had to laugh. Here was rock's ultimate contrarian. I wondered what Bob would have done if I had opened by saying I'd like to talk about anything but his new release. He probably would have started in on the record in detail. Instead, he said, "I don't know if you even want to hit on the records. When people think of me, they are not necessarily going to buy the latest record anyway. They may buy a record from years ago. Besides, I don't think interviews sell records."

When nothing else worked, I asked a lame question about how the tour was going. He suddenly came to life. He said he was upset with critics who had attacked him on this tour for tampering with his old arrangements and for having too slick a stage manner.

"Have you seen the reviews?" he asked impatiently between sips of coffee backstage. *Time* magazine had called the "mocking show-biz turns" in Dylan's show "tiresome." The *Chicago Sun-Times* termed the concert a "sometimes depressing, sometimes exhilarating, sometimes funny cross between *Name That Tune* and *That's Entertainment.*"

"You'll see the show tonight. You'll see the crowd and how they react. Then, read the paper in the morning and you'll see that whoever reviewed it most likely wasn't there or didn't see the same show— maybe he heard it on the telephone. The writers complain the show's disco or Las Vegas. I don't know how they came up with those theories. It's like someone made it up in one town and the writer in the next town read it. I don't know what the reviewers mean half the time. I don't even care."

It was strange hearing that the thirty-seven-year-old Dylan obviously did care about what others thought. "I'm not trying to mock anything in this show," he continued. "We're not equipped to do that. We don't have any props. We're just up there playing my songs. That's all we've ever done. There are so many groups that get on stage these days with smoke bombs or people rising up on twelve-foot stilts. I'm not into that. That's not my scene. I can still relate to a man or a woman on stage who is singing a song that is telling me something—something I need to know. If that's not happening on a stage, I've got better things to do than sit in an arena."

Bob's "Gotta Serve Somebody" album, *Slow Train Coming,* was released a few months later and I thought it was his most important work in years, a collection of gospel songs written from a strict "born again" Christian perspective. I called Wasso about an interview, but he said Bob wasn't doing any. Dylan said he had put everything he wanted to say in the songs. That changed a few months later.

MORE FAVORITE ROAD TRIPS

Colonel Tom Parker in Las Vegas, Summer 1978

It was two years after Elvis's death, but his name—"Always Elvis"—was back on the giant marquee outside the Las Vegas Hilton hotel to announce a convention whose chief lure was the chance to shake hands with Colonel Parker. What Elvis fan could resist that? Plenty of them, it turned out. Sponsors of the ten-day event hoped for three thousand people a day, but less than a quarter of that showed up the day I walked among the rows of souvenir stands that offered everything from Elvis dinner plates to copies of the *National Enquirer* casket photo.

Between smiles for the camera and handshakes, Parker seemed dispirited, a man with a gigantic void in his life. By 10:00 p.m., the photographers and fans were gone. With only a couple members of his old entourage to talk to, Parker finally stood, picked up his cane, and headed toward the exit. At the door, he stopped in front of a giant photo of Elvis taken during his glory years at the hotel. I sensed a moment of vulnerability in this private man. The Colonel was nearing seventy, but he looked even older.

"You miss him, don't you," I said.

Parker turned slowly toward me and his voice cracked in this rare moment of public vulnerability. "Of course, of course," he said, looking back at the photo. "I loved him like a son."

Then he reverted to his old form. "But don't quote me on that. The Colonel doesn't give interviews."

He smiled, patted me on the shoulder, and walked away. A security guard turned off the lights in the room and followed him down the hall. The Colonel had left the building.

Elton John in the Soviet Union, Spring 1979

By the late 1970s, Elton's record sales had slipped noticeably, and in hopes of shaking things up, Elton's advisors suggested that he do a series of concerts in the Soviet Union. As the first Western pop star to tour there, he would be treated like royalty and the publicity would help him back home. Elton invited me to go along as the only US journalist on board. I hooked up with the touring party in London, and then we flew to Moscow and proceeded to Leningrad by train.

Elton performed in a luxurious 3,500-seat concert hall, and there was near pandemonium when he played the Beatles' "Back in the USSR." But the highlight was in the dressing room after the show. We were in the third-floor room when we heard shouting outside. Opening the window, Elton saw a couple thousand fans in the street chanting his name. We assumed they were fans from the show, but someone from the theater told Elton that they hadn't been able to get tickets because admission was limited to people with ties to government officials. The fans in the street were hard-core Elton enthusiasts who risked arrest because they were blocking traffic.

As I watched him wave to the fans below, I remembered Janis Joplin and what she had said about how hard it is to be loved by thousands on stage and then face the world alone. I stood next to him as he listened to the continuing chants of "Elton, Elton." Even on this night of triumph, there was something about Elton that made it obvious he felt terribly alone.

Jerry Lee Lewis in Longview, Texas, Winter 1981

Jerry Lee has always been as brash as he is talented; he once said his only re-gret as a performer was that he couldn't sit in the audience and watch himself on stage. He was so sexually suggestive and unruly in the 1950s that he made Elvis seem tame. His career took a nosedive in the late 1950s when DJs stopped playing his records after it was learned he had married his thirteen-year-old cousin. But Jerry Lee kept fighting, and he eventually resurfaced in country music, putting out some remarkable records before returning to the rock circuit. Along the way, he probably lived as hard as anyone in show business. I've seen him go through most of a bottle of whiskey before going on stage and another bottle afterward.

Those fast-lane excesses caught up with him in the summer of 1981, when two stomach operations left him near death. I phoned him at the hospital and he spoke in a voice so weak I could barely make out his words, but a few months later Jerry Lee was back on the road. I flew to Longview, Texas, to see him at the Rio Palm Isle. The honky-tonk manager said Jerry Lee was resting in the back office. I pictured him relaxing on a couch. But when I opened the door, he was sitting behind a desk taking a long swig of whiskey straight from the bottle. "How ya doin', killer," he said. Turning to his assistant, he added, "Better bring us another bottle."

Bob Dylan in Israel, Fall 1987

On paper, Bob's first concert in Israel seemed a sure success: rock's most acclaimed songwriter playing in Tel Aviv for an audience that strongly identified not only with his socially conscious music, but also with his Jewish roots. And sure enough, the nearly forty thousand fans in a sprawling park on the edge of the city lit thousands of candles in salute and set off flares that brightened the night sky. But the cheers eventually gave way to confusion and disappointment.

Rather than tailoring the material to an audience that had waited decades to hear his early anthems, Bob stuck mostly to newer, lesser-known tunes like "Joey" and "Señor." There was considerable grumbling in the reviews the next morning in Tel Aviv's four largest newspapers. The writers used words like "boring," "monotonous," "flat," and "withdrawn" to describe Bob's manner and song selection. Declared one writer, "Robert Zimmerman, your time has passed."

At breakfast, Bob asked, "How was the crowd?"

I told him the audience had been disappointed that he hadn't done more of his familiar songs. Bob scoffed. He said the same thing I had heard from Bruce. He never wants to feel like the audience is dictating what he should do on stage. Besides, he pointed out, he went to see Frank Sinatra and he wasn't upset that Sinatra didn't do many of the songs from his classic Capitol albums. He said he wanted to hear whatever Frank wanted to sing, and that's how all audiences should approach a concert.

I told him I normally would agree, but this was a special case. These shows were the most eagerly anticipated concerts in Israel's history.

"Okay," he finally said. "What songs do you think I should do?"

I tore a sheet of paper from my notebook and wrote down song titles, starting with "The Times They Are a-Changin'."

The next night I stood with nine thousand other Dylan fans in the scenic Sultan's Pool, which was built by Pontius Pilate and is located at the base of the stone wall that surrounds the Old City of Jerusalem. Rushing on stage with a determined gait, Bob stepped to the microphone and, before even looking out at the crowd, started singing "The Times They Are a-Changin'." He followed with several more songs from my list, including "Like a Rolling Stone" and "Ballad of a Thin Man." The crowd was ecstatic.

Fifteen years later in Los Angeles, I brought my second wife, Kathi, back-stage to meet Bob. I must have seen him a half-dozen times since Israel, but he never mentioned the piece of paper I gave him in Tel Aviv. When I introduced her, though, Bob smiled and said, "Does your husband have a set list for me tonight?"

Paul McCartney in Rotterdam, Winter 1989

When I heard Paul was returning to live shows for the first time in thirteen years, I headed to Rotterdam even though I was suffering from the flu. I interviewed Paul before the concert, and we were scheduled to get together again afterward. I felt so bad that I rested backstage rather than watching the concert. Then, I was disappointed to hear that Paul was going to fly back to London rather than spend the night in Rotterdam. He told me he was going to say that we could finish the interview before the next night's show in Rotterdam, but when he saw how sick I was, he suggested instead that I go home and he'd call me in a couple of days so we could finish the interview. I was nervous because I had a tight deadline and knew that some musicians might not follow through. But Paul called right at the appointed time and I got everything I needed for the story. I was extremely grateful.

Neil Young in Northern California, Winter 1989

I always enjoy seeing Neil. He is someone, like Lennon, who expresses himself freely. The plan this day was to do the interview while he drove his vintage white Cadillac convertible through the woods near his ranch.

"There is a side of me that is always restless, and it's probably something I feel more than ever because there is so much to do and there is less time than there was yesterday," Neil, forty-four, said about halfway through the three-hour drive on the winding backwoods roads. "I've written lots of songs just driving around these old roads like we did today, and when the songs come, you want to get them because they might not come again," he said. "If I feel a song coming on and I'm around people, I can just disappear so I don't lose it. I don't want anything else to get in the way of it."

I asked what would happen if he started feeling a song coming on while we were driving.

Without taking his eyes off the road, he said, "I'd say, 'Sorry, Bob, but the interview is over.'"

CHAPTER
THIRTEEN

When I asked Ahmet Ertegun how he had managed to build Atlantic Records into a powerhouse label with a roster that included Ray Charles, Aretha Franklin, Cream, and Led Zeppelin, he said his secret was to walk around very slowly and hope to bump into a genius. He found one of his biggest stars by accident at a showcase in London for Atlantic's Wilson Pickett. "I was at the bar next to Wilson with my back to the bandstand," he told me. "All of a sudden I heard these fabulous guitar lines. I thought I was listening to someone in Wilson's band, but when I asked Wilson, he said, 'He's not in my band. My guitarist is at the other end of the bar.'" Ahmet turned around and saw Eric Clapton. Six months later, Atlantic released Eric's album with Cream.

In similar spirit, I bumped into a genius and it led to one of my most prized interviews. It was backstage at a Bruce Springsteen concert at the Los Angeles Sports Arena in 1980. I don't usually go backstage unless I am doing a profile on the artist, but my son, Rob, loved Bruce's music and I knew it would be a treat for him to see what goes on backstage during intermission. Once we got there, we literally bumped into Bob Dylan. I introduced him to Rob and expected him to move on, but he stayed by our side. As I saw several people staring at us, I realized why Bob was sticking by us. If he was by himself, he would be a target for anyone who wanted to approach him, but as long as he was talking to someone, others hung back. After about ten minutes, the houselights flashed, signaling the start of the second half of the show. "Hey," Bob said. "I'm doing some more gospel shows in San Francisco next week. Why don't you come up so we can talk about it?"

Bob hadn't done any interviews since *Slow Train Coming,* his "born again" Christian album, had been released the previous year, so this would be a real coup.

Longtime Dylan fans had been severely disappointed by Bob's "born again" tour the previous year because he hadn't done any of his earlier, secular material. There were scattered boos and even some walkouts. In returning to the road this time, Bob was doing a few old songs in the show, but the focus was still on the gospel tunes. At the San Francisco show, many of the people around me raised their hands, palms up, in spiritual bonding as he sang about salvation. I went back-stage afterward, but he said he was too drained to do an interview. Maybe he'd feel better after the next night's show, he said. But he still wasn't up to it the following night. After the third show, he was ready.

When I knocked on his hotel room door at 3:00 p.m. the next day, he looked like he'd just woken up. He was wearing jeans and a wrinkled T-shirt. "Take a seat," he said, gesturing toward a chair. "I've just got to finish this call in the other room." As I waited for Bob to return, I looked around. He was in town for two weeks, so he had clothes scattered all over the place, but an open Bible on the nightstand caught my eye. There were also a couple of books about understanding Jesus. When he finished his call, he sat on a couch opposite me and lit a cigarette. Without even waiting for a question, Bob started talking.

"I truly had a born-again experience, if you want to call it that," he said. "It's an overused term, but it's something that people can relate to. It happened in 1978. I always knew there was a God or a Creator of the universe and a Creator of the mountains and the sea and all that kind of thing, but I wasn't conscious of Jesus and what He had to do with the Supreme Creator."

Bob said he had accepted Jesus Christ in his heart after a "vision and feeling" during which the room moved. "There was a presence in the room that couldn't have been anybody but Jesus." He was reluctant initially to put his feelings into songs or even to tell his friends, but he now wanted to share his experience with others.

"The funny thing," he continued, "is that a lot of people think that Jesus comes into a person's life only when they are either down and out or are miserable or just old and withering. That's not the way it was for me. I was doing fine. I had come a long way in just the year we were on the road in 1978. I was relatively content, but a very close friend of mine mentioned a couple of things to me and one of them was Jesus. Well, the whole idea of Jesus was foreign to me. I said to myself, 'I can't deal with that. Maybe later.' But later it occurred to me that I trusted this person and I had nothing to do for the next couple of days, so I called the person back and said I was willing to talk about Jesus."

Dylan said the friend introduced him to two young pastors in the San Fernando Valley. He said he was skeptical, but also open-minded. "I certainly wasn't cynical. I asked lots of questions, like 'What's the Son of God, what's all that mean?' and 'What does it mean—dying for my sins?'"

Slowly, Dylan said, he began to accept that Jesus was real and that he wanted Him in his life. "I knew that He wasn't going to come in my life and make it miserable, so one thing led to another until I had this feeling, this vision and feeling."

At the same time, Bob showed me that he hadn't lost his questioning spirit. When I asked about the political activism of fundamentalist Christian groups like the Moral Majority, he replied, "I think people have to be careful about all that. It's real dangerous. You can find anything you want in the Bible. You can twist it around any way you want and a lot of people do just that. I just don't think you can legislate morality. The basic thing I feel is to get in touch with Christ yourself. He will lead you. Any preacher who is a real preacher will tell you that: 'Don't follow me, follow Christ.'"

In the Q&A with Bob that I did for the *Times,* I made it clear that it would be wrong to infer that he had become a stereotypical "Jesus freak" interested only in discussing that subject. Once he had expressed his feelings, he spoke with equal conviction about other issues, including the decision to do his old material again. For nearly two hours, he spoke clearly and directly, without any trace of the bobbing and weaving that was made famous by the *Don't Look Back* film. Here are parts of the interview.

Some people would love you to go on stage and just sing the old songs, like a living Beatlemania. Isn't there a danger in that? That's what Elvis Presley ended up doing.

Elvis changed. The show that people always talk about [with] Elvis was that 1968 TV show, but it's not quite the same as when he did those songs in the beginning. When he did "That's All Right, Mama" in 1955, it was all sensitivity and power. In 1968, it was just full-out power. There was nothing other than just force behind that. I've fallen into that trap, too. Take the 1974 tour. It's a very fine line you have to walk to stay in touch with something once you've created it. Either it holds up for you or it doesn't. A lot of artists say, "I can't sing those old songs anymore," and I can understand it because you're no longer the same person who wrote those songs.

However, you really are still that person, someplace, down deep. You don't really get that out of your system. So, you can still sing them if you can get in touch with the person you were when you wrote the songs. I don't think I could sit down now and write "It's Alright, Ma" again. I wouldn't even know where to begin, but I can still sing it, and I'm glad I've written it.

After you had the vision, I understand you attended a three-month Bible course at a church in Reseda [California].

At first I said, "There's no way I can devote three months to this. I've got to get back on the road soon." But I was sleeping one day and I just sat up in bed at seven in the morning and I was compelled to get dressed and drive over to the Bible school. I couldn't believe I was there.

But you had already accepted Jesus in your heart?

Yeah, but I hadn't told anybody about it because I felt they would say, "Aw, come on." Most of the people I know don't believe that Jesus was resurrected, that He is alive. It was like He was just another prophet or something, one of many good people. That's not the way it was any longer for me. I had already read the Bible, but I only looked at it as literature. I was never really instructed in it in a way that was meaningful to me.

Did you start telling friends about it when you went to the Bible classes?

No, I didn't want to set myself up. I didn't want to reflect on the Lord at all because if I told people and then I didn't keep going, they'd say, "Oh well, I guess it was just another one of those things that didn't work out." I didn't know myself if I could go for three months. But I did begin telling a few people after a couple of months and a lot of them got angry at me.

Do you see how people could think some of the messages in the album were heavy-handed?

I didn't mean to deliver a hammer blow. It might come out that way, but I'm not trying to kill anybody. You can't put down people who don't believe. Anybody can have the answer I have. I mean, it's free.

Are the early songs still meaningful to you or do you just do them because people want to hear them?

I love those songs; they're still part of me.

What about some of the new songs? Some seem only remotely religious.

They've evolved. I made my statement and I don't think I could make it any better than in some of those songs. Once I've said what I need to say in a song, that's it. I don't want to repeat myself.

Is music still important to you?

Music has given me a purpose. As a kid, there was rock. Later on, there was folk-blues. It's not something that I just listen to as a passive person. It has always been in my blood and it has never failed me. Because of that, I'm disconnected from a lot of the pressures of life. It disconnects you from what people think about you. Attitudes don't really make too much difference when you can get on stage and play the guitar and sing songs. It's natural for me. I don't know why I was chosen to do it. I'm almost forty now and I'm not tired of it yet.

. . . .

The article was reprinted in scores of papers around the world, and I got hundreds of letters from Dylan fans. Just as fans assumed I knew everything about Elvis, these readers thought I was their connection to Dylan, and I heard from some of them for decades.

CHAPTER
FOURTEEN

John Lennon's house-husband period was over by the fall of 1980, and John and Yoko were finishing up their new album, *Double Fantasy*, as I headed to New York for John's first newspaper interview in five years. This was when John raced into Yoko's office at the Dakota with a copy of Donna Summer's "The Wanderer." I spent the next three days with John and Yoko, a couple of hours each afternoon in their apartment and then each night in a recording studio about ten minutes away on Forty-Eighth Street.

The Dakota is one of New York's most famous residential addresses. Built in 1884, the Dakota has spacious rooms and high ceilings; John and Yoko's living room had the formal but graceful feel of a museum with its Egyptian art, including a sarcophagus that dominated one side of the room. From one window of the seventh-floor apartment, I could see across Central Park and much of the city's spectacular skyline. For the preceding five years, that scene had been John's primary view of the world. He had decided in 1975 to shut down his career to rebuild his strained marriage with Yoko and to spend time with their son, Sean, who was born that October. He also wanted to escape the pressures and expectations of the rock 'n' roll world. Despite his highly acclaimed solo works of the early 1970s, John found it difficult to deal with the ghost of his Fab Four association.

"When I wrote 'the dream is over' [in 'God' in 1970], I was trying to say to the Beatles thing, 'Get off my back.' I was also trying to tell the other people to stop looking at me because I wasn't going to do it for them anymore because I didn't even know what the hell I was doing in my own life," he told me that first day. "What I realized during the five years away was that when I said the dream is over, I had made the physical break from the Beatles, but mentally there was still this big thing on my back about what people expected of me. It was like this invisible ghost. During the five years, it sort of went away. I finally started writing like I was even before the Beatles were the Beatles. I got rid of all that self-consciousness about telling myself, 'You can't do that. That song's not good enough. Remember, you're the guy who wrote "A Day in the Life." Try again.'"

John wasn't a recluse for those five years. He and the family traveled to Japan and elsewhere. He also went out regularly in New York, but he stayed away from the music business and the media. He said he had begun writing again the previous summer, during a vacation with Sean in Bermuda. Excited about the new material, he had called Yoko, who had remained in New York to take care of some business matters, and he played her a tape on the phone. She then wrote reply songs, which she played back to him a few days later. With the songs forming a dialogue, the Lennons went into a recording studio in New York in the autumn to record an album. They were especially excited about "(Just Like) Starting Over," the first single from the LP. Though the title could symbolize Lennon's return to music, he wrote it mainly as a love song to Yoko, an admission of past neglects and a pledge of greater sensitivity.

Moving into the kitchen, where he sat on a wooden table while Yoko prepared a salad to take to the studio, John said "Starting Over" was a plea for men and women to start over. "Sexism is such a big issue, and we haven't even begun to deal with it. There are all kinds of inequities in the world—this race versus that race, this country versus that country—but it's always women at the bottom." Even though the Lennons had caused a stir when they addressed the same point in

"Woman Is the Nigger of the World" on 1972's *Some Time in New York City,* John said he had been as much a sexist at the time as the people he was writing about. "I accepted intellectually what we were saying in the song, but I hadn't really accepted it in my heart. It wasn't a matter of whether I accepted Yoko's opinion—or any woman's—I didn't even consider them.

"In some ways the last five years were almost like a penance, a way to say, 'I understand completely and I'm willing to put my life on the line for this belief.' I don't just intellectualize about it now or go to a group meeting or write a song. I shut up and learned how to cook and be with the baby and allow the feminine side of myself to exist rather than crush it out in fear or insecurity that I wasn't manly enough."

In the limo on the way to the studio, John continued to talk about Yoko, saying she served as an artistic catalyst—questioning, discussing, challenging. He called their musical relationship a partnership, noting that she wrote and sang half the songs on the album. But what about the commercial consequences? There had been so much anti-Yoko feeling because of the breakup of the Beatles. Would his fans accept Yoko as a musical partner?

This time, Yoko spoke up. "I have two concerns in this album," she said. "First, I hope that it reminds people of John's talent. Second, I hope the fact that I am working with him enhances the man-woman dialogue. At the same time, I don't want the situation to become negative because my songs are too far-out or anything. That's hurting the chances of the album reaching as many people as possible. That wouldn't be fair to John. So in selecting my songs, I was conscious about the ones that are not too—shall we say—offbeat. This album is like our first hello. When you say hello, you don't want to complicate things. Maybe in the second or third album, we can experiment more."

John smiled at her words and said, "Yes, this is just starting over. We're going to move forward in the next album. It's going to be even better, so people better get ready."

As she leaned on his arm in the back of the limo, they seemed very comfortable. It was nighttime and everything felt quiet and safe in the car. "It's not really so unusual, you know," Yoko said, mentioning the literary couple Robert and Elizabeth Browning. "Ah," John said.

He started quoting one of Elizabeth Barrett Browning's most famous lines: "How do I love thee? Let me count the ways." Yoko talked about how Robert and Elizabeth had inspired each other. I said that might be a good angle for a story: "John and Yoko, the Robert and Elizabeth Browning of rock." We all smiled.

It was dawn by the time the session ended, so we didn't get together the next day until early afternoon. Once again, John greeted me with a surprise. "Look at this," he said, holding up a framed newspaper clipping. "It's the first write-up ever on the Beatles. I don't even know what paper it is from, but it must have been around 1959, before we went to Hamburg. It's the only copy around anymore. Paul doesn't even have this." However tormented John had felt in the early 1970s about the pressures of being a Beatle, he certainly hadn't lost his affection for the band.

Reading aloud from the brief article as we stood in the kitchen of the apartment, John especially enjoyed the part that listed the names of the band: "'A Liverpool rhythm group, the Beatles, made their debut. . . . John Lennon, the leader, plays one of three rhythm guitars. The other guitarists are Paul Ramone and Carl Harrison.'"

Interrupting the reading, John said, "That was Paul and George. I don't know why Paul called himself 'Ramone,' but 'Carl' was for Carl Perkins. The myth is we all took other names, but I never did. They say I was called Johnny Silver, but I was never called that. What happened was this guy tried to change our name to the Silver Beatles. He didn't like just plain Beatles. So, he asked what my name was. When I told him 'John,' he said, 'Oh, great, why don't you be Long John Silver and the Beatles.' I refused, but he was in control of the dance hall, so I allowed him to call us the Silver Beatles. But that only lasted ten days. It's another myth that we were called the Silver Beatles for months and months."

At the studio, we tended to talk about the new album, the househusband period, and his relationship with Yoko. But the time at the Dakota was like recess for us both. On that second day, he took me to Sean's playroom, where he kept one of his prized possessions, a vintage jukebox. Plugging it in, he punched one Elvis Presley record after another and bopped around playfully.

As Elvis sang "Don't Be Cruel" in the background, John recalled his first and only meeting with our mutual rock hero. It was a story he relished sharing as much as he did his Beatles memories.

"It was probably 1965 and we had a break in LA during a tour. We went up to his house and we were terrified. I can't remember the first moment I saw him, but he looked great. We started singing some of his songs. That's what we always did when we met Chuck Berry or Carl Perkins or any of them."

I asked if Elvis had known how big the Beatles were and if he had felt any hint of competition.

"Are you kidding?" John replied with a laugh. "He knew damn well who we were—from the word go. He was terrified of us and the English movement because we were a threat to him. I heard he was so paranoid all afternoon that he kept practicing things to say to us, asking the guys around him if we were any good. It was like Ali wondering if he could handle Frazier. To us, he was a god. We'd like to beat his record and become the champion, but we would always give him credit. It always hurts and infuriates me when Mick Jagger puts Elvis down. Maybe he's jealous because Elvis was the original body man in rock and it's too near to Mick's game for him to admit that Elvis's movements were at least as good as his and that maybe Elvis could sing a damn sight better than he could."

John's favorite time with the Beatles surprised me—the early days. Hamburg, Liverpool, the dance halls. I'd thought he'd say it was when the band had conquered America. "Naw," he said with a wave of a hand. "We were already blasé. We had the show down. We were already past our peak as performers. It was like Vegas—what we did on stage, I mean. We shook our head on this number and . . . well, you know the rest."

We had never spoken all that much about the Beatles, and John seemed to be amused by my sudden display of interest. He even laughed when I told him the reason I wanted to be Elvis was because of all the screaming girls. Was it the same with him in the Beatles? "That was one of the main reasons you go on stage, because the guy in the band gets the girls," he said with a broad grin. "There's an old joke, but it's true: Sometimes you'd get this girl after the show and you'd be in bed and she'd ask you which one you are. I'd say, 'Which one do you like?' If she said 'George,' I'd say, 'I'm George.'"

This was so much fun that it didn't even seem like an interview. I was just a fan, asking him to name things like his favorite Beatles albums (*Rubber Soul, Revolver, Sgt. Pepper's Lonely Hearts Club Band,* and the white album) and what tracks he'd put on a Beatles greatest-hits package ("I'd favor my own tracks, of course. I'd go with 'Walrus,' 'Strawberry Fields,' 'Come Together,' 'Revolution,' 'In My Life,' 'Hard Day's Night,' 'Help'—stuff like that and some of the early tracks like 'I Want to Hold Your Hand' and 'Day Tripper.'").

John was so into reminiscing that he even came up with a question: What would have happened if the band hadn't broken up in 1970?

In answering it, he said, "We would have probably gone down the tubes and then been resurrected like everything else. I always thought it was best to go out when you're flying high. The popularity was always ebbing and flowing. That's what people forget. It was only during the initial rush that people thought everything we did was right. After that, it was up or down depending on the single or the album or whatever. We could split up in 1970 because we were on top. In fact, it was probably the best thing that ever happened to the Beatles myth. I read this book about Mick where he said after the breakup, 'At last, we're No. 1.' What he didn't realize was that when we split, we created a much bigger thing than if we had stayed. He could never catch up with that."

At the studio that night, I spoke to John and Yoko separately in an adjacent lounge during breaks in the session, and they both most enjoyed talking about each other. John and Yoko both saw *Double Fantasy* as the first in a series of joint albums together. "One of my most important discoveries during the last five years was that Yoko is as important to me as my music," John told me when we were alone.

"The irony is that people say Yoko split the Beatles," he continued. "In truth, it was the Beatles that split John and Yoko. That was more like it. She was buried by the Beatles in a way. It just took a long time because part of us is very tough. But all the shit from those days finally accumulated until what burst was the two of us. I couldn't stand the suffering that came from seeing the way people were treating Yoko. I began to think that if I got away from her, things would be better for her. Although she was the one who eventually kicked me out, my behavior was becoming such that she had no choice. She had to say, 'Get the hell out.'"

I was intrigued by how calmly John spoke about such personal matters, but I also realized that he had needed that fearlessness to make an album as unflinching as *Plastic Ono Band*. He credited Yoko with finally freeing him from the Beatles burden.

"Without her, I'd probably be dead," he said. "She was the one who literally said to me, 'You don't have to do this. You exist outside of the music.' That was a frightening concept for me. My whole security and identity was wrapped up in being John Lennon, the pop star."

I told John I couldn't imagine, as a fan, how hard it must have been for him to simply walk away from music.

"It was the hardest thing I've ever had to do in my life—not make music," he said. "Not because I had this love for music or because I was so creative and I couldn't bear not to be creative, but because I felt that I didn't exist unless my name was in the gossip columns of *Rolling Stone* or the *Daily News* or whatever. Then, it dawned on me that I do still exist."

When I later mentioned to Yoko that John had said she was more important to him than music, she seemed embarrassed and waved her cigarette at me. "I don't know if he really means that," she said. "He tends to get emotional. He's a poet. So, he lives to use extravagant words. Both of us are very honest to our own desires. The only way I can describe our relationship in terms of our art is through karma. Music and art are still very important to me, but if the karmic relationship with someone as close as John isn't right, I couldn't go on with the music or art. I couldn't just escape into art and music. I'd be involved with them for the wrong reasons. To John, I'm his reality, and he's my reality."

We had such a good time over the three days that John invited me to his and Sean's birthday party at Tavern on the Green. I knew what the perfect birthday present for John was. I had mentioned in the studio that there was a great new Elvis photo book by Alfred Wertheimer, who had spent a couple of weeks with Elvis around the time of "Hound Dog" in 1956. John hadn't seen it.

The party was scheduled for noon, and I left the hotel around eleven, thinking I'd pick up a copy of the book at a bookstore. But I had to go to a half-dozen stores before finally finding one, and the party was over by the time I got to the restaurant. I headed back to the Dakota. I didn't want to bother John, so I left the book with the doorman.

At the bookstore, I also picked up a copy of Elizabeth Barrett Browning's poetry in case I wanted to quote more from the poem John had mentioned. He had said he wished he could put those feelings into a song, because it would be the perfect love song. During the flight back, the final lines struck me. In them, Barrett Browning says, "If God choose, I shall but love thee better after death."

I flashed on that final line two months later when I heard the news.

CHAPTER
FIFTEEN

A fter ten years at the *Times,* I was at a crossroads in my personal life. I loved my family, but I was also so obsessive about my work that I found myself devoting more and more time to it. I wanted to be everywhere there was a good story, and that meant I had to choose between being with the family on important days, such as New Year's Eve, or flying up to San Francisco because I had heard so much about Bill Graham's New Year's Eve extravaganza. Sitting in the arena that night, I knew there was no way the trip had been essential, but I also knew that if I had stayed home, I would have spent the whole evening imagining what I was missing in San Francisco. I saw how Bruce gave all of himself to his work and I bought into it. Finally, my wife and I separated.

To get away, I flew to Memphis for a week's vacation and spent the whole time working on some stories I had long wanted to do. I pored over local newspaper articles from the 1950s at the library, trying to get a sense of what the city had been like when Elvis, Jerry Lee Lewis, and Johnny Cash were cutting those landmark

Sun singles. I also interviewed soul singer Al Green and stayed up until almost dawn one night interviewing one of my heroes, Sun Records founder Sam Phillips.

I was exhausted on the flight home and happy to find a row with three vacant seats, which allowed me to stretch out and sleep. I didn't wake up until the wheels were touching the runway in Los Angeles. I was still rubbing my eyes when a stewardess said I was supposed to phone the city desk at the *Times* and KNX radio as soon as I got to the terminal. I assumed there must be some fast-breaking news, perhaps even an accident at the airport. I went to the pay phones and called the paper. A voice said gently, "John Lennon was shot to death in New York, apparently by some crazy fan outside his apartment building."

I was stunned, but not in the same way I had been when I'd learned of Elvis's death. I'd been at home when that news came on television and I'd felt like a part of me died. This time, I thought about how hard John had fought not to end up another rock 'n' roll tragedy. I recalled those lines from the Elizabeth Barrett Browning poem. But there wasn't time to dwell on it. The editor wanted me to write an appreciation of John for the next day's paper and then go to New York to cover the funeral. So, I rushed straight to the office. Normally, I try to outline a story before actually writing it, but this time I just started writing. I wanted the appreciation to be straight from my heart. I wrote about how we were accustomed to tragic deaths in rock—Elvis Presley, Janis Joplin, Jimi Hendrix, Jim Morrison, Keith Moon—but that John's death didn't fit the pattern. He wasn't a victim of rock excesses.

I continued with something John had said just two weeks before by phone. He was excited that the new single, "Starting Over," was already in the Top Ten. "It's still a thrill to hear your record on the radio," he said. "It sort of finally makes the music real to me even though I've heard the song a million times by now in the studio." John was also touched by the way disc jockeys were responding to his return. "When they play the song, the DJs don't have to say anything, but they've been saying all sorts of wonderful things. That makes me feel like they really like it. Yoko and I are so excited that we're going right back in the studio to begin working on the next album. I feel just like a kid again."

I ended the appreciation with what had been my last question to John. I had wanted a feel-good quote to end that earlier story, so I asked him if this was a good time for him. His answer: "The best."

As I finished the appreciation, I noticed that some people from the paper were gathered outside my office. One copy messenger, a girl of nineteen, was seated at a desk, sobbing.

My first thought was "Why is *she* crying? John was *my* friend."

At the same time, it felt audacious to even think that John had been my friend. I had only spent a few days with him over a period of seven years, and maybe John's openness and charm had made everyone feel close to him. Ultimately, it didn't matter. I would later read some dark accounts of his behavior during the Beatles days and afterward, but I was lucky to have known him when he was at peace with himself and the world. Now, he was gone, and I felt the loss deeply.

Six hours later, I was on a plane to New York.

I spent most of the flight writing down thoughts about John and going through the notes from my various interviews with him. In the final interview, we had talked about Elvis, which led to John talking about the concept of death. At the Dakota, he had pointed out all the Elvis records on the jukebox.

"Everybody tried to contact me when he died, but I was still doing my Greta Garbo disappearing act," he said. "I nearly opened my mouth and said something, but I was in the mountains in Japan and that helped me maintain my distance. It's hard for me to speak about death. I have had so much death around me. My mother was killed in an auto accident, Stuart Sutcliffe [a musician and close friend in the early days of the Beatles] died of a brain tumor. So did Len Gray, another guy in one of our groups. Buddy Holly died when I was in art school. They all affected me, but I can't find a way to put the feeling into words. It's like you lose a piece of yourself each time it happens."

Looking at those notes, I thought about how Memphis had mourned so visibly following Elvis's death. I hoped that New York, which often struck me as a cold, anonymous place, would also show some sentiment. I checked into my usual hotel near Central Park and phoned Elliot Mintz, John's friend, who normally stayed across the street at the Plaza. He wasn't in, so I left a message that I was in town and wanted him to tell Yoko that my prayers were with her. Then I put down the phone, laid on the bed, and waited. Finally, Elliot called. "I gave Yoko your message and she would like to see you at the Dakota."

What did that mean? Did she want to see me as a friend or as a journalist who could relay her feelings to John's fans? I picked up my wallet and notebook, but I left the tape recorder on the bed. I didn't want to send Yoko the wrong signal.

I took a cab to the Dakota, where there was a large crowd of fans in the street singing John's songs and staring up at Yoko's window. Elliot was waiting at the entrance to escort me past the security guards. I wanted most of all to hug Yoko and tell her how much I missed John and about how people, including those in my office, were so deeply touched by his music. But I knew how strong Yoko is—it was one of the things John so liked about her, needed from her—and I vowed to stay calm. Elliot led me into the living room and said he'd see if Yoko was ready to see me. Sean, who was five, was in the apartment with Julian, John's son from his first marriage.

When Elliot returned, he led me to Yoko's room. The curtains were drawn and Yoko was sitting up in bed, a cigarette in her hand and the covers pulled up around her. I could see the tear stains on her cheeks. I could also hear the fans below singing, but the words were indistinguishable. It just sounded like mournful tribal chanting.

I didn't know what to say, so I just sat on the bed and reached out and hugged her. I fought hard not to cry myself. Elliot stood next to the bed as Yoko started talking. She told about how hard it was to accept that John wasn't here with us and she said some sweet things about John's feelings for me. Then, she recounted the evening. "It was so sudden . . . so sudden," she said. "We had planned to go out to eat after leaving the recording studio, but we decided to go straight home instead. We were walking to the entrance of the building when I heard the shot. I didn't realize at first that John had been hit. He kept walking. Then, he fell and I saw the blood."

She sighed and leaned back. Finally, she looked over at the drapes and said how sweet the music sounded, how nice the fans were to come by. She said she wished she could speak to them all, but she knew that would be crazy. But I had the feeling that what she said next was what she would have said to them: "The future is still ours to make. The '80s will blossom if only people accept peace and love in their hearts. It would just add to the tragedy if people turned away from the message in John's music."

I asked her if she would like me to put that quote in the paper— the idea of not giving up—and she said that would be nice. She also said she hoped that people wouldn't blame New York City for John's murder.

"People say that there is something wrong with New York, that it's sick, but John loved New York. He'd be the first one to say it wasn't New York's fault. There can be one crank anywhere."

By now, I had my notebook out. Yoko paused, and I could imagine her trying to think of what else John would have wanted her to say. After a slight pause, she said, "We had planned on so much together." She was now crying. "We had talked about living until we were eighty. We even drew up lists of all the things we could do together for all those years. Then, it was over. But that doesn't mean the message should be over. The music will live on."

I was in the room for probably ten minutes, but it felt like an hour. I walked out with Elliot and asked him to go into the hall with me, where I went over the rapidly scribbled quotes in my notebook, making sure I filled in a couple of blanks with what he had heard. Then I took a cab back to the hotel, where I borrowed a typewriter in the manager's office and wrote the story for the next day's paper. I was so concerned that everything be true to Yoko's feelings that I requested that a copy editor read me the headline before the paper went to print, something writers rarely do because the headline choice belongs to the copy desk. But the copy editor understood the sensitivity involved and read me the headline that would appear on page one: "A Time for Love, Not Hate: Yoko Hopes the World Will Let It Be, Let It Be." I was so stressed that I didn't even think about "Let It Be" being a Paul McCartney song. The spirit felt right, so I said the headline was fine.

The next morning I took a cab to the *Los Angeles Times*'s New York office so I could see a copy of the paper. I read quickly through the piece to make sure there were no typos, then picked up the phone to call Elliot. He wasn't at the hotel, so I left a message. Then, I saw a copy of the *New York Post,* which subscribed to the Los Angeles Times/ Washington Post News Service. My Yoko story was splashed across the cover of the tabloid, and I was horrified to see that it was accompanied by a photo of John's coffin. I thought about how terrible Yoko would feel upon seeing that photo, and I was afraid she would think I had betrayed her.

When Elliot returned my call, I mentioned the *Post* photo and asked him to explain to Yoko that I had had nothing to do with it. Elliot was great. He said he knew how some papers work. There was no reason for me to feel guilty. He had called to say Yoko had decided there would be no public service for John. She wanted to avoid the circuslike atmosphere that had surrounded Elvis's funeral. She asked that people join in a silent, ten-minute prayer vigil Sunday, "wherever you are." But New York mayor Ed Koch felt there should be a public tribute, so he invited fans to join Sunday near the band shell in Central Park. I decided to stay and cover the Sunday memorial—and was touched by how the city was moved by John's death. Wherever I walked, I felt the impact. The tabloids ran six to twelve pages a day on John, while every local TV news program opened with more expressions of sorrow and disbelief. There were also conversations everywhere—in the subways, coffee shops, hotel lobbies. The words I heard most often were "sad" and "why?" John's death knocked the wind out of New York City as much as Elvis's had Memphis.

On the day of the prayer vigil, visitors in the heart of Manhattan didn't need to ask for directions, they just followed the crowd. Unlike the hysterical weeping that I'd seen in Memphis in 1977, the audience on Sunday was more subdued, listening to Lennon songs over a loudspeaker. Some held signs, offering messages like "Just Give Peace a Chance" and, inevitably, "We Love You, John." At 2:00 p.m., the crowd began its silent prayer. This was the day's most emotional moment. Midway through the silence, a photographer in the roped-off press area stopped taking photos of weeping mourners and retreated behind a parked truck to cry himself.

One thing troubled me on the flight back to Los Angeles. Had I been honorable in contacting Yoko? I had wanted to express my feelings to her about her and John, but I also hoped deep in my heart that she had wanted me to write a story. I remained anxious until the day a card arrived from Yoko. It read "Thank you," and was signed "With love."

INTERLUDE
SOME FAVORITE QUOTES

There's a debate in journalism over the value of quotes. I once attended a writing seminar given by a *Wall Street Journal* editor who prided himself on almost never using quotes because he thought they slowed the pace of a good story. But I've always enjoyed reading an artist's own words, and I worked hard at trying to get good quotes. I think they help bring intimacy to a profile. Here are some of my favorites.

"When I was twenty years old, I'd get on the back of a motorcycle with some guy who'd been up three days speeding his brains out and was drunk, and I'd be yelling, 'Faster.' Because, let's face it, it was a thrill. Right now, if I saw the same guy, I'd say, 'See ya later, pal.' These days I'm getting on the slowest Honda in town."

—Chrissie Hynde, leader of the Pretenders, in 1984 at age thirty-two, after the drug-related deaths of two of her bandmates and the birth of her first daughter

"My biggest goal isn't to be No. 1. My goal is to be able to think in ten years from now that I'll be able to listen to our third album and not be embarrassed by it."

—Michael Stipe, shortly after the 1985 release of R.E.M.'s third album, *Fables of the Reconstruction*, a much-admired collection that contributed to the Georgia band's status as the godfathers of the indie-rock movement

"After you've been in a band for a long time, you feel like you're on a one-way ticket to the edge. You talk about taking a break, but there are so many commitments that you never get the time. So I finally just went off on my own to Paris. I grew a beard and walked around like Fidel Castro, and it was great because nobody recognized me. I felt like a real person again. I think it's real important to make that contact with reality. Look what happened to Elvis Presley. That was the saddest thing. The poor guy never wanted to end up being locked up in that hillbilly palace."

—Joe Strummer, the Clash cofounder, in 1986, looking back on the time when the British band seemed poised to take over the title of world's greatest rock band. Ultimately, the pressures on Strummer in particular were so great that he let his ego lead him to convince the band to kick out guitarist Mick Jones. It was a move that proved fatal to the Clash.

"In the end, you either cheer people up with your songs or help them exorcise some problems they have—and people need a bit of both right now. The mood of the country as a whole is that things aren't as they are being advertised. Lots of people are going hungry. Even more have had to downscale their expectations. They are confused. They remember everything they heard about this country in school and they wonder what happened to it."

—Steve Earle, soon after the release of *Guitar Town,* a 1986 album that spoke up for the small-town, blue-collar Americans who felt they were being left out of the prosperity of Reagan's America

"Some writer was asking me something once, and Andy Warhol said, 'You're not going to tell the truth, are you? You know you don't have to tell the truth. You can say anything you want,' and that's what I did for years. Unfortunately, I'm still haunted by those lies. People continue to ask, 'Did you really put a rifle to a guy's head?' and 'Do you really have a degree in music from Harvard?'"

—Lou Reed, talking in 1992 about his dislike, ever since the days of the Velvet Underground, of journalists asking personal questions

"People think you are this grand person who has all their shit together because you are able to put your feelings into some songs. They write letters and come to the shows and even to the house, hoping we can fix everything for them. But we can't because we don't have all our shit together, either. What they don't understand is that you can't save somebody from drowning if you're treading water yourself."

—Eddie Vedder of Pearl Jam, days after the death of Kurt Cobain in 1994, when he was suddenly looked upon as the next great hope in rock

"You didn't used to like me, did you?"

—Barbra Streisand's opening words when I sat down with her backstage in Detroit in 1994 during her first concert tour in two decades. (I had criticized her frequently during the 1970s and 1980s for overly dramatic vocals.) But the line was followed by a playful smile. I thought the tour was a revelation. Her singing was graceful, her material purposeful, and her manner endearing. I ended up doing three more interviews with the notoriously media-shy performer, actress, and director, and I enjoyed them immensely.

"I get a little nervous about things like awards and sales. Part of me wonders if all that makes it harder for you to focus on what you should be doing as artists. There are lots of dangers in rock—the lifestyle, the business issues—but the biggest danger is ego and how that can alter the kind of music that you make."

—Thom Yorke, during an interview in London in 1998, soon after Radiohead's *OK Computer* had been nominated for the album of the year Grammy

"Everybody has a ventriloquist act. Rodney Dangerfield has an act. Bob Dylan has an act. I guess it's a question of who's the dummy. Where do you leave off and where does a character begin? I don't know . . . Let's order some food."

—Tom Waits, in a restaurant near his home in Northern California in 1999, responding to a series of questions dealing with just who is beneath all those sometimes crusty, eccentric characters in his songs who come across as part Charles Bukowski and part Captain Beefheart

"I was out of control. I was wildin' out, partying, women . . . I think the business and all the fame and fortune just sucked me in and I had to step back and see I was ruining everything I had worked so hard at building. I finally had to sit down a few years ago and try to picture myself ten years from now and imagine which people I wanted around me, which people were really a positive force in my life. That list turned out to be very small. But the list of people around me at the time could have filled the [eighteen-thousand-seat] Forum."

—Dr. Dre, the greatest producer in rap, reflecting in 1999 on wild and violent times in his life, including breaking another rap producer's jaw. He spent six months in a Pasadena, California, jail.

"I know people are confused by a lot of what I do, but I am too sometimes. That's why I went into therapy. I wanted to understand why Axl had been this volatile, crazy, whatever, for years. I was told that my mental circuitry was all twisted . . . in terms of how I would deal with stress because of what happened to me back in Indiana. Basically, I would overload with the stress of a situation . . . by smashing whatever was around me. . . . I used to think I was actually dealing with my problems and now I know that's not dealing with it at all. I'm trying now to [channel] my energy in more positive ways . . . but it doesn't always work."

—Axl Rose, the mercurial leader of Guns n' Roses, in a 1999 interview about the tug-of-war between his creative and destructive urges

"I don't think music can make you kill or rape someone any more than a movie is going to make you do something you know is wrong, but music can give you strength. If people take anything from my music, it should be motivation to know that anything is possible as long as you keep working at it and don't back down. I didn't have nothin' going for me . . . school, home . . . until I found something I loved, which was music, and that changed everything."

—Eminem in 2000, when his nothing's-sacred mix of sexual and violent imagery had parents asking "What kind of madman is this?" An artist of the highest order, Eminem captured brilliantly the pain of growing up with all the cards stacked against you.

"I heard someone from the music business saying they are no longer looking for talent, they want people with a certain look and a willingness to cooperate. I thought, that's interesting, because I believe that a total unwillingness to cooperate is what is necessary to be an artist—not for perverse reasons, but to protect your vision. The considerations of a corporation, especially now, have nothing to do with art or music. That's why I spend my time now painting."

—Joni Mitchell, one of the half-dozen most-influential songwriters of the rock era, explaining in 2004 why she had (temporarily, it turned out) given up making albums

CHAPTER
SIXTEEN

'd like to be able to say I had a "Jon Landau seeing in Bruce Springsteen the 'future of rock 'n' roll' moment" when U2 made its LA club
debut at the Country Club in March of 1981, that I was perceptive
enough to realize that a twenty-year-old who called himself Bono
was going to incorporate the inspiration and character of Elvis
Presley, Springsteen, Bob Dylan, and John Lennon into a single,
uplifting package. At the time, I just saw an extremely promising
young band. My initial reference point was the Who.

On stage, U2 played songs from its debut album, *Boy,* with the
power and unabashed emotion of Pete Townshend and company.
Rather than the literal aggression of British punk outfits of the time,
U2 documented more subtly the joys and anxieties of adolescence. I
didn't know whether to call the lead singer by his real name—Paul
Hewson—or the nickname he used on the album jacket, but he reached
out to the crowd with the broad, open gestures of a man on a mission.
Like Townshend, he didn't seem to be reaching just for the charts, but
for his audience's heart and soul. His lyrics at times bordered on vague
abstraction, but the sharp, sparkling, trancelike lines of the Edge's

guitar work gave the music both its own identity and a visceral punch.

I met Bono a few days later at Warner Bros. Records in Burbank, and he was eager to see something he had heard about for years in Dublin—an American drive-in restaurant. So I took him to the nearby Bob's Big Boy, a drive-in prototype complete with carhops on weekends. Bono was so interested in American pop culture that it was hard to keep him on the subject of his band, which I found unusual. Normally the only thing artists want to talk about is their music. But Bono wanted to know what it was like living in Los Angeles, with its rich history of movies and music. Once he learned that I had met many of his heroes, he wanted to hear stories about them. He was particularly interested in Elvis, Lennon, Dylan, Cash, and Springsteen. By the time we got back around to U2, he was on his second ice-cream-and-hot-fudge cake.

Even then, he was asking as many questions as I was, including how I had found out about U2. When I told him I had read about them in a roundup of new psychedelic rock bands in one of the British pop magazines, Bono declared, "I don't know why they settled on 'psychedelic.' I don't identify with that music at all. Our music has mood and atmosphere, but it's not drug oriented. I find drugs very boring. The '60s bands that had an effect on me were the classic ones—the Who, the Beatles, Stones, Cream, Dylan. I remember seeing films like *A Hard Day's Night* and *Help!* and loving the excitement and celebration."

He said U2 hoped to bring some of that classic spirit back to music. "It just seemed like it went away in the 1970s," he continued. "Everything suddenly seemed soft and professional, instead of warm and raw. I could relate to the raw energy of the Sex Pistols, but that, too, was ultimately limited. It had emotion again, but only one emotion. We wanted more dimension. We wanted power *and* sensitivity."

Listening to him, it was hard to fathom that he was just twenty. Bruce was twenty-four the first time I'd spoken to him, and he was nowhere near as certain about his path or as sophisticated about the music industry as this intriguing young man was. I asked if he was discouraged that the "I Will Follow" single was getting so little radio airplay. "No," he said, taking the last bite of the ice cream cake. "I'm in no hurry. I'm not even sure our music is good enough for radio right now. We're just starting out. We're willing to take the time. We're not just here for a couple of weeks. We want to do a lot of shows in America so that people can find out what we're about. It may take another album, even a third album, before we connect with America, but I know it's coming."

As cocky as the words sounded, Bono had a winning humility. When I dropped him off at the record company, I wished him well, but I had no idea what was ahead. Lots of terrific bands had failed to make it big in America because they hadn't fit within the narrow boundaries of rock radio. Why should U2 be any different?

I was puzzled by U2's second album in the fall of 1981. The lyrics were vague on *Boy,* but it wasn't a major problem because the elusiveness fit the uncertainty of the album's youthful theme. Besides, the dazzling instrumental textures captured your allegiance. In *October,* however, the introspective lyrics explored spiritual matters in a way that was too abstract and the music wasn't uplifting enough to compensate. I felt U2 could still deliver live, but I couldn't see them realizing their dreams unless they wrote better songs.

They lived up to that challenge in *War,* the 1983 album that spoke in convincing and concrete terms about political and religious turmoil. Key songs on the album were prayerlike calls for peace from men who were disillusioned with the religious and political discord at home. The turmoil took on a special meaning for Bono because his mother was Protestant and his father was Catholic. Several of the album's songs, including "Sunday Bloody Sunday" and "New Year's Day," picked up radio airplay, causing enough of a buzz to get the band a featured slot at the gigantic US Festival. U2 didn't headline the three-day event, which drew 250,000 fans to a motor speedway just east of Los Angeles, but they stole the show with a passionate performance during which Bono carried a white flag of peace some thirty feet to the top of the stage scaffolding.

It was a spectacular set, and I couldn't wait to see them a few months later at the twelve-thousand-seat Los Angeles Sports Arena. Inspired by the attention they were getting, U2 displayed even more firepower, with the Edge's guitar, Larry Mullen's drumming, and Adam Clayton's bass forging together with both force and elegance.

Bono roamed the stage, looking for new ways to connect with the cheering fans. At one point, during an instrumental part of a song, he left the stage only to reappear, with the white flag on a staff, on the arena's balcony level. The idea was reasonable enough; Bono wanted to create a symbolic bond with the audience by having fans march along with him. But he only got six feet before a guy yanked the flag from the staff and raced away. Eager to find another way to bring down the barrier between performer and audience, Bono climbed over the balcony rail and dropped ten to fifteen feet into the arms of fans on the ground level. It was one of the most dramatic moves I had ever seen a pop star do, and also one of the most questionable.

I was troubled. In his eagerness to inspire, Bono could hurt himself and lead others to do the same thing. Indeed, two fans at the arena did follow Bono's lead and leapt from the balcony, only this time there were no outstretched arms to greet them. There was also a chance the audience would start looking forward to his wild-man antics more than his music. I ended my review by saying, "When you have music as exciting and as purposeful as U2, you really don't need a sideshow as well, especially a potentially dangerous one."

On the day the review appeared, Bono called. "I am going to heed what you say," he said. "The band has been trying to stop me from the 'antics,' as you call them, for a long time, and I just didn't listen. But you won't see me jumping off balconies or climbing up scaffolding anymore. The music is enough, and I realize that."

Over the following months, Bono and I talked periodically about the band and its progress. One day, he phoned after seeing Springsteen in Dublin, and he spoke for several minutes about how inspirational it was, especially the way Bruce reached out to his fans to establish a sense of community. "That's what we want to do, as well," he said. "It's what I, in my clumsy way, had been trying to do with the white flag. But I see how Bruce does so much with just the music and his words to the crowd."

We also spoke a lot about the new music. I was expecting the band to build off the economical songwriting and commentary of the *War* album. But Bono was quick to correct me when I told him I could envision U2's next album being its breakthrough *Born to Run*. He said the group had thought about trying to follow *War* with another series of anthemish, arena-ready tunes in the style of "Sunday Bloody Sunday," but they didn't feel ready to make that step. That's why they'd brought in producers Brian Eno and Daniel Lanois to help them develop a stronger musical vocabulary. The band wanted to be able to make music that was more multilayered and graceful, music that was ideally tailored to the sometimes complex themes running through the band's songs. They were committed to growth even if it meant the music on the new album might not be as accessible. Don't be surprised, he said, if it took two or three more albums for U2 to come up with its *Born to Run.*

I wasn't sure I understood exactly what he was talking about, and I'm not sure the follow-up album, *The Unforgettable Fire,* clarified it. The new album left me confused. There were two brilliant tracks: "Pride (In the Name of Love)," which was the first single from the album, and "Bad," a dramatic number that reminded me of the intensity of John's *Plastic Ono Band* period. The latter song stressed the role of faith in overcoming insecurities and doubts. In a key segment, he just shouts these words:

> *Dislocation.*
> *Separation.*
> *Condemnation.*
> *Revelation.*
> *Dislocation.*

It was a powerful, even hypnotic sequence. For the most part, however, the album didn't reach out to the listener with the immediacy and color that I had expected from U2. Despite my mixed feelings, in my review I pointed out that the high points were as glorious as anything we'd hear all year in rock.

Two days before the band headlined the Long Beach Arena that year, Bono called to thank me for standing by the group. He said a lot of critics had just focused on the sound of the album and how it didn't seem to have the immediate impact *War* had. He spoke again about having seen Springsteen and how he felt U2 was starting to build that same sense of community at its shows. The Long Beach concert, indeed, was a revelation. In the show, Bono kept his promise of sticking to music rather than high-wire antics. Still, he prowled the stage and he sang about isolation with an almost cleansing power. At the end, he seemed drained. As if needing physical contact at that moment, he called a fan to the stage for a long embrace as the band finished the song.

The quiet, reflective tones of several of the songs seemed absolutely essential live—a part of the necessary evolution of a band that was trying to live up to its own lofty ideals and expectations. I phoned Bono the next day and I tried, very gently, to tell him how close the band was to some fragile territory—a time when they could either step up to the level of the Beatles or Springsteen or become intimidated by some of the "holier than thou" criticism that was starting to be leveled at them. He was already ahead of me. He knew that for every person who was touched by the spiritual qualities of "Pride," there would be someone who felt U2 was being pompous and self-righteous. People argued that Bono had no right to refer to the late Reverend Martin Luther King Jr. in lyrics that spoke about trying to live a virtuous life.

Every great artist goes through periods when his or her image and integrity are questioned, I told him. Springsteen had been widely accused of being just "hype" after *Time* and *Newsweek* both put his photo on their covers, and Lennon had had to combat backlash against his "bigger than Jesus" remarks. The only thing you can do, I said, is trust in your music. The worst thing you can do is start compromising yourself, because then you lose everything. I don't know why I felt that I could help Bono, but I kept reminding myself he was still young, and I had seen how hard rock 'n' roll could be on people.

I sometimes felt like a conspirator in writing about U2, but I believed in the band—just as I believed in Springsteen and Dylan and a few others. I found that I often didn't recognize musicians I was familiar with when they were profiled in other newspapers and magazines. All too often, the writers seemed to mold the artists to fit their stories. I wanted to present my subjects as faithfully as I could so I would win their trust and enable readers to get an accurate picture of them. One thing about U2 that consistently intrigued me was their spiritual leanings—how they were anything but self-righteous believers.

"That's a funny thing about rock," Bono said when I asked him about the group's themes. "Spirituality is a topic that is taboo for some people, but I don't think what we are saying is of interest only to Christians. I hate a lot of what I see—people who go around claiming they have the only answer and they are free from sin. It's such a sham when people go around holding the Good Book to their breast or holding the baby up to the TV. It's tragic that people have turned faith into an industry. It's also tragic that the name of Jesus, which is precious to me, gets trampled on. They use it like a little badge."

What I didn't put in the stories were some of the goals Bono expressed during our informal chats. He said critics of the band would really freak out if they knew what he would like to do eventually: talk about issues in the world, including poverty. He said he knew he was only a rock 'n' roller and that his power was limited, but he felt there must be a way to use all the emotion that he felt to make a difference in the larger world.

CHAPTER
SEVENTEEN

The River was Bruce Springsteen's attempt to welcome everyone into his community, while the follow-up, *Nebraska,* was designed with a smaller audience in mind. The 1982 collection was part history lesson and part social outcry. Set in a barren, 1930s musical framework that mixed the fierce folk-country commentary of Woody Guthrie with the clear-eyed populism of John Steinbeck, the album was a desolate examination of the way social forces strangle some people so completely that they either lose their will or strike back savagely.

None of this made sense from a commercial standpoint. Following the success of *The River,* the natural move would have been to come back quickly with another highly accessible collection of songs. Turning instead to something as dark and challenging as *Nebraska* said a lot about Bruce's creative heart. "It's the opposite of the cynical thing that is so dominant with a lot of people these days," Jon Landau told me in one of our many conversations about Bruce. "He has the capacity to inspire people, to make them feel good so that they go away from the show feeling elevated." Though *Nebraska* sold only a fraction of what *The River* did, it was a brilliant work that is likely to be seen decades from now as a remarkable reflection on the social casualties of the increasing American indifference toward the underclass that accompanied the Ronald Reagan years.

Bruce was as fiercely proud of *Nebraska* as John had been of *Plastic Ono Band,* and I saw his *Born in the U.S.A.* album in 1984 as the equivalent of John's *Imagine* collection. Bruce again touched on some of the brooding themes of *Nebraska,* only the inviting E Street Band accompaniment gave the music a far more accessible tone. The title track reminded me of the economical, unadorned writing style of John Fogerty. It may have sounded like a patriotic anthem, but it was a savage denunciation of America's role in the Vietnam War—accompanied by a compassionate look at the men who lived through that nightmare only to return home to a bleak future.

Eager to know more about Bruce, I headed to his hometown of Freehold, New Jersey, to talk to people who had known him as a youngster and to try to put myself in his place on the streets of the decaying city. The first thing I tried to discover was whether the town matched the stories Bruce told us about it on stage.

Walking through Freehold, and the nearby town of Asbury Park, was like walking through hundreds of American hometowns that have been strangled by changing times with the closing of a factory or the rerouting of a highway. It was easy to imagine Bruce walking these streets, ducking into the sandwich shop here and the dime store there, daydreaming about the escape that was eventually glamorized in "Born to Run."

I went to the modest, wood-frame house where Bruce lived with his parents and sister until he was eighteen, and the present residents told me fans regularly stopped by to take photos. Bruce's parents had moved to Northern California years earlier, but Bruce's aunt, Dora Kirby, was still in Freehold, and she spoke of Bruce like, well, a loving aunt. "When Bruce came on the TV [in the 'Dancing in the Dark' video], I just kissed the screen," she said, beaming. "He was just so wholesome. I never worried about Bruce because he was, and still is, a good boy. Even though he's in a business that has all kinds of problems, I knew he'd never lose the wholesomeness that was instilled in him as a boy. You know, when I see Bruce on stage, I always get the idea that he's preaching. He's telling them that they can do the same thing he has—that they can make something of themselves if they work at it."

Born in the U.S.A. spent seven weeks at No. 1 on the national sales charts and led to sellout crowds in arenas and stadiums. It's no wonder that politicians tried to win his endorsement, but Bruce wanted to remain an independent voice. He was, however, becoming increasingly outspoken on stage. At a show in Oakland that fall, Bruce opened with "Born in the U.S.A." and introduced "Reason to Believe," a song from *Nebraska,* by saying, "Here's a song about blind faith. That is always a dangerous thing, whether it's in your girlfriend or if it's in your government."

Later, when introducing the solemn "My Hometown," Bruce took an even harder swing. "There's a group of people in this area called the Berkeley Emergency Food Project who are trying to feed people—people who have been cut down by the injustices in our social system and by the economic policies of the current administration." Watching him on stage that night, I remembered his aunt's words. I, too, started to see Bruce as a preacher.

Bruce's marriage to actress Julianne Phillips in the spring of 1985 caught everyone by surprise. But, for all the joy he brought to others, Bruce had long felt a void in his life and it was eating away at him during the final stages of the *Born in the U.S.A.* tour. I met him in Greensboro, North Carolina, in connection with a coffee-table book I was doing on him for Rolling Stone Press. On stage that night, which was just a few months before his marriage, Bruce looked like a rock 'n' roll version of Superman. He had become a fitness buff, devoting hours to the gym. Still, I sensed a longing in him that I hadn't noticed before. Midway through the set, he told the audience about how he used to think that he would never return to his hometown, but that he found he often went back to Freehold. "When I was a kid, I think I was afraid of belonging to something, because if you admit you belong to something, that means you've got some responsibility," he said.

After the concert, Bruce sat in one of the arena's team locker rooms, looking exhausted. In researching the book, I had spoken to a mutual friend who told me he thought Bruce was going through an important transition; after years of devoting all his energy and emotion to music, he was feeling a need for others in his life. When I mentioned it to Bruce, he nodded and talked about seeing a friend from one of his earliest bands at a recent show with his wife and three children. He realized that he envied his friend and his family.

"I guess relationships have been [hard for me] just because I've traveled on my own for my whole adult life, and it was difficult to settle into something and make those types of sacrifices," he said. "I guess the most precious thing anybody has in the end is their time. That's what you can't bargain with . . . and you never know when it is going to run out. I've changed quite a bit. It's not a question of wanting to do less. It's just more a question of wanting to round out your life."

In committing himself to a relationship, Bruce, I thought, was closing his eyes and taking a major leap of faith. Deep down, this classic loner—who liked nothing more than the solitary moments he spent riding across the country on a motorcycle—must have worried if he'd be able to live up to the challenge. He shared some of that questioning two years later, in 1987, when he delivered *Tunnel of Love,* an album that was in places as dark and despairing as *Nebraska* had been. The songs spoke about longing for marriage, but fearing that it may only be an elusive, heart-shattering dream. The most gripping song, "Brilliant Disguise," is a chilling reflection about commitment. The song asks how a person is to know if a relationship is true or built on mutual self-deception. In an especially sobering moment, a husband and his wife go to a gypsy fortune-teller who says their future is bright, but he later wonders whether the fortune-teller had lied. I marveled over how Bruce was constantly improving as a writer, capturing in this song the psychological combat of *Tunnel of Love* in such intimate and dramatic ways. I also couldn't help but wonder how Bruce could record those songs while he was still married to Julianne, but then maybe it was his way of communicating with her.

Months later, I thought about those songs again when the *National Enquirer* ran a headline declaring, "Bruce Springsteen's Marriage in Trouble." The accompanying article said the problem was that Bruce wanted children and Julianne thought the timing was bad for her career. The piece also said she was furious about the time Bruce was reportedly spending on the road with singer Patti Scialfa, the latest member of the E Street Band.

My initial reaction was disbelief, but there was no doubt once paparazzi in Italy got photos of Bruce and Patti on a hotel room balcony in their underwear. It was the only time I recalled Bruce doing something in bad taste. I was disappointed, yet I also felt for him. He had been stymied in his dream of finding his own family, and he must have been humiliated by the tabloid coverage. He apologized to Julianne in a public statement, but it was too late. The couple was divorced in 1989.

After the *Tunnel of Love* tour, Bruce and the E Street Band joined Sting, Peter Gabriel, and others on an Amnesty International tour. I attended the opening show in London as well as a few other dates, and I noticed a growing friendship between Bruce and Sting. Bruce is immensely articulate one-on-one, but he was less comfortable expressing the goals of Amnesty International at press conferences. In contrast, Sting was a master, and I could see how Bruce admired him. More importantly, Sting, who is two years younger than Bruce, had already left one of the biggest rock groups in the world, the Police, so he could more freely explore his creative instincts. I suspected that Bruce coveted that same freedom.

CHAPTER
EIGHTEEN

Michael Jackson's *Thriller* was well on its way to becoming the biggest-selling album in the world when attorney John Branca phoned me early in 1984. He said Michael was going to do a book for Doubleday and that Michael wanted me to help him with it. Of course, I was interested. Michael was the hottest recording artist in the world, and the book would be a great career opportunity. I was also intrigued by him and at having the chance to see what it was like at the center of so much attention. I had first met Michael in the early days of the Jackson 5, but about all I remember from the evening was that Michael was anxious to get through my questions so he could go back to his room and watch cartoons.

The next time we met was when Michael was on tour with four of his brothers in 1981. Michael and the brothers had left Motown in a dispute over creative control, and Michael launched a remarkable phase two of his career with the spectacular solo album *Off the Wall*. On the tour, I had found Michael to be one of the most fascinating artists I had met in music. There's often a gap between a performer's public and private sides, but rarely had I felt it was as pronounced.

For all his charisma and authority on stage, he had a Bambi-like shyness and fragility away from the spotlight. As he sat in the rear of the tour bus the day after the concert, he seemed anxious, frequently lowering his head when speaking.

When I asked why he didn't get his own house like his brothers, he said he couldn't imagine not living at home with his mother in Encino. "Oh no, I think I'd die on my own," he said. "I'd be so lonely. Even at home, I'm lonely. I sit in my room sometimes and cry. It is so hard to make friends and there are some things you can't talk to your parents or family about. I sometimes walk around the neighborhood at night, just hoping to find someone to talk to. But I just end up coming home."

. . . .

After I told Branca I was interested, he said I needed to get the blessing of Jacqueline Kennedy Onassis, Michael's editor at Doubleday. She wanted to see some samples of my writing, so I sent my interview with Michael plus my last interview with John Lennon and the subsequent coverage of his funeral. I liked the Lennon stories, especially because they felt so personal. Two days later, Onassis called from New York. She loved the stories, especially the Lennon ones. She said they made her feel close to John and identify with Yoko. I could hear her voice break. Only then did I realize that she was drawing a connection between Lennon's death and her first husband's assassination. I hadn't even thought of that parallel.

After getting Onassis's approval, I met Michael at a studio in Hollywood, where he was rehearsing for the Jacksons' upcoming Victory tour. "I heard you talked to Jackie," he said in his soft, high-pitched voice. "Isn't she just wonderful? That's the only reason I did the book. I don't want people knowing all about my life, but I couldn't say no to Jackie." He said he had lots of free time on the road, so I should just come out every few weeks and join him and we could talk about the pictures.

Pictures?

"Don't ask me what's going on in the world because (a) the cynics will attack me and (b) some people will act as if God has spoken. The people I'm trying to reach are in between. I hope they judge for themselves."—John Lennon (with Robert Hilburn), in a New York studio in 1980. (Photo by Bob Gruen)

"Thank you very much, ladies and gentlemen. Good evening. My name is Wayne Newton. I've got a brother named Fig."—Elvis Presley, shown in concert at the Inglewood Forum in 1974.
(Photo by John Lockwood/LAT)

"I listened to Alan Lomax field recordings for hours and that's what I wanted to do with my music, too: Tell real, human stories." — Johnny Cash (with Robert Hilburn), at Folsom Prison in 1968.
(Photo by Jim Marshall)

"I don't think I'll be perceived properly till 100 years after I'm gone. I don't think anyone has even caught on to 'Blonde on Blonde' yet."—Bob Dylan, on stage in San Francisco in 1979.
(Photo by George Rose/LAT)

"I was never caught up in trying to 'top' the last album. The only thing you can hope to do is grow so that you can do your best work in a new time."—Stevie Wonder, in Los Angeles in 1978.
(Photo by Ken Hively/LAT)

"My whole life came alive that night, musically, emotionally, everything."—Elton John, about his US debut at the Troubadour in 1970. Here he and Bernie Taupin go over ticket requests for his return to the club in 1975. (Photo by Tony Bernard/LAT)

"It's beautiful at the shows when people join together . . . It's only when you step back outside . . . that you see all the craziness."—Michael Jackson, at Dodger Stadium in 1984. (Photo by Ian Dryden/LAT)

"They used to book me only one night a week because I was making enough in one night to pay for everything, but it was a drag. The most fun I have is when I'm playing."—Janis Joplin, backstage in San Francisco in 1968. (Photo by Jim Marshall)

"When you're young, there is a bit of the expectation that fame is a way to achieve a life without complications. But it's a lie, and I realized that fairly quickly."—Bruce Springsteen, in Bloomington, Minnesota, in 1978. (Photo by George Rose/LAT)

"People sometimes feel helpless, but we shouldn't forget how resilient we are. We are built to be strong."—Patti Smith, at a photo shoot in West Hollywood in 1978. (Photo by Tony Bernard/LAT)

"Songwriting really is a mysterious process . . . because we're asking people to expose themselves. It's like open heart surgery in some way."—Bono, at the Country Club in Reseda, California, in 1981. (Photo by Martha Hartnett/LAT)

"It's important that we educate our people as well as entertain them . . . how the black person feels about his situation in America or in the Western World."—Chuck D, in Los Angeles photo shoot in 1994. (Photo by Patrick Downs/LAT)

LEFT: "Happiness has nothing to do with validation from other people. The important thing is being happy with yourself." —Kurt Cobain, in concert at the Inglewood Forum in 1993. (Photo by Larry Davis/LAT)

RIGHT: "Music gave me a reason to hold my head high at a time little else did." —Jack White, on stage in Los Angeles in 2007. (Photo by Lawrence K. Ho/LAT)

"Rap is not just dance music. It's about knowing yourself, knowing who you are and knowing who is trying to bring you down." —Ice Cube, at a photo shoot in Los Angeles in the early 1993. (Photo by J. Albert Diaz/LAT)

I hadn't gotten the impression from Onassis that she wanted a picture book. She had talked about doing the story of Michael's life, an autobiography. I wondered what I had gotten myself into.

You couldn't turn on the radio or TV in Kansas City around the July 6, 1984, start of the Victory tour without hearing something about Michael and the army of Michael look-alikes around town—at the airport, major hotels, and, of course, Arrowhead Stadium, where forty-five thousand fans would scream their approval when their hero stepped on stage. I hadn't seen as much excitement over the start of a tour since Elvis's opening in Las Vegas.

The day before the first show, I sat with Michael in his hotel room as he watched TV news reports about the tour. He loved it whenever newscasters interviewed excited young fans. He'd squeal with delight if a youngster was dressed like him, wearing either a sequined white glove or white socks and black loafers. He was so full of adrenaline that he even danced around the room. To help pass the time, he decided to go see the film *Gremlins* at a suburban theater. "Watch," he said as his bodyguards led us down the hall. "They're going to take us down the back way, the same way they do the president." When we got to a van with darkened windows, Michael asked the driver to go around to the front of the hotel so he could see the dozens of fans who had gathered. He giggled with excitement as the van roared past the unsuspecting youngsters. Michael loved the adventure of getting to the movie as much as the film itself.

Earlier, I had had a similar "public" experience with Michael in Los Angeles. I went with him to a bookstore on Hollywood Boulevard that specialized in show-business histories. Sometimes a bodyguard would arrange for the store owners to temporarily close their doors so Michael could walk around in private. But Michael and I went alone on this day, and he spent nearly a half hour in the store, looking at books about movies and pop music. He kept glancing nervously over his shoulder the whole time to see if anyone was watching him. But there were only a couple of customers and they were looking at books in another section.

Finally, Michael decided it was time to go and as we walked out the front door of the shop, he spotted some teenagers a half block away.

They were walking slowly our way. Michael started walking to the car. Suddenly, he looked over his shoulder again and started running. "Come on," he said. "They've spotted us." When we got to the corner, I paused and looked around. There was no one following Michael, but he loved the thrill of the chase—even if there wasn't a chase. Safely inside his car, Michael said, "This is why I hate to go out in public. People just won't leave you alone."

As he pulled out of the parking lot, I happened to see the teenagers that Michael thought were after him. They were still strolling down Hollywood Boulevard, pausing every so often to see whose star was laid in the cement beneath them.

· ·

The opening-night concert in Kansas City was a resounding success. Michael shone most when he was on stage without his brothers. You'd think that would make the other Jacksons feel awkward, but they spoke of Michael's triumph as their own; they may have been the only ones in the stadium who still saw it as a Jacksons show rather than a Michael Jackson show. They walked around afterward accepting congratulations, even though many of the fans who spotted them in the hotel really were trying to find out how they could get up to Michael's room. Extra security guards were brought in to keep weeping fans from roaming the halls in hope of sighting Michael.

Eventually, the fans had given up on trying to find Michael's room, but more than a hundred of them stood in the street beneath his window, hoping he'd wave to them. They got their wish. One thing Michael could always find time for was cheering fans. He spent much of the second day in his hotel room, looking at photos of fans. As the tour photographer put one after another on the floor in front of him, Michael howled with laughter when he saw young imitators in their sequined jackets and gloves.

Every time I asked when we should start talking about the book, he said we had plenty of time to do that, but first we should have fun, which for him was sitting on his bed and watching cartoons. Michael was nearing twenty-six.

. . . .

During one of our first meetings he said, "You like Bruce Spring-steen more than me, don't you." Bruce's *Born in the U.S.A.* album was on top of the pop charts, and Michael knew I was a fan. I answered by saying that he and Bruce were entirely different artists, both great in their own way. But he was just teasing me when he mentioned Bruce. He didn't really see him as a threat to his own King of Pop dreams. Michael was serious, however, when he brought up another rival.

"Have you seen *Purple Rain* yet?" he asked as soon as I entered his suite on one trip. "Is it any good?"

Michael and Prince were natural rivals. They were born just months apart in 1958 and both grew up in the Midwest.

I said the Prince movie was fun, but it was far from great. In many ways, it was just another pop-star vehicle. It was the equivalent of, say, Elvis's *Jailhouse Rock.*

"*Jailhouse Rock?*" Michael responded with alarm. I don't think he liked me linking Prince with the man whose crown he sought. I explained that I thought the Prince film was being overpraised by critics, that it was little more than a conventional pop movie just as *Jailhouse Rock* had been a conventional pop movie in the 1950s.

"Michael, it's not magical," I said.

Michael looked relieved. But Prince's name continued to come up, and I sensed that Michael was testing my allegiances.

. . . .

Though I never told Michael this, I was far more impressed by Prince, the artist, than by Michael in the pre-*Thriller* days. The first time I saw Prince was early in 1981, and I described his performance in a review as "frequently electrifying" in the sexually aggressive tra-dition of Presley, Jimi Hendrix, and Mick Jagger. He was born for the stage, spontaneous in a way Michael wasn't, and his music had deeper and more consistently provocative themes. In the debut LA show, he had bumped and grinded his way around the stage, clad only in black bikini briefs and thigh-high stockings.

Prince wasn't just confronting sexual taboos. He was also helping reunite the power of rock and the urgency and pulse of black music. His ninety-minute show reminded me of David Bowie's bold and memorable 1972 show at the Santa Monica Civic Auditorium, which was one of the best debuts I had ever seen. Prince wasn't getting much radio airplay at that time, but he did have a hit with "I Wanna Be Your Lover," a charming slice of early Motown–pop soul that featured the head-scratching lines about wanting to be someone's mother, brother, and sister. When Prince returned the following year to the Santa Monica Civic, he was stronger than ever, and I continued to compare him to Bowie. Like Bowie, Prince used music chiefly as a backdrop for a larger purpose: to celebrate the freedom of the individual.

The first thing Prince wanted to know when I interviewed him in the fall of 1982 was why I kept comparing him to Bowie.

Prince was every bit as eccentric as Michael during that interview. He seemed to cringe as the door of his West Hollywood hotel room opened. Like Michael, he had enormous charisma and confidence on stage, but in person he was painfully shy. Sitting on the floor next to a dim lamp, the young singer's doleful eyes suggested the sad resignation of a fugitive cornered after a long chase. Prince disliked interviews, but he had agreed to do four to promote his new Warner Bros. album. I was the first of the four to see him. When the interview was over, Prince waited until the door opened, then turned off the lamp and sat in the dark. Very theatrical, I thought.

The next day I got a call from Bob Merlis, the publicist at Warner Bros., asking what had happened. I said I thought the interview went very well. Merlis replied that Prince had found it too draining and headed back home to Minnesota without doing the others.

I didn't see Prince again until he was a surprise guest at one of the Victory tour shows.

While standing backstage before the show, I noticed a van with darkened windows pulling into the arena. It was Prince coming to check out his rival. I walked over to Michael's trailer, hoping I could see them together, but it didn't happen. Prince stayed in the van for nearly twenty minutes until Michael was on stage. Then he stepped from the van and walked to the backstage ramp and watched from the wings, giving no sign of emotion even when Michael went through the moonwalk. As Michael started the final number, Prince headed back down the stairs and got into the van and sped off.

Michael watched the charts anxiously to see how long the *Purple Rain* album would stay at the top. When it finally fell from No. 1 after twenty-four weeks, Michael proudly reminded me that *Thriller* had been No. 1 for thirty-seven weeks.

I tried to kid him back by warning that there was always next time for Prince, but Michael just giggled. He said his next album was going to sell twice what *Thriller* did.

CHAPTER
NINETEEN

O nce the Victory tour got rolling, I met regularly with Michael on the road and became increasingly aware of his isolation and his obsession with fame. I had been on tour with scores of bands and seen musicians spend much of their time rehearsing or thinking about improving the show. I had seen others lost in a drug stupor or preoccupied with lining up girls for the night. But I had never seen anyone sit around for hours talking about his own stardom, wanting reassurance that he was the biggest star in the world, or looking at photos of screaming fans in the audience.

When we finally sat down to talk about the book, I wanted to know his feelings—and I'm sure that's what Jackie Onassis wanted, too—but Michael had something different in mind: a book with large photos and as few words as possible. Michael also spoke lovingly about a host of famous movie stars, including Elizabeth Taylor, Katharine Hepburn, and Jane Fonda. He said he got inspiration from them and how they were the only ones who understood him, yet I sensed that being linked to the film stars was part of a game plan to make him seem even more famous. It was easy to see why he would later marry

Lisa Marie Presley. What bigger trophy for the self-proclaimed King of Pop than to be married to the daughter of the King of Rock? What puzzled me was why Lisa would marry Michael and later swear they had sexual relations "just like a normal couple."

Michael implied that he'd had lots of sexual experiences in the early days of the Jackson 5, but when I asked him about supposed encounters with Tatum O'Neal, his eyes got big as he told me about the time at the Roxy that she had actually put her hand on his knee under the table. He hinted that his relationship with Brooke Shields was more serious, but what I saw at his postconcert party in Los Angeles left me with doubts. Rather than staying at the house in Encino, Michael had booked a suite at a downtown hotel. Brooke and her mother showed up early, but sat for more than an hour in chairs near the door. Michael, meanwhile, was in his bedroom a few feet away, pillow fighting with a half dozen five- and six-year-olds. He did come into the living room to say hello to a few celebrity guests, but then went back into the bedroom to watch cartoons—all out of Brooke's sight. Finally, Brooke's mother had had enough and they both left.

After I quit trying to get Michael to talk on the record about his personal life, I thought the rest was going to be easy. But he had trouble telling me enough to even fill out a decent caption. When I picked up a photo of an elderly African American man from the top of the stack of photos, I asked Michael who it was. I laughed when he said, "That's Prince," but it was true. One of his grandfathers was named Prince, and he had worked as a railroad porter for decades.

I asked Michael how he felt about his grandfather.

"I love him very much," he said in that high voice.

Okay, I said, we'll put that in the caption.

But Michael's eyes widened. "Oh, no," he said, "that's too personal."

The scene was repeated with photo after photo. The exception was a photo of his mother. He said he adored his mother; he couldn't imagine anyone having a more loving parent. It was a different story when we got to his father. He spoke about his father's dedication to making the Jackson 5 a success. Then he gestured to me to turn off the tape recorder and started telling me things about his father—the words were dark.

"But you've got to promise me," he said, "you'll never tell anyone what I said."

It was the only time I was around Michael that I saw fear in his eyes. Nothing he said made me understand his uneasiness. I could only imagine what he left out.

The cities blurred—Chicago, Philadelphia, Houston, New York, and finally Los Angeles—and the adoration at the shows was amazing. But what did it mean? Could I ever picture him matching the cultural depth of Elvis, the Beatles, and Dylan? Michael was unquestionably a dynamic performer, and the best of his tunes were powered by irresistible rhythms. He was doing more than anyone since Berry Gordy to make black music a dominant strain in modern pop music. Many of the biggest stars in pop, from Prince to Justin Timberlake, owe much of their style and inspiration to Michael. But there was also a limit to his relationship with his fans.

When I spoke to Michael's older admirers—those in their late twenties and early thirties who had been following him since the Jackson 5 days—their "love" of Michael didn't seem to have much to do with his dancing, his singing, or his songwriting. They simply "loved him"—his "innocence," his "sweetness." There was little of the ideological bond that Bruce and U2 were building with their fans. Bruce's and U2's fans were bound by what the artists stood for—their themes and their inspirations—and the intensity of those relationships was compounded when Bruce and Bono reached out by actually sharing their thoughts with the audience.

In fact, there was a noticeable distance between Michael and his fans, partly because he couldn't reach out to them. I thought about how much more powerful he could be as a performer if he actually spoke to the audience the way Bruce did. I even suggested one night to Michael that he try it. "Oh, no," he said. "I can't do that." I think the words he used next were "I'd be too frightened." Michael said he tried to block out the audience when he was on stage so he didn't become self-conscious. The next night, Michael did pause between songs to try to speak to the crowd. But he only got a few words out before he quickly went back into his shell.

After that night, I gave up on trying to talk to him about the show. I had enough of a challenge just getting him to come up with information for the book. But one photo did trigger a reaction: a photo of him from his teen years. "Ooh, that's horrible," he said, turning the photo face down. Michael said that period in his life was so traumatic that it had changed his personality—his face was covered with acne and his nose was so large that people couldn't even recognize him anymore. Instead of being frisky and outgoing, he suddenly— around age sixteen—started to keep to himself. He'd look down at the floor when talking to people or just stay in his room when visitors came to the house.

"My skin broke out real bad and my face got fatter," he said on one of the many nights that we ended up talking about things that he didn't want in the book. "I used to hate looking in the mirror. I was so unhappy." Michael said he went to various doctors, hoping for a cure for the acne, but nothing seemed to help. He started studying nutrition and went on a vegetarian diet, which did help. But the shyness and resentment didn't go away.

"People want to keep you small and that's not fair because you are human," he said. "You have a right to get bigger, but it's like the whole world is saying, 'How dare you grow up on us.' It's as if you betrayed them." He also told of having people come to the house looking for little Michael and they would look right past him, never picturing that the cute little kid had turned into *this*.

The more Michael spoke, the more I began to see a human side to him—how fame seemed to be the only thing that he could count on. He had sacrificed much of his childhood in pursuit of fame and then, when the record sales had slipped and his appearance had changed, he felt rejected. Now, he had fought his way back to unimagined heights and he hungered for more. Michael became so emotional some nights that he had to stop himself to fight back tears. But he wanted that side of him to remain private. He wanted the fans to think of him only as glamorous.

Finally, it was time to send an outline of the picture book to Doubleday, and Onassis was not pleased. She flew out to Los Angeles to confront Michael.

Though the meeting at his house was supposed to have been secret, a dozen or so photographers showed up at the Jackson gate at precisely the time she arrived. I remember looking at the photographers through a window with Michael and him complaining about them intruding on his life. It was only later that I learned that someone in Michael's camp had tipped them off Michael was flattered that President Kennedy's widow would want to work with him. To Michael, it was another confirmation of his stardom.

But Michael's anxiety took over as soon as Onassis arrived. He told me that I should talk to her for him and he raced upstairs.

Onassis told me she wanted a more substantial book, and I told her that Michael didn't want to do a traditional autobiography. Onassis then suggested that Michael talk at length about things that interested him. What about a chapter on the wallpaper in the house? What about another on his wardrobe? I thought that was a terrible idea. Millions of people were already wondering if there was anything to him beyond the glitz, and a shallow book about him fawning over clothes and wallpaper would just confirm their suspicions.

A few weeks later, I got a call from Branca's office thanking me for my part in the project, but saying that Doubleday was going in another direction. To fulfill the contract, Michael apparently let Doubleday put together a traditional autobiography—just what he had argued against in the beginning. But it was either that or risk a public falling out with Onassis, and Michael coveted the association.

Moonwalk eventually appeared, and it was typical show-biz fluff. It felt like something a ghostwriter put together after reading everything already written about Michael. I had to laugh at the line "another love was Brooke Shields. We were romantically serious for a while." I thought back to the postconcert party in Los Angeles, when Michael hadn't even stopped the pillow fight games long enough to sit down with Brooke.

• •

Because of the book project, I didn't write about Michael for the *Times* for the rest of the 1980s, with the only exceptions being Michael's landmark 1985 purchase of the publishing rights to the Lennon-McCartney song catalog and the 1988 Grammy Awards ceremony where *Bad,* Michael's follow-up to *Thriller,* was nominated for five awards, including album of the year.

I was disappointed with *Bad* because I could see Michael's obsession with sales and fame costing him the artistic impulses that had made *Thriller* such a defining work. Determined to top the sales of *Thriller,* he put together a collection that was designed to fit into various radio formats, and it ended up hollow. Because of his enormous fan base, *Bad* sold well by most standards; it stayed at No. 1 for six weeks in the fall of 1987. Next to *Thriller's* thirty-seven weeks at No. 1, however, it was a dramatic decline, and I imagine it felt like a disaster for Michael.

Things didn't get any better with the next album, *Dangerous.* The 1991 collection sold almost as many copies as *Bad,* but it was even less distinguished. Michael came no closer to regaining the qualities that had made his music so striking. The joke in the industry was that the album should have been called *Desperate.* The next CD, *Invincible,* in 2001, sold only two million copies.

Meanwhile, Michael had bigger problems than declining record sales—the charge of child molestation. He denied allegations in 1993 that he had sexually molested a thirteen-year-old boy over a period of several months, and criminal charges were never filed. He settled a civil case with the boy's family for millions of dollars in 1994. And there were new charges, which led to a jury trial. Michael was found not guilty, but his future was in question.

When I surveyed twenty-five of the industry's sharpest minds in 1995 to determine music's top recording artists, Michael wasn't one of them. His showing was so bad that he even finished third among artists with the same surname—far behind sister Janet and country star Alan Jackson. Said one executive of the man who still called himself the King of Pop: "He's wounded as a commercial property." Another summarized, "Over."

The main problem, according to the panel, wasn't a backlash against the child-molestation allegations, but that Jackson had gone in the public mind from being the King of Pop to the King of Hype. One panelist summarized my feelings exactly: "The thing he doesn't understand is that he'd be better off in the long run if he made a great record that only went to No. 20 on the sales chart than if he hyped another mediocre record to No. 1. The thing he needs is credibility." None of this meant that there wasn't still enough public fascination with Michael to make him a huge concert draw. The record executives just didn't think he was a good investment as a record seller.

On the day after the article appeared in the *Times,* Michael called me at the paper. He sounded wounded and asked how I could have written such cruel things about him. I pointed out that I was quoting others, not stating my own opinion. Michael said they were just jealous, they were trying to hurt him, and they were lying. I responded that they were telling the truth. The line went dead. Michael had hung up.

But maybe Michael was stronger than I thought. After enduring much ridicule and humiliation, he returned to the pop scene at age fifty in 2009 by announcing concerts in London. And that public fascination and affection were strong enough to sell out fifty nights at the O_2 Arena. Whether he could make another great record, however, was another question.

The question, of course, was never answered. Michael died on June 25, 2009, after suffering cardiac arrest in a Holmby Hills mansion, not far from the house where I interviewed him nearly four decades earlier. He was fifty.

. . . .

As soon as I heard about Michael's death, I thought about my favorite moments with him during the Victory tour—moments when he set aside his fixation on fame and showed an endearing generosity. This— along with his best nights on stage—was when Michael, for me, was the strongest and most magical.

Because of his painful teenage years, Michael went out of his way to pay his respects to various former child stars, inviting them to the shows and sometimes having them join him for dinner in his hotel suite. He wanted to show them they weren't abandoned or rejected as he had been. I joined him during a tour stop in Texas, where he spent three hours at dinner with Spanky McFarland of "Our Gang" fame.

Michael kept telling Spanky, then in his midfifties, how much he loved watching the "Our Gang" shorts and that he was inspired by seeing young people doing childhood pranks on television. He even said he often went to see Spanky's star on the Hollywood Walk of Fame.

Michael also found time to visit children's wards at hospitals. During one encounter with some terminal cases, the mood was so tender that his manager Frank Dileo, who could be a tough negotiator, had to leave the hospital room so the children wouldn't see him tearing up.

I thought about Michael's desperate need for affirmation and about how in our evenings together he would sometimes break into tears while telling about his loneliness and the hurt of the earlier rejection. I also thought about the unsettling TV interviews and reports of painkillers of recent years.

In the days after Michael's death, I watched the parade of people on TV news and talk shows stressing how Michael had been in great shape and was looking forward with confidence to the 50 London shows he'd scheduled starting in July 2009.

In the best scenario, Michael would have triumphed in London, not only erasing his mountain of debt, but restoring for him the sense of invincibility that fame once represented for him. Failure, however, could have left him even more wounded and vulnerable than ever.

I imagined Michael's anxiety mounting day by day, even hour by hour, as he wondered if he could live up to what could be his make-or-break moment.

There must have been days where he felt that he could do it in London. With a series of breathtaking performances, Michael could reclaim his crown and stand forever alongside Elvis Presley and the Beatles in pop music lore.

But what if he was wrong?

What if he wasn't strong enough, physically and emotionally, to pull off the marathon series of shows?

What if he couldn't live up to expectations?

What if no amount of love could make him feel safe again?

Maybe in the end, the pressure was just too much for his already broken heart.

INTERLUDE
MOMENTS TO REMEMBER

THE ALLMAN BROTHERS BAND. Even after the 1971 motorcycle-accident death of guitarist Duane Allman, this Southern band had the tightest instrumental attack of any I've ever heard. The Allmans traveled with so much cocaine in their early days that two different members and one of their roadies all offered me some the same afternoon. I had never taken cocaine, but I tried to sniff the powder after the third offer—just to be one of the guys. I figured I must have done it wrong because I didn't feel any different. But when I called a friend a few minutes later, he said, "Why are you talking so fast?"

DAVID BOWIE. I interviewed David several times during the 1970s and he was always provocative and fun, always eager to share his feelings about cultural shifts. But he seemed distracted when I spoke to him in 1983 in Dallas, where he was rehearsing for his first tour in five years. He was hesitant when answering questions, frequently stopping to revise his remarks. When I woke up the next morning, I found a four-page handwritten message from David under my door. He apologized for being "inarticulate" earlier and outlined some of the books he was reading and social changes he saw ahead. "It could be a wonderful future," he said. "I just wish I could have been a bit more wonderful in the interview."

GEORGE HARRISON. I gave George enough low marks on his solo albums that I understood when he told his US publicist he'd talk to anyone at the *LA Times* except me. But that tension made things ticklish on the night in the late 1970s when I was urgently trying to track down a rumor about a Beatles reunion. After calls to sources close to John, Paul, and Ringo proved fruitless, I was forced to search for George himself, who happened to be in town. When a woman answered the phone, I identified myself only as being "from the *Los Angeles Times*." I didn't want to give my name in case George was still upset over the reviews. I waited as the woman apparently put her hand over the phone for a few seconds and spoke to someone. Finally, she asked, "Who did you say this was?" After I told her, she again put her hand over the receiver for a few nervous seconds before telling me, "Just a second." When George took the phone, he denied the rumor. There would be no Beatles reunion concert, he said, adding that I could use the same quote the next time the rumor came up. It would save me the trouble, he chuckled, of having to track down his home number.

MADONNA. I'm not generally a fan of her music, but Madonna Louise Ciccone is one sharp cookie. She may be the only person I've ever interviewed who gave such good quotes that every single one was worth using. I met her for the first time just before the release of the *Like a Virgin* album in 1984. On the way to the publicity office at Warner Bros. Records in New York, I picked up a huge Prince cutout stand-up poster from a friend in the building. As soon as I entered the office, she shouted, "Where did you get that? I want one!" I thought her interest in Prince was appropriate because she seemed equally brash, sexy, and hugely ambitious. When I asked if she identified with him, she replied, "Sure, he's competitive, from the Midwest, . . . a screwed-up home, and he has something to prove. I can relate to all that—totally."

ELVIS COSTELLO. I was an early champion of the Englishman who turned ridicule and revenge into an art form in the 1970s and 1980s. I admired how he poured energy and emotion into every line of every song. But I finally found myself on his wrong side. It was in 1986, when he opened a five-night stand at a 1,700-seat theater in Beverly Hills. He planned to perform a different set of songs each night, drawing from his diverse catalog. I made it clear in the review that I thought he was an artist of immense stature, but I thought the opening-night show was a disappointment because it seemed like simply a greatest-hits exercise. Elvis was irate. In the first show after the review appeared, he complained that no one could get a favorable review in Los Angeles unless he was Bruce Springsteen, forgetting that he had gotten nothing but good reviews from me for years. I was pleased to find that he didn't hold a grudge when we next met by accident in London.

RICKIE LEE JONES. At her best, Rickie Lee combines the fearless introspection of Joni Mitchell with the colorful literary bite of Tom Waits. But the comparison that came most to mind when I saw her in concert in Berkeley in 1982 was Janis Joplin. Coming on stage in sheer, lacy lingerie, Rickie seemed to be operating close to her emotional edge: taking lusty swigs from a Jack Daniel's bottle, embracing band members for assurance, and delivering some embarrassingly incoherent chatter between songs. In my review, I declared that this hadn't been a concert, it had been a psychodrama. I was afraid for her. I was even more alarmed at Rickie Lee's concert in Pasadena a few nights after the review came out. A fan, who apparently had read the review, walked to the edge of the stage and held up a present: another bottle of Jack Daniel's.

When I interviewed a sober, clear-eyed Rickie Lee two years later, she looked across a coffee table at me and said, "I was full of fury when I read your review of the Berkeley show. When people do good things, there's a small note about it. But when you mess up, there's three pages." Rickie paused, then added, "But the main thing I felt was shame because everything was true." About the fan in Pasadena, she continued, "I couldn't believe it. It was like a cartoon. I thought, 'These people will see you to the grave—just as long as you keep performing for them.' It made me feel scared and hostile because of the way they were responding to what was a part of me, but not the only part. The idea of me being the last one in the club was true at one time, but how long can you live that way before you die of cirrhosis of the liver? You change or you die. I change."

THE JESUS & MARY CHAIN. The Mary Chain was one of my favorite outfits from across the Atlantic in the 1980s, but their Southern California debut in 1986 was a sloppy, drunken mess and I scolded brothers Jim and William Reid in my review, saying that they owed it to their music and fans to put on a more disciplined set. A few nights later, the Reids walked on stage at the Roxy sober and delivered a knockout set. I assumed for months that they had responded to my review, only to discover when I interviewed them in London what had really happened. They had shown up at the club at about 9:30 p.m., expecting to have a few drinks, as usual, to combat their nerves before going on stage at midnight. To their horror, they learned that the set was scheduled for 10:00 and they didn't have a chance to get drunk; the review had had nothing to do with it.

LEONARD COHEN. I interviewed Leonard at every opportunity, including at the Zen Center on the edge of the tiny resort village of Mount Baldy, outside of Los Angeles. It was 1995 and Leonard had been living in a cabin no larger than a budget motel room for about two years, so involved in the center's lifestyle that he got up every morning at 3:00 a.m. to begin preparing the day's first meal for Joshu Roshi, a spiritual leader. After our talk, Leonard, who had traded in his stylish suits for modest robes, invited me to stay for lunch, which was one of his soup specialties. I watched him labor over the various vegetables for more than an hour until he was satisfied. Afterward, he walked me to my car. When I opened the trunk, he noticed an open package of Fig Newtons that I kept for an occasional treat. Eying them, Leonard, speaking in a slow, deliberate style that seemed in keeping with the Zen Center itself, asked ever so politely, "Could I have one of those Fig Newtons?" Being the generous guy that I am, I offered him the whole package. "Oh, no," he said, pointing to his spartan lifestyle. "Just one will be fine." As I drove away, I could see in the rearview mirror that he was staring fondly at it, presumably thinking about whether to take a bite now or save it for later.

PJ HARVEY. This British singer-songwriter dreaded interviews so much that her publicist had to arrange for us to meet briefly for coffee to make sure PJ was comfortable before letting me talk to her at length. I passed the audition, because she agreed to do a formal interview a few months later in London. She was twenty-five in 1995, and she wrote about sexual and spiritual longing with the soul-baring intensity of Sinéad O'Connor. We met in a hotel lobby a few hours before PJ headed to Paris to begin an important two-month tour.

"I feel I am filled with complete opposites," she said early on. "Half of me loves doing what I do and the other half wants to just be really quiet and on my own in the country." As time went on, she seemed to loosen up and she spoke at length about her music and background. When I suggested at the end that I thought she had done really well, she said a soft thank you. "But it's hard on the inside. If you are an observant person, you will notice that I have picked most of my fingernails away during the interview." As she held her fingers up in the dim lobby light, I could see the skin around her nails was swollen and raw.

CHAPTER
TWENTY

hen "Rapper's Delight" began getting airplay in Los Angeles in 1980, I never imagined the new sound could assume as significant a cultural role as rock had. The novelty record by the Sugarhill Gang had more words than a *New Yorker* short story, but they just sounded goofy to me. If "Rapper's Delight" was an indication of what this highly energetic New York street sound was like, rap sounded like nothing more than some weird offshoot of disco. I changed my opinion two years later when I heard "The Message" by Grandmaster Flash and the Furious Five. It examined the tensions of inner-city life so vividly that it felt like a documentary film. I was so impressed that I named "The Message" my single of the year in 1982, as did many other music critics.

I started hearing about other New York rappers, including Kurtis Blow and Afrika Bambaataa, but it wasn't until three young men from Queens put together a string of knockout hits that rap had its first superstars. Run-D.M.C., a trio featuring Joseph Simmons, Darryl McDaniels, and Jason Mizell, rapped about everyday life. They broke into the R&B Top Ten in early 1986 with "My Adidas" and then made a major step toward the rock mainstream by reworking Aerosmith's "Walk This Way." The group went on a national tour, which included stops at the Long Beach Arena and the Hollywood Palladium. I wasn't at the Long Beach concert, but the show was all over the news the next day after forty-one people were injured in gang violence. It was the first that many adults in Los Angeles had heard of rap, and they didn't like what they heard. Overnight, the music was on trial.

The uproar reminded me of the reaction against rock 'n' roll in the 1950s. It was hard back then to find anyone in the media defending rock, and I wanted to do what I could to give a new type of music a fair hearing, so I tracked down Run-D.M.C. the day after the Long Beach concert.

Run—Simmons—so nicknamed because he talked nonstop, appreciated the chance to tell his story, and he explained that the trio were trying to be positive role models—antidrugs, antigangs, antiviolence—and they had been as surprised and disturbed as anyone when fighting broke out at the show. Run said the problem wasn't the music, but the widespread gang activity in Southern California. He said there was a lot of juvenile lawlessness in New York, but it wasn't so much tied to gangs. He felt that the city fathers in Los Angeles either didn't know the extent of the problem or didn't want to admit it, so they blamed it on rap. I had heard about gangs in parts of the city, but I didn't think it was any worse than in other urban areas.

I followed the group to Columbia, South Carolina, for its next concert. I went from the airport to the group's hotel, where Run was pacing in his room, underscoring his words with the same sudden arm gestures that he used to dramatize his lyrics on stage. He was excited because he had just received a telegram from the Los Angeles Street Scene Committee—which sponsored an annual, free downtown concert series—asking if Run-D.M.C. would perform at the two-day September event. The telegram said the committee would like to explore the possibility of making this year's program a fund-raiser for antidrug and antigang projects.

"Some of my [fans in big cities] haven't been around anything positive because of some of the areas they live in and their parents don't have anything positive to offer them," Run told me. "I come from the middle class and I'm fortunate enough to have good parents who did set a good example. I knew by the time I was ten what was good and what was bad, and I always try to be on the good side." He invited me to New York to meet his parents and do a comprehensive story on the group. The more he talked, the more I saw the parallel between rock in the 1950s and rap in the 1980s, and the more I wanted to defend the music against the wild accusations surrounding it and its audience.

When I got to the ten-thousand-seat arena, there was no hint of violence. I spoke with dozens of young fans, and they backed up Run's comments. They thought the group's music and image were positive, and they didn't express any concern for their safety even though police stood guard nearby and there was a metal detector at the door.

A month later, the Los Angeles Street Scene Committee withdrew its invitation to Run-D.M.C. even though the group's latest album, *Raising Hell,* had already sold more than a million copies. The decision was based in part on City Hall's uneasiness. Deputy mayor Tom Houston declared, "I'll be damned if we'll have them."

I thought the attack was unfair. I headed to New York to do another feature on Run-D.M.C. There, I met Run's brother, Russell Simmons, a young entrepreneur who was the leading force in convincing the record industry that rap had a future, and Rick Rubin, who would become the first great record producer in rap. Russell and Rick co-owned Def Jam Records, which was located near Bleecker Street in Greenwich Village, the same Bleecker that in the 1960s was the home of the folk-music movement that produced Bob Dylan. Rap was still mostly underground around the country, but on Bleecker Street, it felt like a genuine revolution. Wherever I walked, I could hear the music's chantlike vocals and sharp, percolating rhythms coming from car radios and boom boxes.

Race was certainly responsible for part of the opposition to rap, and writing about the genre was garnering me a lot of hate mail and hate calls. The message was: Write about real music; leave rap to the ghetto. Some readers wrote letters to the publisher, asking him to stop promoting this "trash."

What I found in the Simmons brothers couldn't have opposed this notion more starkly. They took me to their old neighborhood in Queens to meet their father, Daniel, a supervisor of attendance for the New

York City school system. Daniel was a quiet, proud man who once went to jail for his civil rights beliefs. His two-story house, with candy kisses in a bowl on the living room table and family photos on a nearby desk, had warmth stamped all over it.

"It bothers me when these parent groups attack Joey and the boys and say they cause violence, because I see the good they do," he said, sitting on a sofa in the living room. "I have more children staying in school on the basis of Joey than on the basis of what I can do. They give a hundred-dollar savings bond to the child in every graduating class who has the best attendance, and Russell gives more bonds to the children who have shown the most improvement in reading and math."

While I was at the house, Russell said he had just signed a deal with Columbia Records that meant millions for Def Jam. "This is just the beginning," he said confidently. "Give us ten years and rap will be the music business." He wasn't far-off. Rap did lure away so many young rock fans that history may eventually show that rock has never fully regained its influence.

I'd stop by the Def Jam offices every time I went to New York because Simmons and Rubin kept coming up with important new acts, including the Beastie Boys, whose *Licensed to Ill* was the teenage outrage record of 1986, and L.L. Cool J, the young Romeo of rap. But the act that most interested me was Public Enemy. Led by a self-proclaimed "rap activist" named Chuck D, the group's music started where "The Message" left off. Its black-consciousness message was more consistently and pointedly political than anything else on the scene. The group's 1987 debut album, *Yo! Bum Rush the Show,* didn't sell with the speed of those of other Def Jam acts, but there was a power and seriousness about the album that demanded attention.

I met Chuck at the Def Jam offices. He was in his early thirties, which was considerably older than the other artists on the label. Like Run-D.M.C., Chuck (his real name is Carlton Ridenhour) came from a lower-middle- to middle-class background in the New York suburbs. His interest in politics was sparked by his mother, an activist in the 1960s who sent him to a summer study program where some of the teachers were former Black Panther Party members and the emphasis was on an intense examination of black culture. He grew up listening to Motown, but his music was mostly inspired by records like "The Message" and the commentary of earlier groups like the Last Poets.

"But no," he said with a smile when I asked about some of the violent imagery on the record. "I'm not urging anyone to go pick up a gun. I use UZIs as a metaphor for the brain . . . to point out how words can be more powerful than bullets. You have to use strong messages at first to grab people's attention. If I had just said 'My brain is powerful,' no one would have thought twice about it. I say UZIs and they pay attention, but you could tell what the song was about if you paid attention. Some people just heard that one word and said, 'Oh, it's about mindless violence.'"

Chuck was smart, serious, and ambitious, and I could see him bringing a respectability to rap and having the potential, even, to be the Bob Dylan or Bob Marley of the movement. In my most optimistic moments, I could see Public Enemy joining Bruce and U2 at the forefront of pop culture. Chuck looked pleased when I mentioned Dylan because he felt more of a connection with rock than with the R&B hits of the late 1980s. He pointed out how rock and rap both grew out of black music and shared the same aggressive, questioning attitude. He had done some shows with the Beastie Boys in Europe before almost-all-white audiences and found that they picked up on lyrics faster than black audiences in the United States. "With a black crowd, they will only pay attention to the words if you prove to them that you are what is happening," he said. "When I first started out, I was happening kinda slow, but now I am at a level where I am in the top block and what I say is important. That's why the message on the next album is going to talk about even stronger, deeper issues." The title: *It Takes a Nation of Millions to Hold Us Back.*

I made arrangements to meet him later at a recording studio a few blocks away where he spent much of the night working on the new collection, which was released in the spring of 1988. But when I got there, I couldn't convince the guard at the door that I had an appointment with Chuck. If I were him, I'd have been suspicious of this unlikely, middle-aged white guy, too.

I stood outside in the cold for a half hour until someone from Def Jam recognized me. Inside, I listened to some of the tracks from *Nation* and was impressed by the merging of two of the most radical grass-roots genres of music in post-1960s pop: punk rock and rap. As suggested by songs titled "Mind Terrorists" and "Louder Than a Bomb," there was an edge of rage as Chuck lashed out at forces that he felt hurt the black community, both external (government oppression) and internal (drug users and pushers). But he also reached out to a wider audience by trying to clarify some of the confusion caused by the rough imagery on the debut collection. He declared in one song, for instance, that he's not a hooligan or a racist.

"It's important that we educate our people as well as entertain them," he said after almost everyone else had left the studio. "We also have to let others know how the black person feels about his situation in America or in the Western world. That's one reason there is so much confusion over rap. White audiences think they are familiar with the black experience, but they aren't. That's why they find the language and symbols sometimes shocking. And sometimes they are shocking because we are trying to get people's attention."

Director Spike Lee underscored Chuck's cultural importance by making Public Enemy's song "Fight the Power," from *Fear of a Black Planet,* the musical centerpiece of his film *Do the Right Thing,* the brilliant, widely debated look at racial tension in an inner-city neighborhood. I placed *Nation of Millions* at No. 5 on my list of best albums of the year. I should have placed it at No. 1, as it was surely the *Highway 61 Revisited* of rap.

CHAPTER
TWENTY-ONE

Even more so than the Concert for Bangladesh and the "We Are the World" single, the Live Aid concerts in London and Philadelphia in July of 1985 represented a breakthrough in rock activism—and it felt good. It wasn't just rock fans who were caught up in the spirit of the benefit concerts that raised an estimated forty million dollars for famine victims in Africa. There was talk everywhere I went in London in the days after the show, which was broadcast throughout Britain in its sixteen-hour entirety by the BBC. "Wasn't it fantastic?" a hotel porter in his fifties said to a desk clerk as he returned to work the day after the show.

"The experience made me feel good about rock 'n' roll. It made me feel good about people again," said a woman in her thirties who had been disillusioned by the killing of John Lennon, the breakup of the Clash, and a widespread decadence in rock. Richard Williams, one of my favorite rock critics before he switched to sportswriting, picked up on the national mood in his Live Aid review in the *London Times*. The concert, he wrote, felt like "the healing of our own nation."

After years of being identified as rebels and mavericks in the public mind, rock's biggest figures had finally entered the Age of the Good Guy. David Bowie—who had been the epitome of cool cynicism during his Thin White Duke days a decade earlier—chuckled when I brought up the "good guy" reference the day after the concerts. But he agreed that times had changed. "I think that a lot of the causes and things we are caring about now are the same as we cared about in the '60s," he said. "It may just be that we're better dressed now . . . and better able to deal with them." Talking about his own music, David added, "I think it has evolved into what you might call a brighter lot. One loses a lot of the darkness in his music when you learn the thing you should be doing is quite simple. To help is enough."

The Live Aid broadcasts were seen by an estimated 1.5 billion people around the world. Some musicians also expanded the importance of the day. In a spontaneous aside during his performance in Philadelphia, Bob Dylan suggested that American farmers needed some financial help, too. Willie Nelson, who had been thinking the same thing, followed up on Dylan's remark by joining with Neil Young and John Mellencamp to organize the first Farm Aid concert on September 22, 1985, at the University of Illinois Memorial Stadium in Champaign.

Live Aid was also a pivotal moment for Bono. U2 was too new to be given a closing, showcase spot on the bill, but the quartet's brief, two-song set in the middle of the afternoon was a showstopper, the moment when the boys of "I Will Follow" became men. Thousands waved symbolic white flags as U2 opened with "Sunday Bloody Sunday." During "Bad," Bono saw that it would be difficult to bring a fan on stage for the kind of embrace he had done at the Long Beach Arena, so he jumped off the stage to dance with a girl.

Watching, I realized that Bono was starting to step into the role he had long spoken about to me in private: He would use his position in rock as a bully pulpit.

U2 lived up to all its promise two years later in 1987's *The Joshua Tree,* a musical declaration of faith. It became my favorite album since Springsteen's *Nebraska.* The music was more tailored and assured as the Edge, Adam, and Larry expanded upon the moody textures of earlier songs like "Bad" and reached out for new, bluesier touches. Bono's lyrics were more consistently focused, and his singing underscored the band's expressions of disillusionment and hope with newfound power and passion. While biblical images abounded, the songs, most notably "I Still Haven't Found What I'm Looking For," "Where the Streets Have No Name," and "Running to Stand Still," were human tales of reaching for your ideals while battling moments of doubt and despair.

Bono had been urging me to come to Dublin for years, saying it was the only true way to understand the group. I went that spring to spend a couple of days with the band before the start of its eighteen-month world tour. Because anticipation about the album and the tour were overwhelming, I assumed I'd find the band in a celebratory mood in its rehearsal hall, but the band's excitement was tempered by its concern about the effect of this enormous escalation of popularity. They were all too aware of how so many rock heroes had either destroyed themselves or lost their competitive edge after reaching such mass acceptance. Now they were going to be tested.

After rehearsal, Bono took me down to his favorite part of the old capital city: the decaying and mostly deserted Grand Canal locks. The neighborhood of stone-arched alleys and brick streets is near the River Liffey, which splits the city into the working-class north and the more fashionable south. "This is the same canal that many of the great Irish poets wrote their best works by," Bono said as we walked along. "But that was up in the part of town that they call the Lazy Acre, the bohemian center of Dublin. This is Irish Town, a forgotten place. They are trying to tear it down and put up new buildings. But to me, it is the heart of Dublin."

The Grand Canal was so far off the beaten path that it was ignored by tour books, but Bono found inspiration there. "Things are moving fast," he said, turning up the collar of his black leather jacket to shut out the cold damp as he headed back to the studio. "It's like a brush fire at the moment. Dublin is our anchor, I suppose. You get so high sometimes when you are on stage and you need to come down, and you really do that in Dublin. The people here don't allow you to act like a rock star. It's a reminder of how important family and friends are, how very much we need them to keep us from being swallowed up in the pop world. . . . I want to hold on to who I am."

On the last night of rehearsal, the Dalton Brothers, the band's alter ego on nights when its members wanted to play some country or other cover tunes, stepped to the microphones before a crowd of friends and family they'd convened in the studio. The choice this night was Curtis Mayfield's gospel-tinged "People Get Ready." Bono's voice had a gentle, prayerful edge and there was a hush among the crowd. The atmosphere was sentimental. Most of these people had known the band for years, and they sensed the group was at a crucial point. I asked Niall Stokes, editor of *Hot Press,* the leading Irish rock publication, about the differences he'd noticed over the years. The big thing, he said, was that Bono had become far more political. "There was a time when a discussion of politics would have seemed irrelevant to him. He was more interested in spiritual issues. Now, they have become more political and the new album is an awareness of that."

. . . .

The Joshua Tree **hit with gale force.** It spent nine weeks at No. 1 in the United States and earned the band the cover of *Time* magazine—a mark of cultural command that linked them with the Beatles, Dylan, and Springsteen. The group was so touched by the response to the album that it turned the tour into an homage of sorts to many of its own heroes. They played a Beatles song ("Helter Skelter") at one show and made another tip of the hat to the Beatles' rooftop concert in the film *Let It Be* by playing "Where the Streets Have No Name" in a video shoot on top of a hotel in Los Angeles. U2 also wrote and performed one song with B.B. King and Bono collaborated on another with Bob Dylan.

I tried to spend as much time as I could with the band on the tour, which was chronicled in a revealing but also controversial film titled *Rattle and Hum*. Director Phil Joanou captured the spirit of the band well, not only its passion on stage, but also its fascination with American musical influences. But when the film was released in theaters, many fans and critics saw it as an act of self-glorification. It was bad enough, the complaints went, that U2 was trying to be the moral conscience of rock, but the band was now trying to suggest that it was at the level of Elvis, the Beatles, and Dylan.

Bono was aware of the mounting criticism when he accepted the album of the year Grammy for *The Joshua Tree*. "It really is hard to carry the weight of the world on your shoulders, . . . [saving] the whales, . . . organizing summit meetings between world leaders, but we enjoy the work," he said sarcastically at the awards ceremony in New York. As the audience laughed, he turned serious. "It's hard, however, when fifty million people are watching, not to take the opportunity to talk about things like South Africa, what's happening there, and remarkable people like Bishop Tutu."

We had breakfast the next morning at a coffee shop near Central Park and Bono talked again about the thin line between inspiring people and turning them off by appearing sanctimonious, and he worried that another album with the crusading zeal of *The Joshua Tree* might turn many people away from the band. He hated being a caricature in some people's eyes, but he understood what contributed to it. Bono talked about some side projects he was considering. He mentioned writing a film script, a novel, some short stories, and essays on world affairs. He also wanted to travel more and raise his voice for the disadvantaged around the world, especially in Africa, where he and his wife, Ali, had spent time in a refugee camp. As I listened, I admired his ambition and heart, but I also worried that he might be spreading himself too thin. I pointed out how Kris Kristofferson's songwriting had suffered when he started making movies. Bono acknowledged the point, but I could see he wasn't convinced.

I had seen so many bands torn apart after achieving creative and/or commercial heights. The reasons weren't always the same, but the Beatles, the Band, Creedence Clearwater Revival, and the Eagles had all failed to make it through even one decade without splintering. Would U2 be any different? It had only been seven years between the group's first album and the Grammy Award for *The Joshua Tree*.

I voiced my concern. I asked Bono how many great songs he had written so far. Before he could answer, I asked how many great songs Bob Dylan had written, and Cole Porter, and John Lennon. I told him that if he put all his energy into his music, he could be one of the all-time-great songwriters. Think of what George Gershwin left behind, I said. Think of Hank Williams. "Would anything else they could have done been worth it, if it meant the end of their songwriting?"

He just sort of looked down at the table and finally said that the activism actually helped inspire him as a writer. It was something he needed to do. He couldn't see setting it aside.

I told him I wasn't talking about the activism. I was talking about the movies and the books and plays.

I couldn't tell I if had encouraged him or offended him.

Bono never mentioned the conversation again, but I got my answer eight years later when Bill Flanagan, in his book *U2: At the End of the World,* described me as Bono's "conservative conscience." He said the songwriting lecture in New York "still rattles around in Bono's head."

CHAPTER
TWENTY-TWO

I t was hard to know what to make of N.W.A's *Straight Outta Compton* when it came out in 1988. The raw imagery in a few of the songs was so ugly and violent that even some big-name East Coast rap artists thought it was irresponsible (though they wouldn't say so publicly because they didn't want to appear soft). The controversy escalated when an FBI official warned that one song, "Fuck tha Police," could lead to violence against law enforcement officers around the country. But the more authorities attacked the record, the more young people, black and white, rushed to buy it. Despite getting no mainstream radio airplay or MTV exposure, *Straight Outta Compton* sold five hundred thousand copies in six weeks—and the buzz was spreading across the nation. N.W.A wasn't trying to infiltrate the big-time record business by copying what was already popular on the radio. The rappers wanted to create their own style, which gave them immediate independence. Because the record was released on their own label, they didn't have to tone down the language to satisfy major-label sensibilities.

I connected with them through their manager, Jerry Heller, an industry veteran I knew through his brief affiliation with Elton John. He suggested that the best way to get an interview was to just show up at N.W.A's concert at the Celebrity Theatre in Anaheim. I arrived at about 4:00 p.m., figuring the group would be doing a sound check. But I couldn't find Jerry, and two of the guys, MC Ren and DJ Yella, were out somewhere in search of food. Eazy-E was on the phone and totally disinterested in talking to me. Dr. Dre was checking out the turntables in the auditorium. My first impression was that the group was trying to be like the Sex Pistols—so rude that everyone was offended.

But Ice Cube, nineteen, proved eager to talk. He came from a tough area of Los Angeles, but he'd had a stable childhood. His parents worked in blue-collar jobs at UCLA and instilled in him the importance of education. He graduated from Taft High School in the San Fernando Valley, where he was bused daily, and then studied architecture briefly before devoting himself to the group. His forte was words. On the touchy issue of "Fuck tha Police," he said the music was aimed at young people in the hood and they understood the language and message of the song. He wasn't trying to "educate and inform" in the manner of Chuck D, but he did feel rap was a positive force for young people because it provided an outlet for their frustration.

Security guards pressed handheld metal detectors against everyone who entered the 2,500-seat theater and checked purses for weapons. To reduce the chances of anyone showing gang colors, hats, bandannas, and rags were prohibited. The atmosphere was calm as the crowd listened to the opening acts, but the intensity increased sharply when N.W.A walked on stage and went into "Gangsta Gangsta" and "Fuck tha Police," two of the most explosive tunes on the *Compton* album. I made sure my backstage pass was still stuck on my jeans so I could get to safety in case of trouble—and my heart skipped a beat when a fight broke out during "Dopeman," another graphic song.

I saw this as a moment of truth for N.W.A and for rap. If the group was after sensational headlines, it would welcome the outburst. But if Cube was as responsible as he said he was, the group would try to put down the uprising. I waited anxiously for the answer—one eye on the group and the other on the backstage door. Cube's response was encouraging. He stopped the song to address the flare-up. Speaking in the same angry tone he used in his songs, he shouted, "If you want to fight, come up here on stage. This ain't [the movie] *Colors*. . . . You didn't come to see a fight, you came to see a concert." With the help of security guards, order was quickly restored.

I came away from Anaheim a believer. This was a group that was playing a dangerous game, but you couldn't deny the artistry of Cube's words and Dre's exquisite beats.

The reaction against my article on N.W.A was fierce. A high school principal in Orange County was among the dozens of callers. He said rap music was encouraging students to defy authority and every story about the group only empowered the troublemakers. He said if I kept promoting rap, there could be blood on my hands. Even my mother—who was so supportive she defended me when her neighbors tried to put down Elvis or Dylan or the Rolling Stones—said she thought I was going too far with N.W.A. "Tell me," she said in a hushed tone one day. "Tell me, you really don't like that stuff. Go back to writing about Elton or Bruce."

. . . .

Race can be a tricky thing, especially for someone who grew up in the South in the 1940s. When I was living on the farm before starting school, I spent most of my days playing with a couple of black boys who were my age. But there were limits. We could play in the fields and in the barns, but they couldn't come into the house with me. When we went to movies, they had to sit upstairs. When I started second grade in Los Angeles, I was seated next to a black girl. I casually mentioned it to my folks that evening and they were not pleased. I always thought of my mom as the most generous person in the world. She was always helping out at church and putting money in Salvation Army pots at Christmas, but she went to the school the next day and asked that I be moved to a different seat.

Years later, my mother looked back on the incident with regret. She became much more tolerant with age. Her real awakening was in the 1960s, when she became enthralled with John and Robert Kennedy. I think part of it was that she, as a Catholic in a heavily Protestant part of Louisiana, gently felt the sting of prejudice. So, she celebrated Kennedy's victory as the first Catholic president, and she sympathized when the Kennedys addressed the evils of segregation.

For my part, I spent most of my California school days in virtually all-white schools and communities, first in Del Mar, then in the San Fernando Valley. I knew about civil rights problems in the South and cheered the efforts to overcome segregation. But in Los Angeles, I didn't have any real contact with African Americans for years. The same was true in the workplace, first at my newspaper job in the San Fernando Valley and then, for the most part, in the public relations post at the Los Angeles Unified School District.

Spending time with Chuck D and Ice Cube and listening to their music not only helped me understand the creative merits of rap, but it also helped me understand what was going on in urban ghettos. To most Americans, the country seemed to have come a long way since the protests and riots of the turbulent 1960s and the nightmare surrounding the assassination of the Reverend Martin Luther King Jr. For years, Americans had been cuddling up with Bill Cosby, *Sanford and Son,* and *Good Times* on TV. Michael Jackson was the King of Pop. One of 1988's best-selling records was by the son of the first male black soloist at the New York Metropolitan Opera. The light, upbeat song by Bobby McFerrin would also win the Grammy for record of the year: "Don't Worry, Be Happy."

N.W.A challenged all that, which made the music appear to white America to be all the more exploitive—and threatening. The paradox of N.W.A was that the factors that made the group's music seem alien even to mainstream rappers were the same elements that gave the music its significance and strength: a view of the inner-city African American experience that was rarely presented elsewhere.

In retrospect, even the socially conscious side of black music in the 1960s had been temperate. Stevie Wonder and Curtis Mayfield were by nature idealistic. In the tradition of Reverend King, they wanted to reach out to blacks and whites and bring them together. Record companies encouraged moderation because they didn't want anything that was controversial enough to sacrifice radio airplay, the key to reaching a wide audience. The trend culminated in the early 1980s when Paul McCartney and Wonder joined together on "Ebony and Ivory." The exception was James Brown's 1968 "Say It Loud—I'm

Black and I'm Proud," a furious cry for self-affirmation that was aimed almost exclusively at black audiences.

This gap between the perception of LA race relations and the reality was highlighted by the LA riots of 1992 in the aftermath of the acquittal of the police officers involved in the Rodney King beating a year earlier. Those traumatic days and nights of looting and burning opened a lot of eyes in Southern California, where the homicide rate in ghetto neighborhoods was four times the national average and where residents saw nowhere to turn; they felt like the victims of both the gangs, whose members numbered in the thousands, and the police, who were supposed to protect them. The verdict, which ran counter to the tape that seemed to confirm that the officers had used undue force, confirmed that the system had failed the people it purported to protect. Suddenly, the music of N.W.A and Ice Cube assumed an eerie air of prophecy and the media sought Cube out, hoping for insights into what had happened.

· ·

Ice Cube refused more than a hundred requests for interviews after the rioting started. Discouraged by earlier media criticism, he worried that his words might be taken out of context again. Because of our relationship, however, Cube met me in his manager's office, which was just a few stoplights from where white truck driver Reginald Denny was pulled from his vehicle and beaten by a crowd of rioters. The area had the feel of a fortress. Barbed wire was stretched across the top of an iron fence that protected a warehouse across the street, while bars fronted the doors and windows of almost every house on adjoining streets. Inside the office, there was an eerie calm. The curtains were drawn and the only noise was the hum of the air conditioner as Cube searched for the latest news report on TV.

Cube began by saying he hadn't been surprised by the decision in the King case. "I knew it was going to be not guilty as soon as they moved the case to Simi Valley," he said. "What happens is that America looks at black men in two ways. You have the nice black man, like a Bill Cosby, and you have the bad black man, . . . the person you see going to jail at night on the news. To most Americans, especially in a place like Simi Valley, it is one or the other. If Rodney King was seen as a good black, then the officers would have been found guilty, but all through the trial, they kept saying that he was a monster, . . . a wild animal, . . . plus he had a past criminal record. To the jurors, he was a bad black, so anything done to him was justified."

As he continued, I thought about the rows of burned-out buildings I had passed on Crenshaw Boulevard on the way to Cube's office.

"The media and authorities like to concentrate on the looting and say it was just a bunch of criminals or thugs out there, but there were all kinds of people out there, women and children, . . . poor people who wouldn't have to loot if they had the money to buy things. That's why, to me, it was a protest. It was a protest against the conditions and the injustice, not just the verdict, but the years of injustice. The looting that was done in South Central was nothing like the looting done by the savings and loans. You take everything that happened in fact and it was just a smidgen of what has happened to blacks all these years."

Unlike many rappers, Cube didn't try to embellish his background with vague references to gang ties—something that might have been tantalizing to suburban teens who embraced the tough, gangsta rap style. Despite the persistent scowl in album cover and publicity photos, Cube had a disarming smile and spoke lovingly about his fourteen-month-old son. "I grew up a lot once I was on my own," he said of his solo career. "When I was younger, I thought the best thing to do was to be the hardest rapper you could, . . . 'I got a thousand guns . . . ' and all that. But if you stick to that, you become a comic book. I wanted to be more sincere with my lyrics, more truthful."

Just before I left, Cube said he had a new song he thought I might like. It described a day where nothing goes wrong, where nobody gets killed. The song, "It Was a Good Day," was released the following spring, and it became a hit on both the rap and pop charts. Its success sent a welcome signal to hard-core rappers that they could step away from the relentless confrontation and macho bravado without losing street credibility.

CHAPTER
TWENTY-THREE

Even though I spent most of my time covering rock, I never lost my love of country music and was delighted by the success in the 1970s of my outlaw buddies Willie and Waylon, the moody but immensely talented Merle Haggard, and Johnny Cash. Between them, they had more than 120 Top Forty country singles in the decade alone. Haggard at one point had nine straight No. 1 hits. Willie and Waylon also sold strongly in the pop field, with Waylon's 1979 *Greatest Hits* collection and Willie's 1978 *Stardust* both topping the five million mark.

But nothing lasts forever, and country music record execs and radio station programmers started turning away from anyone identified with country music's honky-tonk past. My Big Four, along with other veterans like George Jones and Loretta Lynn, continued to have a chart presence, but Kenny Rogers was the new model. Instead of strong individuals singing meaningful songs, the top slots on the country charts in the 1980s were generally filled with creditable vocalists who either imitated the old country greats or buried all traces of emotion under lush arrangements in hopes of picking up pop as well as country airplay.

So it was heartwarming to see nearly twenty thousand people at an arena in Chicago giving a standing ovation to four of the true country greats: Willie, Waylon, Johnny, and Kris Kristofferson. Standing next to each other on stage one night early in 1990, they represented a Mount Rushmore of country music. But there was a melancholy edge to the evening. Cash's sales had fallen off so much in the late '80s that he had been dropped by Columbia Records. The same label was breaking Nelson's heart with suggestions about how to make his music more commercial, and RCA had said farewell to Jennings. Kristofferson had tried to combine acting and songwriting, but the acting had proven much more viable for years. The fact that they were all appearing on the same bill, as the Highwaymen, was another sign of their status. Johnny, Willie, and Waylon used to be able to sell out an arena by themselves, but they now needed to band together to generate that much drawing power. On stage, they looked upbeat. Inside, they were all struggling with the thought that the tour could be a last hurrah.

The game plan for me was to see the opening show, then to travel with Waylon on the bus ride to Detroit. I'd then ride halfway to the next night in Minneapolis with Willie, then the rest of the way on Kris's bus. John preferred to sleep at the hotel after the shows and then travel to the next city the following morning. I'd catch up with him at the hotel in Minneapolis. The customized buses—which cost between three hundred thousand and five hundred thousand dollars each—traveled together out of a spirit of kinship and so that help was available in case of trouble.

Sitting opposite Waylon and his wife, Jessi, on his Silver Eagle bus, I couldn't help but think of all the times I had heard him sing Bob McDill's song "Amanda" and marveled at the line about the pleasures of being in a hillbilly band. All four of the Highwaymen were over fifty now, and the lines in their faces showed the toll of all those nights of music and tour buses and planes and chasing dreams. With Waylon's help, I figured out that they'd spent a collective 115 years on the road. During that time, they'd collectively had twelve marriages and truckloads of pills, whiskey, and weed.

"I think it's the freedom," he finally said to explain the line in the McDill song. "Being in a cowboy band is a way of getting through life without having to give in—and the jeans are part of it. People used to tell us to dress differently, sing differently, make records differently because that was the way to get ahead in Nashville. But we weren't interested in just getting ahead. We fought and we won."

The conversation about the changes in country music went on for a half hour, but Waylon eventually returned to the McDill song that he had sung hundreds of times on stage. "You know what other line hits me every time I sing it? The one about a gentleman's wife. I think of Jessi. She was what made me finally quit drugs. I looked at her face one day and I could see what I was doing to her, the pain I was causing. Nothing else had been enough—the fact that I almost ruined my voice, that I couldn't even see straight some nights on stage."

He said he wanted to spend more time with his ten-year-old son, Shooter, and hoped to start booking his tours in the summer so the boy could be on the road with him. "It's funny how your dreams and goals change over the years," he continued. "You know what my ambition is now? I want to live to see what he becomes. All of my other children are grown now and doing well, but there is something special about him. I guess it's the fact I had him so late in life that I realized I have to give him a lot real quick."

On Willie's bus the next night, Gates Moore, the driver, didn't like the way the ice was forming on the side mirrors as he headed to Minneapolis. If the temperature on this chilly, late-night run dropped even another degree or two, "Gator" feared the roads would become so dangerous that he'd have to reduce his speed to twenty miles per hour or less, which could add four or five hours to the more than twelve-hour trip. But none of this bothered Willie as he sat back in the lounge area. He spends more than two hundred days a year on the road, so what difference was it if this trip took a little longer? He's more comfortable on the bus than in hotel rooms, which is why he often stays in the hotel parking lot rather than going inside with the rest of the band, most of whom travel on a separate bus. Besides, nothing seemed to bother Willie. This was back in his heavy marijuana-use period, when Willie gave new meaning to the term "mellow." I had the feeling that if a thief tried to hot-wire the bus, Willie would give him the keys and then return to the rear of the bus and pick out a new tune on his guitar. At least, this was the public Willie. On this night, even Willie had the blues.

Nelson had sold more records than any of the Highwaymen during the 1970s and 1980s, but his sales had dropped off dramatically and his record company wasn't happy. Even though Nelson was one of the greatest songwriters and singers in all of pop music, they wanted him to "update" his sound. And Willie, in his mellow way, went along because he wanted to be a team player. He in effect had turned over creative control to a producer and simply gone in and done the vocals. Willie wasn't pleased with the results.

"Here, let me play it," he said as the bus headed through the night. "Maybe you could tell me what you think." I listened to it, then told Willie I thought the music lacked his usual soulful touch. It was what he wanted to hear. He reached into a bag and pulled out another cassette. This time, Willie sang with winning character and ease on a series of country music standards; it was an album that captured the feeling of a real, live honky-tonk. I liked it much, much better, and I could see tears welling in Willie's eyes when he said the record company didn't have any interest in it. How sad to think that this man who had made millions of dollars for his record label was considered just another hired hand.

Even with this setback, I couldn't picture Willie ever wanting to leave the road. Unlike Waylon, he was addicted to it. When I asked him if he ever got tired of it, his spirits lifted. "There's something in me that just needs to keep moving," he said, staring through the bus window into the darkness. "I worked a lot of sit-down jobs in the early days out of necessity, but I was always wishing that Hank Thompson or one of those big bands would hire me so I could step onto the bus with them—and I've never wanted to get off."

When I caught up with John at his hotel, I wondered how much longer he'd be able to tour. Though he was roughly the same age as Waylon and Willie, he seemed far frailer. His jaw was severely swollen, the aftermath of some recent dental work, and his spirits were low. He said he felt so far from what was happening in Nashville that he wondered if he'd be able to get a record contract if he was just starting out. "I think the only job I'd be able to get would be singing in a coffeehouse somewhere because that's where I could sing songs that mattered to me," he said between sips of a protein drink that June made for him. "I sure couldn't get into singing most of the things you hear on the radio."

John said he enjoyed singing with the others, but that he mainly hoped the shows would make a difference in the country music world. "You've got thirty-three songs on the show and I think they are all important," he continued. "The reviewer in Detroit said something about it being a nostalgia thing, but it really isn't. The songs are just as now and as alive as they ever were because a good song is about real life and real emotions and those things don't get out-of-date."

The tour did well enough that the Highwaymen went back on the road for more dates, but it didn't do much to change minds in Nashville. Waylon would only have three more singles make the country chart after 1990, and none made the Top Ten. His health deteriorated quickly. I saw him for breakfast in 2001, and it was hard seeing him struggle to make it down the hall with a cane. I think he noticed my expression as I walked with him back to the hotel elevator after breakfast because he turned to me and said, "Hey, I'm a lucky man. My dreams did come true." Waylon died in February of 2002. He was sixty-four.

Kris mostly stuck to films after the Highwaymen and he kept in great shape. He moved to Hawaii with his wife, Lisa, but made periodic returns to the music business, whether it was to join the cast at a Dylan tribute concert in New York or duet with Jerry Lee Lewis on a video for a new Lewis album. Wherever he went, he was a humble and passionate spokesman for high quality in music, lavishing great praise on other musicians. In truth, Kris's role in the evolution of songwriting in Nashville was as important as that of anyone of his generation.

Willie stuck it out for years on Columbia, then started recording for various labels, doing country music, some reggae, and even jazz. Though his impact on the country charts was minimal, he kept touring and playing the music with his friends—a link for millions to a country music era that had passed.

John, meanwhile, suffered through more health problems, but he eventually found someone who still believed in his music: Los Angeles–based rock and rap producer Rick Rubin. I spoke to John on the phone soon after he started working with Rick in the mid-'90s, and he was jubilant. The plan was to work with Rick on picking some songs from all fields, from country and rock to gospel and folk. John was so excited after the first album was finished that he sent me an early copy along with a note asking what I thought. He was especially curious about whether I thought his old fans would relate to his new direction. I told John it was the best thing he had done in years and that if his old fans didn't relate to it, he'd pick up a whole crop of new fans that would. I was so happy for him that I sent him occasional lists of songs I thought he should consider recording. One of the songs he did record was Don Gibson's "(I'd Be) A Legend in My Time." The first two Cash–Rubin collaborations won Grammys, one for best folk recording of the year and the other for best country recording.

The pair was just about to start work on the third album when John fell on stage during an October 1997 concert in Flint, Michigan. Doctors told John he had a neurological disorder called Shy-Drager syndrome and had only a couple of years to live. Even so, John and Rick slowly began preparations for the next album and John's health gradually improved enough for him to finish the project. It was for the fourth album, 2002's *American IV: The Man Comes Around,* that Rick brought John the Trent Reznor song "Hurt." John didn't know what to make of the tale of self-despair, but he eventually found his way into the music and delivered a performance so stirring that it gave even Rubin and Reznor chills listening to it.

. . . .

Seeing the turning of a page in country made me think about the issue of longevity in rock. It had been almost a quarter century since Mick Jagger declared that he couldn't imagine singing "Satisfaction" at thirty, but he was nearing fifty in 1990 and singing the song in stadiums around the world. Once they passed thirty, Keith Richards and other rockers proclaimed that if their heroes, bluesmen, could keep playing indefinitely, why not them? It made sense, and it helped me forget my own age. But I was particularly sensitive because I was now fifty—and I got a good-natured telegram reminding me of it from Bruce Springsteen, a fellow Libra, but ten years younger.

From the time of my start at the *LA Times,* I had been conscious that I was covering a musical field whose core audience was in its teens and twenties. I watched my high school and college chums increasingly lose interest in rock in their late twenties. Whereas they'd once lived for the next great record, they now didn't have time to keep up with new sounds and personalities. At most, they stuck with some of their old favorites—which meant I got a lot of calls for tickets when the Stones or Dylan came to town. Otherwise, I usually found myself alongside twenty-two-year-olds when checking out new bands.

When I raised the matter of longevity with Paul McCartney, the ex-Beatle laughed and said, "I wonder what Pete thinks about that line: 'Hope I die before I get old'? But, of course, we all thought the same thing. In fact, I remember the time when I thought twenty-five was too old to be in a band. The reason twenty-five stood out for me was that Frank Ifield [a British pop singer of the time] was twenty-five and he seemed too old to ever be in a rock band."

But Paul saw things differently when he turned twenty-five. "By the time we were twenty-five, we were at the height of our Beatle-mania powers, so it seemed like we could go on another five years or so," he said. "Then thirty arrived and we all felt pretty good still, . . . looked all right, . . . so thirty-five started to be the marker. By thirty-five, I was into Wings and forty seemed to be the end. Now I'm not sure. Maybe fifty?"

I also tried to talk to Bob Dylan about aging in rock, but he was nearing fifty and everyone wanted a story about what it was like for rock's most celebrated living figure to reach that milestone. He turned down all requests. He knew writers would take advantage of the birthday to reflect on his life and his art, but they'd have to do it on their own. Besides, he always said he hated looking back. And what could he say about the present? He continued circling the globe, recycling old hits, but it was hard to imagine him creating anything that recalled the brilliance of his early work. His albums continued to be praised politely by critics, but his audience was shrinking. It had been twelve years since one of his collections, *Slow Train Coming,* had reached the Top Ten, and even many of his old fans shook their heads at the snarling version of "Masters of War" he did on the 1991 Grammys telecast that was almost impossible to decipher.

Maintaining his media silence, Bob spent most of 1991 touring.

And yes, I put in my bid for an interview, but the word was no. Bob said he wanted to get past the May 24 milestone first. As politely as I could, I kept renewing the request every few weeks until, in October, I got word that Bob was ready to talk. Could I join him in Chicago and maybe spend a couple of days on the road? Could I? I would have hitch-hiked there if necessary.

. . . .

The scene surrounding Bob in Chicago had changed a lot since 1974 when he had embarked on the tour with the Band. This time, there was nothing in the papers about his show on the campus of nearby Northwestern University and there wasn't a camera in sight when I checked in to the Ambassador East, one of the city's grand old hotels. He was playing before 3,500 fans at McGaw Hall, a basketball gym-cum-auditorium.

Bob called my room at about 2:00 p.m. "I heard you wanted to come out and see some shows," he said in his raspy voice. "I'm going out early today so maybe you can ride out later with Jeff." He was referring to Jeff Kramer, who oversaw his touring plans. *Damn,* I thought. If the whole idea of the trip was to spend time with Bob, why wouldn't he invite me to go out to the show with him? So he really caught me by surprise when he added, "Then, if we're not too tired, we can go out to some clubs tonight if you'd like. There are some cool blues places."

At this and other college shows, he was playing mostly to young people who weren't alive when "Blowin' in the Wind" was written. There was little of the raucous exuberance in the hall before the show that I remembered from earlier tours. The mood was mostly curiosity—about Bob and about the 1960s. The students spoke about the show in the same spirit they would have if they were about to hear an honored novelist or historian deliver a lecture. For most of the concert's first hour, the audience simply watched politely. They didn't become responsive until "All Along the Watchtower," a song that several students later told me they knew through Jimi Hendrix's version or, in some cases, U2's recording.

Jeff and I got back to the hotel just as Bob's bus arrived. As the band members filed off and headed to their rooms, Bob stood on the sidewalk, shifting his weight back and forth in the cold and staring into the distance. Finally, he looked over at me and asked, "Wanna hear some blues?"

Bob was bundled up and no one recognized him on the walk to the nearby bar. He took a seat while a trio went through some familiar licks. During a break, Bob's bodyguard braced as a middle-aged man in a business suit walked up to Bob and put an arm around him. But the smile on Bob's face said it was okay. "This is Arnie," he said, introducing me to the visitor. "We went to high school back in Hibbing."

Bob seemed bemused as Arnie told me about some of their adventures from long ago. "Back in English class, Bob wrote me a note: 'Arnie, I'm going to make it big. I know it for sure, and when I do, you bring this piece of paper and for two months, you can stay with me, no matter where I am at.'" Arnie looked at me and said, "I still have it at home."

Bob laughed. It was good to see him relaxing.

Arnie continued. "I took off and joined the navy and Bob went down to the University of Minnesota and the next thing I know, he's got this record out."

Knowing that Bob didn't like talking about his personal life, I kept expecting him to step in and change the subject, but he just listened as I asked Arnie if he had many of Bob's albums ("some") and what his favorite songs were ("Slow Train Coming" and "Lay, Lady, Lay").

I asked Arnie if he would mind if I used his last name in the story—and that's when Bob did interrupt. "Naw," he said, protectively. "Don't drag him into all this."

I knew what Dylan meant. For years, journalists and fans had hounded everyone ever connected with Bob, eager for tidbits. Bob didn't want Arnie to have to endure the intrusions as well.

Finally, Dylan, his bodyguard, and I left the bar and headed for a nondescript diner a few blocks away. Bob ordered a bowl of soup and asked what I had learned talking to the students at the concert. I summarized my notes for him.

"Older people—people my age—don't come out anymore," he said, starting on his second cup of coffee. "A lot of shows over the years was just people coming out of curiosity and their curiosity wasn't fulfilled.

They weren't transported back to the 1960s. Lightning didn't strike. The shows didn't make sense for them and they didn't make sense for me. A lot of people were coming out to see 'the Legend' and I was trying to just get on stage and play music."

Bob shifted restlessly in the chair. There were a dozen people in the place and no one seemed to recognize him. Finally, I saw the diner manager walking our way. He asked for a photo or an autograph. Bob begged off. Maybe tomorrow, he said before shaking the man's hand.

The next day, Bob invited me to ride on the bus with him and the band to the show at the Dane County Memorial Coliseum on the University of Wisconsin campus in Madison. A snowstorm snarled traffic, so it took the bus four hours instead of two to get there. Bob made a little small talk with members of the band, but mostly sat in the back, either sleeping or drawing in a notebook. On stage, he struggled for inspiration. Despite a standing ovation at the end, he couldn't wait until he was back in the bus and on his way to the next town. The heater was on in the bus, but he still sat bundled up in a rumpled sweatshirt and jacket at a small table in the front.

"That was a useless gig," he said flatly. I mentioned that the audience had seemed to enjoy the show, but he wouldn't have any of it. "Naw, it just wasn't there. Nothin' wrong with the audience. Sometimes the energy level just doesn't happen the way it should. We didn't invite this weather to follow us around."

Then Bob lapsed into silence. I could feel my time with him passing like the miles on the highway. Bob was headed to South Bend, Indiana, for another concert, but I'd get off in Chicago and catch a plane home. The night before at the diner, he'd warned about the toll the road takes. "You sometimes hear about the glamour of the road," he said. "But you get over that real fast. There are a lot of times that it's no different from going to work in the morning. Still, you're either a player or you're not a player. It didn't really occur to me until we did those shows with the Grateful Dead [in 1987]. If you just go out every three years or so, like I was doing for a while, that's when you lose touch. If you are going to be a performer, you've got to give it your all."

I tried to lighten things up by mentioning all the fuss of the media wanting to interview him when he turned fifty. He smiled as I tossed out several of the clichéd headlines that would have accompanied those stories.

"Mr. Tambourine Man Turns 50!"

"Bringing It All Back Home."

I still had his interest so I went with my best shot:

"Knockin' on Heaven's Door."

Bob laughed out loud at that one.

The band members retired to their bunks, so it was just the two of us. Bob once told me that song ideas came so fast in the 1960s that he didn't want to go to sleep because he was afraid he would miss something. But he said those days were over. In fact, he was thinking about setting his songwriting aside for a while.

He said he wanted to make a record of old blues and folk tunes that still meant a lot to him. But I brought him back to the song-writing issue. I asked him if the problem was that he had run out of ideas for songs.

"Once in a while, the odd song will come to me like a bulldog at the garden gate and demand to be written," he said. "But most of them are rejected out of my mind right away. You get caught up in wondering if anyone really needs to hear it." He paused before adding, "Maybe a person gets to the point where they have written enough songs. Let someone else write them."

It was well past 1:00 a.m. when we pulled into Chicago, about a third of the way to South Bend. When the driver stopped to let me off at a motel near O'Hare International Airport, Bob got off and walked across the street to a truck stop for some fresh coffee. He sat at the counter, where he was unnoticed among a handful of truckers and motorists taking a break from the icy highway. When added to the fact that so many of the old fans were increasingly disappointed in Bob and that he seemed to have lost his lust for writing, the diner scene struck me as a downbeat moment you might see in a film about him. I asked if he would welcome a movie based on his life. "Absolutely not," he said, almost contemptuously. "No one knows too much about [my life], so it's going to have to all be speculation. Who was it that said fame is a curse? There's a lot of truth in that." Looking around the diner, he added, "Look at Elvis—he's bigger now than when he was living. He lives on in people's minds. But you wonder if people are remembering the right things about his music, rather than all the stuff that people wrote about him."

Earlier on the bus, Bob had talked about enjoying the role of the traveling musician, partly because he finally felt somewhat freed from the prison of his 1960s mantle. But how much longer will he still want to spend so much time on the road?

"There's no one to my knowledge who isn't surprised by their longevity, including myself," he said. "But it's very dangerous to plan because you are just dealing with your vanity. Tomorrow is hard enough. It's God who gives you the freedom, and the days you should be most concerned with are today and tomorrow. It's one thing to say, 'There's a new record out and people are responding to the new songs,' which is encouraging. But that's not the case. There's no new album, and it's hard for me to know just what that means, why people come out and what they are looking for or listening for in the old songs. Maybe the same things I was looking for when I wrote them."

As we said good-bye, I thought about Bruce Springsteen's song "Glory Days" and wondered if Bob's were over. If so, what did it tell us about the future of rock 'n' roll?

CHAPTER
TWENTY-FOUR

Bruce's retreat from the front lines of rock 'n' roll following his divorce and the breakup of the E Street Band was as dramatic—and as necessary—as Lennon's house-husband period and Dylan's disappearance after his motorcycle accident in the 1960s. It was a time for mending and renewal. Above all, he wanted the relationship with Patti to work. The first of their three children, Evan James, was born in the summer of 1990, and the couple was married the following June.

Bruce eventually began work on what would be a two-album project, and we got the first glimpse of the new music at two benefit concerts for the Christic Institute, a public-interest law firm, in late 1990 at the Shrine Auditorium in Los Angeles. It was a key moment for Bruce because his fans were demanding to know how all the changes in his personal life had affected his music. A lesser artist might have retreated into the safety of his best-known numbers, but Bruce respected his audience and his art too much. He knew he had to address the issue of change in the show. I saw the first signal of Bruce's intent in his dress—he had his shirttail hanging over his faded jeans rather than sporting the suits he had favored on the *Tunnel of Love* tour. I sensed that the old Bruce was back.

The two new albums, *Human Touch* and *Lucky Town*, felt disjointed, but *Lucky Town*'s "Living Proof" was the most personal song he had ever written and, maybe, the most powerful. In it, Bruce spoke of the joy of becoming a father and finally filling that long-aching void of family.

> *Like the missing words to some prayer that I could never make*
> *In a world so hard and dirty, so fouled and confused*
> *Searching for a little bit of God's mercy.*
> *I found living proof.*

When I sat down with him for his first print interview in four years, Bruce said, "I tried Patti's patience pretty regularly. I think I was just trying to re-find myself and dig up the guts to try to move ahead, and I was having a hard time doing that. 'Living Proof' is about the birth of our first son. It was just this unbelievable feeling of unconditional sort of love for Patti and the baby.

"It was probably the single most powerful thing I ever felt, and I understood why I ran from it for so long, because along with it came this enormous fear, probably the fear of loss, the fear of showing your cards, admitting something is that important to you and that you can't have it unless you show yourself," he told me. "Part of it is you are with somebody who makes you feel safe enough to do that, and Patti just gave me that particular confidence."

Bruce often used interviews to clarify his feelings about himself and his music. But I never sensed it more than I did on this June 1992 afternoon in Hollywood as he spoke in his slow, thoughtful way during breaks in rehearsal with his new band. As he leaned forward on a lounge sofa, he wanted to explain why something had gone wrong in his life, which was hard for someone who was obsessed with doing things right.

"When I was young, I truly didn't think music had any limitations," he said. "I thought it could give you everything you wanted in life, and music did that for me—more than I had ever dreamed of. But you eventually get to a point where you realize there are other things you need . . . things that music can't give you. That's when you have to put down the guitar and step into the real world."

Some artists find it difficult to speak about moments of doubt and insecurity, but Bruce felt that being open and honest was part of his bond with his fans. "I just kind of felt lost for a little while after the *Tunnel of Love* tour," he said. "I went through the divorce, and anybody who has been through that knows it is tough. You lose a lot of faith in yourself and your ability to connect with people."

Bruce frequently stopped and tugged at his shirt or rubbed his hands together.

"The point is, everything about you doesn't grow at the same pace," he continued. "You can become very capable in a certain area, even to the point of doing something so well that you are heavily rewarded and everybody applauds and tells you that you are great. But you can be completely unable at the same time to function in almost every other way. In my case, I wrote a lot about community and relationships, yet personally I lived very internally. But eventually you notice that your friends are starting to get married and you even see some of the fans at the shows have kids on their shoulders, and you feel you are missing something important in your life. That's when you have to see if you can live up to the words in some of your own songs. For me, that step took almost ten years."

As Bruce spoke, I thought about how I, too, had reached a point a few years earlier when I fell in love again and vowed this time not to let my job obsession compete with my marriage. I realized that I didn't need to be out at a club every night in search of the next great artist. For one thing, most of the nights were wasted. Great artists don't come along every day, and I found it helped my writing to get away from the scene periodically so I could come back to it fresh.

Bruce rejoined the band on the rehearsal stage, and it felt odd to see him in the company of strangers. Instead of the E Street guys, he had a new group, anchored by the sole E Street survivor, Roy Bittan, on piano. Despite the lineup change, the music sounded energetic and full-bodied. The first show was two weeks away in Europe.

I didn't see the European shows, so the first time I saw Bruce and the new band was in August at the Brendan Byrne Arena, just across the Hudson River from Manhattan. It was Bruce's New Jersey turf, and I got there early enough to spend an hour walking around the parking lot, sampling the mood of the fans. Bruce had sold out eleven nights at the twenty-thousand-seat arena, but the homecoming had its bittersweet side. One fan was turned off by Bruce's dumping the band and moving to LA. Another didn't care for the new material. The one point of agreement: They wanted Bruce to play the old songs.

The response was enthusiastic as Bruce arrived on stage and there was a surge of energy as he went into "Better Days," an upbeat but anonymous song from one of his new albums. The fans reacted respectfully to two other new songs, but you could feel them holding back. It wasn't until he turned to one of his classics, "Darkness on the Edge of Town," that the crowd responded with its old fervor.

That same pattern—polite applause for the new songs and euphoria for the old—continued through the rest of the opening set. The reaction was more consistent in the second half, when Bruce focused on old material. The fans loved it, but I thought he was going against his own principles. Bruce often said he admired artists who did their new material in concert even when it was clear the audience just wanted to hear the familiar tunes; otherwise you are just selling nostalgia.

I wrote in my review that Bruce was being too timid by doing only fourteen of the twenty-four new songs in a thirty-song, three-hour performance. I closed by saying the worst thing that could happen if he changed it was that some fans would fall away and he might sell out only six nights instead of eleven the next time he played the Byrne Arena. "Faith" is a word that Springsteen uses a lot in his music, and I felt it was time for him to put faith in his own new work. I was pleased a few weeks later when Bruce played the Los Angeles Sports Arena and changed his song selection. Best of all, he closed the opening set with "Living Proof."

I didn't see Bruce personally in Los Angeles, but I assumed my review had prompted him to change the focus of the show—and lots of unhappy Bruce fans apparently thought the same thing. When *Backstreets,* the Bruce fanzine, asked readers to name their biggest disappointment of the year, lots of them felt my review had ruined the second half of the tour. Bruce sent me a playful note about it.

· ·

U2 went through its own heavy soul-searching in the early 1990s, though it was less public. Even though the *Rattle and Hum* album sold 7.5 million copies around the world, all the criticism over what was seen as the band's budding megalomania and self-importance shook Bono, Edge, Adam, and Larry deeply. In private, they agonized over their musical direction and personal goals. After some frustrating months in Dublin, U2 headed to a Berlin recording studio where the future of the band was on the line. They emerged from the period of self-doubt in the winter of 1991 with *Achtung Baby,* a triumphant change of pace. Instead of the uplifting songs about man's highest ideals, the themes tended to be darker and more desolate. The music, too, moved from eloquent and ethereal to frenzied, contemporary dance currents. In the process, U2 showed more dimension—elements of mystery and self-parody. On the surface at least, Bono no longer seemed to be preaching, but rather questioning motives, including his own. I went to London to talk to the band as it worked on a video and prepared for its world tour.

"We had some serious problems when we got back to Dublin after *Rattle and Hum,*" Larry said during a break in shooting the video. "A lot of our fans were confused by the movie and they started asking what we were all about and where we were headed—and that's good because we needed to sit down ourselves and think about those questions. There were times [since *The Joshua Tree*] where priorities got confused. There were times when you weren't sure what you were meant to be doing. Are you a musician? A rock star?"

The more he talked, the more I sensed that Larry was relieved that U2 was still together.

"We had to start from scratch in a way . . . get in touch with ourselves musically," Larry continued. "If we didn't come up with the right answers, it could have all been over because I think we all care enough about U2 to end it before we just make a joke of it. Everything was on the line. We didn't want *Rattle and Hum* to become our *Let It Be.*"

It was a sobering parallel to the 1970 documentary about the Beatles that telegraphed the recording studio friction between the bandmates that would eventually cause the band to dissolve. The strain in U2's case wasn't between individual members, but over the group's image and sound. Though Larry and the others stand by the film, they acknowledged that there were misjudgments in letting what was conceived as a small-scale project grow into a wide-screen spectacular that opened in nearly 1,500 theaters and was backed by a massive Hollywood film ad campaign.

Paul McGuinness, the band's manager, was also at the video shoot, and he was quick to take the blame for the extensive campaign. "I never realized what an enormous thing a movie campaign could be," he said. "All across America for a couple of weeks, you couldn't turn on your TV without getting U2 in your face. I think a lot of the band's old fans found it distasteful. The aftermath, quite honestly, was that no one wanted to hear about U2 for a while."

On the following day, the band was at the Zoo, a clothing store on Carnaby Street, to get scenes for the video of "Even Better Than the Real Thing," a song from the new album. The band performed the song in the store window while fans outside watched through the glass. The glass between the band and the audience was designed to underscore the song's theme about how fantasies and things that are untouchable can be even more intoxicating than the actual experiences.

As the camera began rolling, Bono—dressed in a shiny leather outfit and wearing dark glasses in a teasing poke at rock clichés—moved with many of the twisting and turning gestures that had become his trademark on stage. As the record played over a sound system in the street, Bono pressed against the glass, as if trying to make contact with the girls who were reaching for him. During the instrumental break, he noticed a woman's jacket on a sales rack and grabbed it. The jacket was much too small, but he put it on and began strutting around the floor. Fans on the street whooped it up. They weren't used to seeing U2 in such a playful mood.

Afterward, the Edge said one of the things the band had wanted to do with the new album was to show that there is another side of the group, especially of Bono. "People see him as this very serious guy who is always carrying the weight of the world around on his shoulders and that's not the whole picture. He's also a very funny guy and I was hoping we could get more of that into what we do. We wanted to get away from all that U2 earnestness on this record—not to come up with a 'new image,' but to show ourselves more accurately."

Adam, too, had an interesting take on the transition from *Rattle and Hum* to *Achtung Baby*. He said everyone had returned to Dublin in a fairly crazy stage. "I think it was a period of deciding whether being mega was any way I wanted to live my life. I think it was definitely a time for me to ask, 'Is this a path that is worthwhile pursuing?' We had all been on the move for the last ten years and it was our first chance to sit back for a few months and try to put everything into perspective. It was the first time people who had bought houses or been married could live in those houses for more than two or three months—and it was very comfortable. We all had to decide for ourselves how important U2 still was in our lives . . . whether there was really a commitment."

Edge, Adam, and Larry were all so talkative at dinner that I didn't notice until near the end that Bono had been unusually quiet. When I pointed that out to Edge, he said that was part of the plan—for the others to take some of the pressure off Bono so he wouldn't be the target of so much criticism. That's one reason the band refused to do interviews when *Achtung Baby* was released. They wanted the music to speak for itself.

I finally cornered Bono and we talked for a while off the record. He confirmed what the others had said. Finally, he agreed to let me quote him. It was after I asked about "Acrobat," one of my favorite songs on the album. It deals with personal contradictions and doubts— the distinction between the lofty ideals of U2's music and his own difficulty in living up to those ideals.

"I have learned to embrace the contradictions in life, and that's one of the messages of the album," he said. "There was a time when they were tearing me apart because I am not able to live up to a lot of the things I believe in. There was a reason we opened *Rattle and Hum* with 'Helter Skelter.' That's the way our lives felt sometimes. There were times when things could have unraveled. Even on *Joshua Tree,* heads left people's bodies, and not just the four members of the band, but some of the people around us. It's hard to talk about that and the reasons behind the songs on the album without sounding like a guest on one of those [confessional] TV shows, but there were definitely times when the fire you are playing with can destroy you before you even know it's there. But there is a thing that makes us strong. You can call it faith, you can call it lots of things, but it helps pull you through."

I turned off the tape recorder, but Bono wasn't finished. "Basically, for the first half of the '80s there was a slight ostrich element about us and that was good. We were on a spiritual sojourn and we discovered a lot of good stuff that keeps you strong and opens your eyes a bit. But there was a point then where you have to actually walk into the real world and it kind of went a bit wrong. I had a few bad experiences, really bad experiences, and some of that is what you hear in the album. If the first chapter of U2 was innocence, this one is about innocence lost."

INTERLUDE
SOME OF THE
SUPERFICIAL ARTISTS

There are lots of ways to rate rock 'n' roll performers, but Bob Dylan's system makes as much sense as any. Under it, artists fit into one of three categories—the natural performer, who does the best they can within their limits on stage; the superficial performer, who shouldn't be on stage in the first place because they've got nothing original to tell you; and the supernatural artist, who, in Bob's words, "is the kind that digs deep and the deeper they go, the more gods they'll find."

While I was always looking for the supernatural artists, I probably spent most of my time listening to superficial ones because they represented seventy-five percent or more of the rosters of the major labels. Thus, they become the villains in a critic's world—especially the bestsellers, because you want to see all those pop fans listening to more valuable artists. What's especially disheartening is when an artist with the potential to be a natural or a supernatural descends to the superficial ranks because of a hunger for greater and greater success. The post-*Thriller* Michael Jackson was the most flagrant example of this downward spiral in the modern pop era. Garth Brooks was another.

I first saw Garth when he opened for Reba McEntire at an outdoor raceway near Bakersfield, California, in late 1990—and he reached out to the audience with a winning, underdog spirit that made me think he might become the Bruce Springsteen of country. He didn't have an outstanding voice, but he sang about working-class values and dreams with a disarming vulnerability that made me—and probably everyone else at the raceway—root for him. It must have been like that everywhere because Garth went on to sell more records than anyone ever in country music, but he began in the mid-1990s to show signs of the kind of obsession with fame that brought down Michael Jackson. He also began crafting elaborate plans to invade the pop world.

I noticed the shift when I spent a couple of days with him in 1996 as he met with record merchandisers in the Midwest. I had already heard disturbing whispers from Nashville that Garth's success was because of marketing—that he was a better strategist than singer or songwriter. On the flight to Detroit, Garth was furious at *Life* magazine because the publication hadn't given him the cover as promised and had falsely listed him as having been a marketing major in college. When I asked what he had majored in, he said, "Advertising." I told him it might have been an honest mistake because most people would probably see the two as related. No, Garth insisted. He had been betrayed. I, too, fell into the "against us" camp when I started complaining that his music was becoming slick and hollow. After I panned his *The Life of Chris Gaines* album in 1999, he joined George Harrison in putting me on his "no interview" list.

Rod Stewart was a less dramatic example. His solo albums from the early 1970s, notably *Gasoline Alley* and *Every Picture Tells a Story,* revealed a wonderful singer with a raspy, soulful voice that captured beautifully the poignant quality of a song such as Tim Hardin's "Reason to Believe" or the bittersweet strains of his own, nostalgic "Maggie May." By the end of the decade, however, he was turning out such novelty fare as "Da Ya Think I'm Sexy?" Though Rod, a likeable enough guy, probably saw the humor in the No. 1 single initially, there was something about the public fascination with the song that caused him to become a strutting caricature of himself on stage.

Here are some ways I tried to point out to readers the hollowness of some particularly grievous high-profile pop stars.

With his near-constant bumps and grinds, Stewart's concert Monday night at the Inglewood Forum too often seemed like one of those male exotic dancer shows at Chippendales.

—On Rod Stewart in December of 1981

Barry Manilow, who opened a 15-day engagement Sunday night at the Greek Theater, is probably the biggest selling male singer in America. It's not a comforting thought.

—On Barry Manilow in August of 1978

Two important elements you won't find in his interpretations: subtlety and nuance. If critics employed the Bolton approach, every other word would be *italicized* or **CAPITALIZED** and followed by an exclamation point!

—On Michael Bolton in July of 1992

Mariah Carey's sold-out concert Thursday at Staples Center, the opening U.S. stop on her first tour in seven years, brought to mind an old math rule: Anything times zero equals zero.

—On Mariah Carey in March of 2000

It was wanna-be night Friday at the Forum.

We had an opening act that featured an actor—Keanu Reeves—who wants to be accepted as a rock musician.

Then we had a headliner led by a rock star—Jon Bon Jovi—who wants to be an actor.

Even I got caught up in the spirit. For much of the long, dull evening, I wanted to be anywhere else.

—On Bon Jovi in October of 1995

CHAPTER

TWENTY-FIVE

E very decade has produced at least one force in rock that consensus deems great, and an impressive array of contenders stepped forward in the early 1990s—Pearl Jam's Eddie Vedder, though his early aversion to the spotlight alienated a large segment of the rock audience; Nine Inch Nails' Trent Reznor, who fell prey to drugs at a crucial moment in his career; the Smashing Pumpkins' Billy Corgan, who has the talent, but not the disposition to lead; and Rage Against the Machine's Zack de la Rocha and Tom Morello, who went the way of the Clash and called it quits. That left Nirvana's Kurt Cobain.

We've all heard about one band blowing away another band on stage, and that's what happened when I saw Nirvana open for the Red Hot Chili Peppers at the Los Angeles Sports Arena in December of 1991. The Chili Peppers were a symbol of irreverence and innovation on the local rock scene in the mid-1980s, thanks to a combination of a slacker, goofball sensibility and trailblazing punk, funk, and hip-hop strains. But the songs were too marginal to make the band in any way essential. In contrast, I felt every word mattered when Kurt stood at the microphone and sang about life in the new teenage wasteland. He captured romantic complexities and youthful insecurities in songs that were blessed with grunge urgency and a melodic pop accessibility. Nirvana played for only thirty-five minutes, but it was mesmerizing. I was too drained emotionally to even give the Chili Peppers a chance.

I spent weeks trying to get an interview with Kurt and was told on the record that he just wasn't talking to the press until he had some new music to discuss. Privately, though, I heard he was in no condition to do interviews. There were whispers of drug use and deeply rooted psychological problems. So, I was surprised to get a call the following September from Danny Goldberg, an old friend who managed Nirvana. He asked if I still wanted to interview Kurt. Knowing what my answer would be, he had already arranged for a meeting that night. Danny, one of the shrewdest people in the music business, said Kurt wanted to address rumors that were circulating about him. I wouldn't have much time with him, though, because he was ill.

To help break the ice, I brought along an advance copy of the new PJ Harvey album because I had read that Kurt and his wife, rock singer Courtney Love, both loved the new British singer-songwriter.

When I arrived at his apartment in the hills above the Hollywood Bowl, Kurt was sitting in the living room holding Frances, his four-week-old baby. Kurt looked frail as he leaned forward to shake hands. His voice—so powerful on stage—was gentle. There was almost a pleading in his eyes, though I didn't know what he was pleading for.

"Isn't she gorgeous?" he said, holding his daughter.

Courtney hovered nearby as Kurt talked about the joys of being a father. He knew that rock 'n' roll was supposed to be this macho world and that stars rarely mentioned their children in interviews because they used the time to push their new records. "Well, I don't have a record to push right now," he said. "Frances is more important to me than any record."

Is this what Kurt wanted to tell us fans in his first formal interview in almost a year? That he's a happy dad?

After a few minutes, he gave the baby to Courtney, who took her into another room. Kurt was uneasy. He lowered his head. I tried to break the ice by telling him I received more mail about Nirvana than any group in years, but he didn't respond. Something else was clearly on his mind, and he finally just blurted it out.

"I guess I must have quit the band about ten different times in the last year," he said, looking at me. "I'd tell my manager or the band, but most of the time I would just stand up and say to Courtney, 'Okay, this is it.' But it would blow over in a day or two. The music is usually what brings me back."

I assumed Kurt was talking about the pressures of the music business. Growing up, he had had an unstable home life in Aberdeen, Washington, and he felt like an outsider at school. He gravitated to the punk music scene because he despised the commercial hard rock of the day that the other kids were into. His new popularity made him feel so anxious. It was hard to balance the acclaim with his deep sense of unworthiness. But this wasn't where he was headed at all.

After another pause, he said, "The biggest thing that affected me was all the insane rumors, the heroin rumors . . . all this speculation going on. I felt totally violated. I never realized that my private life was such an issue."

Lots of rock artists use drugs as a badge of honor, so it was interesting to hear Kurt speak about the reverse. His remarks were aimed at refuting a *Vanity Fair* article that had quoted Courtney as saying she and Kurt had gotten high the night earlier in the year when Nirvana had performed on *Saturday Night Live* and that she was on heroin. The quote was scandalous because Love was pregnant with Frances at the time. Courtney denied she knowingly took heroin while pregnant, but the magazine stood by its story.

Kurt started cursing at the magazine and saying it had ruined his life.

"I don't want my daughter to grow up and someday be hassled by kids at school," he blurted out. "I don't want people telling her that her parents were junkies."

Then he paused and added more gently, "There's nothing better than having a baby. I've always loved children. I used to work summers at the YMCA and be in charge of, like, thirty preschool kids. I knew that when I had a child, I'd be overwhelmed, and it's true. . . . I can't tell you how much my attitude has changed since we've got Frances. Holding my baby is the best drug in the world."

Kurt said he hated the idea of people thinking of him as a "fucking stereotype of the wasted rock 'n' roller." He also didn't want to be a bad role model for his young fans. "I don't want to have anything to do with enticing drug use," he said. "People who promote drug use are fucked. I chose to do drugs. I don't feel sorry for myself at all, but have nothing good to say about them. They are a total waste of time."

He said he had dabbled with heroin for years, partly because of the glamour associated with rockers like Keith Richards using it. Then the drug use changed dramatically for "about three weeks" after *Nevermind,* the band's seminal 1991 album, was released, he said, reaching for a cigarette. "Then I went through a detox program, but my stomach started up again on tour. [Cobain had recurring, severe stomach pain.] I was vomiting really bad . . . couldn't hold anything down. We went to this doctor who gave me these tablets that were methadone. By the end of the tour, I had a habit again . . . and I had to go into detox again to straighten myself out again. That took a really long time . . . about a month. And that was it."

Kurt said he was feeling good enough to think about something he had felt was impossible only a few months before: recording another album. But he wasn't sure about any more long tours. "I would rather be healthy and alive. I don't want to sacrifice myself or my family."

I was so pleased with how the story turned out that I would have urged the editors to run it on a Sunday because the paper's circulation on that day is much higher than on the weekdays. Danny, however, asked if I could run it as soon as possible because Kurt wanted to get the word out. I didn't know why the timing was so important until I later learned that the Los Angeles County Department of Social Services was looking into Frances's case because it had heard all the reports of drug use. The article appeared just before a hearing, which was ruled in the Cobains' favor.

I realized the interview was a setup, but I believed Kurt's love for the baby was real and I could imagine myself doing the same thing in similar circumstances. Still, I felt I had to make it clear to Danny that I was disappointed. So, I phoned him and lodged an obligatory complaint. What concerned me the most was Kurt's condition. Was he truthful about being drug free? Danny, who was usually candid, replied, "I hope so, Bob, I hope so."

· ·

In the months after talking to Kurt, I kept asking myself whether it was rock 'n' roll pressures that made great artists like him and Janis struggle with drugs or whether there were seeds in their troubled backgrounds that would have led them to drug excesses even if they hadn't become musicians. I thought about Elton John, who struggled for years with those pressures even though he appeared to be the sanest of rock stars. We spoke off the record a few times about his drug problems. Finally, in the summer of 1992, he was ready to speak publicly.

"We were thinking of calling this the 'sober' tour," Elton said as we sat in the living room of his six-thousand-square-foot condo in Atlanta, his new home base in the United States. "I get up at 6:30 in the morning now, which is kinda funny because there was a time when I'd be going to bed at 6:30 or, more likely, I'd still be going strong. I used to stay up sometimes for days at a time—concerts three nights in a row without any sleep. It was really Elvis Presley time again. Rock 'n' roll isn't a normal life. You get cut off from people, isolated. It's easy to lose your values and self-respect. I got to where I didn't know how to speak to someone unless I had a nose full of cocaine. Nothing would satisfy me. I used to complain about everything, right down to the color of the jet." Elton had fallen in love with rock after hearing "Heartbreak Hotel" as a child, and he once told me he had walked away with tears in his eyes after meeting the bloated and self-destructive Elvis.

It was his first interview in three years, and he was looking forward to his first tour in ages. One thing I always admired about Elton was that he always told the truth in interviews, no matter how unflattering. I could tell now that he was as anxious to tell about his descent and rebirth as I was to hear it. He hoped his sobriety would inspire others who were in trouble. He began by apologizing to me and to his fans for having pretty much dropped out of sight. He said things had careened so far out of control by the late

1980s that he had to change. "I didn't want to die angry and bitter and sad, and that's what I had become, physically ugly, spiritually ugly, a slob, a pig."

Elton leaped up and raced to a nearby room, returning with a photo of himself from the late 1980s. In it, he looked like a hollow old man, severely overweight, with gray hair and expressionless eyes. In person, even discounting the hair weave, he looked years younger— upbeat, trim, and with a sparkle in those eyes.

I had thought Elton's recovery began around the time of his emotional public support for Ryan White, the Indiana teen whose heroic battle against AIDS made headlines around the world. But Elton said even that wasn't enough motivation for him to turn his life around. It wasn't until shortly after Ryan's death, when John's lover at the time told him he was checking into a detox center. Elton's first reaction: anger. "I thought, 'God, you can't sort your own problems out,'" he said. "But that's the way I was."

Even so, Elton went to Arizona to visit his friend at the clinic. The meeting didn't go well and Elton returned to London, thinking the relationship was over. "I stayed in my room and I cried, and I used off and on for two weeks. But I eventually realized how much I cared about this person and how much I admired him for doing it. I thought, 'This person tried to do something for himself and here you are just sitting here, fat and haven't washed for weeks, vomit all over your dressing gown.'" Elton said he returned to Arizona, where he and his friend went to a counselor to discuss their relationship. They went through an exercise where they drew up a list of complaints about each other. Elton's friend wrote his list, and it included Elton's drug use, excessive drinking, sexual activity, and bulimia. Elton was embarrassed by how minor his complaints were—things like his friend not putting away his compact discs.

Elton recounted how he had checked in during the summer of 1990. The experience was humbling, and he almost checked out twice. "I packed my suitcase on the first two Saturdays and I sat on the sidewalk and cried," he recalled. "I asked myself where I was going to run. 'Do you go back and take more drugs and kill yourself, or do you go to another center because you don't quite like the way someone spoke to you here?' In the end, I knew there was really no choice. I realized this was my last chance."

At my urging, Elton tried to look back on how he had become hooked on drugs. He spoke about having an addictive personality and how he'd always run away from problems. "When everything happened to me in 1970, I was just a little boy in a way, and you can see that in the photos," he said. "Suddenly, I could do whatever I wanted for the first time. I felt as if I were free and to a certain extent I was, but as soon as I started taking the drugs, I became a prisoner of my old insecurities and doubts. I couldn't deal with all the emotions it brought up."

Since the hospital stay, Elton said he regularly attended recovery program meetings where everyone was urged to talk about their problems. Throwing himself into the process, Elton went to more than five hundred meetings, sometimes three a day. All of that probably helped him talk so freely about his missteps in the interview. When I asked what he thought had been missing in his life during all those years, he paused and looked down. Then he said something in such a whisper that I didn't catch it. When I asked him to repeat it, he said, "Love. I wanted someone in my life to love me."

The desire to live a normal life is what made him take a chance on marriage.

"Even though I knew I was gay, I thought this woman was attractive and that being married would cure me of everything wrong in my life," he said of his 1984 marriage to sound engineer Renate Blauel. "And my wife did love me. But it didn't change my way of life. I wasn't a sexual philanderer during the time, but I certainly didn't stop taking drugs and alcohol and when you take that amount, you can't have any relationship. In the end, we ended up in this big house with separate bedrooms, never seeing each other. It was very sad. I wasn't being honest." Elton and Renate were divorced in 1988.

Elton lowered his head, then looked back at me. "She is one of the few people in my life that I haven't actually been able to make amends to for my behavior because I don't think she is quite ready to," he said. "I know she is very kind and still sees my grandmother. But I haven't seen her since we divorced or heard from her. I think she is very much hurt by it and I can understand why. I think she genuinely loved me . . . the real me, which she could see in glimpses, but you were dealing with a nightmare."

Elton finally found the love he was looking for with filmmaker David Furnish, and they were married on December 21, 2005, the first day that same-sex marriage became legal in England.

I hoped music, Courtney, and Frances would pull Kurt through, too.

CHAPTER
TWENTY-SIX

Nirvana's new album, *In Utero,* was a more demanding and revealing work than *Nevermind,* and it convinced me that Kurt was the next great figure in rock. On the fall 1993 album, he seemed to be both reaching for that leadership role and running away from it. "Go away!" he screamed at one point, seemingly to the world at large, but then he reached out with some of the most vulnerable and affecting lyrics ever to come from a punk-spawned band. His songs favored random but powerful images rather than cohesive narratives with tidy rhymes. His writing style captured a generation of young people whose attention spans were conditioned by video games just as Dylan's lyrics had captivated a generation in search of direction. Kurt was the poet of dysfunctional youth, and young people embraced his songs the way they had Bruce Springsteen's and U2's.

I flew up to Seattle and hoped to find him in a good mood as I drove to his house about fifteen miles outside of town. The warning from the record company was that you never quite knew with Kurt. Everyone spoke of him as gentle and sweet, but they said there were mood swings. I took that to mean drugs. I didn't know what to think when Kurt walked into the room wearing a black, thigh-length thrift store dress over flannel long johns. I wondered if he was having fun at my expense. Kurt seemed to be very much of a new generation at age twenty-six and here I was, at fifty-four, old enough to be his father. Was the dress his way of saying "You just don't get it and never will," or was it a statement against the antigay attitudes he abhorred in rock and rap? Kurt had been frequently tormented in his hometown, a rugged logging community, because he didn't seem manly enough. He was thin and frail, and he cared more about art and music than sports.

He didn't reveal his motives until I asked him about it. "Wearing a dress shows I can be as feminine as I want," he said. "I'm a heterosexual . . . big deal. But if I was a homosexual, it wouldn't matter either." As it turned out, that wasn't the only statement Kurt wanted to make. He loved the new album and was looking forward to going on the road. Yes, he was nervous that the stress of touring might bring back his stomach problems, but he said he'd been in good health for months, ever since he started taking new medication and exercising nightly.

Around midnight, we were talking about some of the songs on the new record when he suddenly stopped and—out of the blue—asked me if I had ever heard the record the Go-Go's had made about me. When I said no, he looked a little sheepish—as if he was suddenly nervous. I had heard the band wrote a sarcastic song about me during its early days, but I'd never actually heard it. He said he'd go see if he could find it. He seemed so defensive that I felt he was afraid the record might offend me, and I guessed he was going to say he couldn't find it. But after a few minutes he yelled from the other room, "I've found it. Come listen." Sure enough the record poked fun at me. I was a fan of the Go-Go's and got a kick out of the single. When I laughed, it seemed to trigger a feeling in Kurt that I was an okay guy—that he could trust me.

When we got back to the living room, Kurt started talking in detail about his childhood. When he discussed the dreariness of life in Aberdeen, he reminded me of Bruce Springsteen talking about growing up in Freehold, New Jersey, and Axl Rose telling about life as a restless, repressed teenager in Lafayette, Indiana, and even John Lennon talking about missing his mother in Liverpool.

I noticed at one point that Cobain was no longer wearing the dress; he must have taken it off one of the times he left the room. It struck me that he was finally comfortable—that we had moved from "interview" to "conversation." I would never be as close to Kurt as I was to Johnny Cash or John Lennon. Maybe that was a factor of age, or maybe it was simply Kurt's basic mistrust of people. Yet he was always friendly and gracious. As he spoke, Kurt wrestled with his role in music.

"Sometimes you wonder," he continued, "if anything has changed. Just because everyone starts wearing flannel shirts doesn't mean they think about the world any differently. If we had changed things, you'd hear a lot of better music on the radio, wouldn't you? I can't deal with all that . . . the future of grunge in America and all that. All I can do is worry about our band and keep from becoming another rock 'n' roll cartoon."

But what about those kids who are really into the music and look to him as a role model? What could he say to them?

"Well, you do learn things, and one of them is that happiness has nothing to do with validation from other people," he said. "The important thing is being happy with yourself . . . finding something that is important to you and sticking with it no matter what anyone says."

I asked him if that had worked for him, if he was happy with himself now.

Kurt stood up, walked over to the window, and stared into the darkness, then came back and sat on the floor.

"The truth is you've got to really be tough because there are all kinds of forces that are always trying to get you to do things their way, trying to tell you that you are throwing your life away if you don't follow their advice. I remember, back when I was moving between relatives, that I lived with my dad again for about a week and in that week he made me pawn my guitar and join the navy. I took the tests and I guess I scored pretty high because two nights in a row this recruiter came over and tried to get me to sign. I remember going downstairs trying to decide what I should do with my life, and I came to the realization that I'd better go back and get my guitar. To them, I was just wasting my life. To me, I was fighting for it."

As I headed down the driveway, I looked back at the house and saw Kurt at the door. "Drive carefully," he said. I wondered how much of his toughness was true. It's one thing to talk about it in the safety of his house, but I wondered about what would happen when he got back on the road. I hoped the worst was over.

. . . .

Courtney Love had a lot to celebrate as we sat in her Beverly Hills hotel room in April of 1994, days before the release of *Live Through This,* the superb album she made with her band, Hole. She had just moved into a new lakefront house in Seattle with Kurt and Frances, who was nineteen months old. And the album was expected to go a long way in combating the idea that she was little more than a provocateur with shrewd media instincts and charisma—someone whose true talent was hooking Cobain. So I was surprised when she suddenly broke into sobs.

It was Courtney's first interview since Kurt had suffered a near-fatal overdose the month before in Rome, and she was haunted by the incident. She wouldn't talk about any of it on the record—the rumors about Nirvana having broken up or Kurt having overdosed another time or his having checked in to a recovery program. Privately, though, she said she was deeply frightened. She said she couldn't get the image of him lying "blue" on the floor from her mind, and she worried that she had contributed to his despair by sometimes talking about her interest in other rock stars as a way to make him jealous. She even mentioned musicians she had thrown at him.

Courtney was known for being a great talker. The joke among rock writers was you didn't have to worry about questions when you interviewed her—just be sure to have plenty of recording tape. And she had lots to talk about. Her background was in many ways as troubled as Kurt's. Her parents had divorced when she was quite young, and she was in and out of foster homes in her early teens and sent to a juvenile detention center after stealing a KISS T-shirt from a department store. By fifteen, Courtney had discovered rock 'n' roll and started a journey that would take her over the next decade from New

York to San Francisco to Minneapolis in search of the right musical partnership. On the side, she danced in strip joints. In Los Angeles, she finally teamed up with guitarist Eric Erlandson and Hole was born. The group made its debut at a small club on Hollywood Boulevard, then later signed with Caroline Records. The pop press in London crowned Hole the Next Big Thing and within months she was dating Kurt.

Hole's first album, 1991's *Pretty on the Inside,* was also powerful, but it was on a minor label and sold only sixty thousand copies. The new one was on Geffen, Nirvana's label—which again caused skeptics to ask whether Courtney wasn't just riding Kurt's coattails. There were even charges that Kurt helped her write the songs, though he's not listed as cowriter on the album.

Courtney was used to being attacked for her relationship with Kurt. As soon as they started dating, rumors of drug use led to a troubling comparison: Love and Cobain as Generation X's Sid Vicious and Nancy Spungen. The Rome overdose heightened the flame around the couple. Love had flown to Rome early in the previous month to spend a few days with Kurt after he cancelled part of a European tour because of illness. She woke in their hotel room to find him unconscious, having taken some of her prescription tranquilizers and alcohol.

"He was dead . . . legally dead," Courtney told me, as if trying to exorcise the memory from her mind. "He was in a coma for twenty hours . . . on life support. They thought he was never going to come out of it." When he did, he was transferred to another hospital, a move that attracted hordes of photographers. Trying to prevent anyone from getting a ghoulish photo of him as he was lying on the stretcher with tubes in his nose, Courtney kicked at a photographer who had a clear shot. Looking at me, she said she now regretted it. "I wish Kurt could have seen [a photo of himself] because if he had he would never get into that situation again."

Talking to Courtney, it struck me that something was going on with Kurt—maybe that he was hooked on heroin again. I asked her about it just as the phone rang. She took it in another room, but I could hear her saying something like "You've got to find him." When she came back, she started sobbing again. Kurt was missing. She thought he was back in Seattle, but he wasn't at the house.

Love tried to get back on track and talk about the album, but she kept breaking down. A Narcotics Anonymous handbook sat on a table next to her new CD. Frances was in a room down the hall with her nanny.

"I know this should be the happiest time of my life and there have been moments where I felt that happiness," she said. "But not now. I thought I went through a lot of hard times over the years, but this has been the hardest."

Courtney called a couple of times after the interview to fill me in on the search for Kurt. They were long, hysterical rants—telling me how much she loved him and she wished she could have done more to help him and that she was sure he was okay because he would never do anything to hurt Frances. One late night she spoke for so long that she fell asleep with the phone in her hand.

Three days after the interview, the news of Kurt's death was broadcast on the radio. He had shot himself in the head.

For the third time I attended a rock star's funeral, and I felt there was a connection. To me, Elvis Presley, John Lennon, and Kurt were all great artists, though I often had a hard time convincing a lot of people when it came to Kurt. Millions of adults dismissed him as a spoiled, whining poser. He was a symbol of everything that was wrong with a slacker generation they saw as ungrateful and unmotivated. They couldn't comprehend how someone so successful could complain about stardom.

Unlike the sympathy and mourning in Memphis and New York City, the mood in downtown Seattle reflected the adult contempt. From a street corner, you could see the opposing sides in maybe the most severe generation gap in rock since the 1950s. In one direction, some five thousand young people were leaving a park where they had stood for two hours in the evening chill to pay respects to the man whose melancholy melodies and urgent vocals mirrored their own deepest feelings. Looking the other way, the rest of the city seemed as cold as the night itself—not just indifferent, but actually hostile. One man in his midforties shocked me when he said, "They ought to pass out shotguns to all the rest of them."

When Courtney learned I was in Seattle, she invited me to the house, where a few friends had gathered before going to the church for the services. Courtney didn't have the strength to attend the memorial, but she sent a tape that contained excerpts from Kurt's suicide note. It suggested a Cobain even sadder than we had imagined. He said he had long ago lost the thrill of music. "I haven't felt the excitement for so many years," Courtney read from the note, her voice trembling. "I feel guilty beyond words about these things. When we were backstage and the lights go out and the manic roar of the crowd begins, it doesn't affect me. The fact is I can't fool you, any of you. It simply isn't fair to you or to me. The worst crime I can think of would be to trick people by faking it and pretending as if I were having 100 percent fun."

I joined Courtney and a couple hundred people who gathered privately a few blocks away at Seattle Unity Church. Soft chamber music played over the sound system as mourners took their places in pews lined with childhood photos of Kurt. Dressed all in black, Love read from the Bible and then again read from the suicide note. At the end, mourners listened to a tape of some of Kurt's favorite music, a tape he played when he was trying to find reassurance. The opening selection especially touched me. It offered a clue to what the man who brought comfort to a generation of young people turned to himself in times of need. It was John Lennon's Beatles song "In My Life," the celebration of times and places in one's life.

How perfect and how sad: John Lennon and Kurt Cobain. John conquered his worst demons and fears; Kurt never gave himself a chance. Kurt's death once again made rock 'n' roll feel like a lonelier place. A big part of the music's future was gone.

CHAPTER
TWENTY-SEVEN

ruce Springsteen was still at a crossroads in 1995. He could count on many longtime fans turning out when he toured, but not all. A sizable number were turned off by the absence of the E Street Band. Album sales fell from sixteen million for *Born in the U.S.A.* to about a million each for *Human Touch* and *Lucky Town*. The gap suggested he had crossed a line, like the Rolling Stones and the Who before him, to where older fans and potential young ones no longer thought of his music as relevant. There were new heroes for young rockers to embrace. On the alternative rock front, Nirvana's Kurt Cobain became a hero to many by rejecting the hero role. Even though Nirvana's *Nevermind* sold ten million copies in the United States, Kurt disliked everything attached to the "rock star" image in America, whether the star was a glam rocker like Axl Rose or a more traditional figure like Bruce. He brought punk rock's suspicion of success to a whole generation of rock musicians. They saw the traditional path to stardom—major labels, hit singles, colorful videos—as a series of demeaning compromises. At the same time, U2 was beginning to beat

Bruce on his own turf, both in Bono's reaching out to his audience and in songs that tackled contemporary issues.

The safe thing would have been to call the E Street Band back together. Instead, he released an acoustic album in November, *The Ghost of Tom Joad.* Drawing inspiration from John Steinbeck's *The Grapes of Wrath,* Bruce updated the novel's themes about the inhumane treatment of migrant workers in 1930s California by singing of the nation's current attitude toward the mass of illegal immigrants. In retrospect, I saw Bruce's "Streets of Philadelphia" and its AIDS message as his reconnection with the social observer-commentator of *Nebraska. Tom Joad* represented the next step. It also gave Bruce time to set aside for a while the question of an E Street Band reunion. All he needed to make the new songs work was his voice and a guitar.

Down to the lobby sign warning that late arrivals would be seated at the discretion of the management, Bruce's performance of *Tom Joad* at the intimate Wiltern Theatre in LA had more the feel of a one-man play than a concert. "A lot of these songs were written with a lot of silence and they need silence to work," he said after the opening number. "So if you like singing and clapping along, please don't."

Like the album, the concert was evidence of a veteran artist moving forward, and Bruce opened boldly by playing eleven of the album's twelve songs. He was putting everything on the line. He even combed his hair back rather than hiding his slightly receding hairline. He sang in a voice so gruff and pointed that it stripped the songs of any trace of comforting melody, in much the way that conditions had stripped the songs' characters of hope.

My phone always rang often after a Bruce concert, but the comments this time weren't all enthusiastic. Some callers complained about the absence of a band and others felt cheated because Bruce didn't do the hits. Several seemed to be saying they had given up on Bruce. To me, however, *The Ghost of Tom Joad* was Bruce's best album since *Tunnel of Love,* and I put it on top of my annual top-ten list.

Was Bruce going to face a melancholy fate like Dylan, where he would play mostly small halls? Would he miss the bigger crowds? Would he feel like his glory days had passed? And what did his fans

think? Was Bruce still hot copy? Critics were divided. *Details* magazine, which took pride in being the voice of the young and ultra-hip,
called *Tom Joad* "a sad attempt" by Bruce to reinvent himself as a
tasteful acoustic folk singer. But *Rolling Stone* called the album among
the bravest works by anyone in the 1990s. Then again, *Rolling Stone*
was accused of "adoring" Bruce almost as often as I was. At any rate,
I wanted to see what was happening in the heartland. I checked
Bruce's itinerary to see what show would offer the clearest insight into
his status. I saw the usual tour stops—Chicago, Detroit, New York,
Atlanta—but then spotted the perfect site.

It was dark and snowing the afternoon I arrived at Youngstown,
Ohio's Stambaugh Auditorium, just ten minutes from the mills that
stood silently at the western edge of town as ghostly reminders of
better days. There were only four names on the press list—me, repre-
sentatives of the Cleveland and Akron papers, and the entertainment
editor of the *Youngstown Vindicator*. The only TV crews were from the
local stations. If Bruce had taken a break during his *Born in the
U.S.A.* days to play a small hall in a town he had just written a song
about, an army of writers and TV crews would have followed him.

I thought about this as I saw Bruce walking through the theater,
checking out the acoustics. He was forty-six, and he no longer resem-
bled the hungry young rocker on the cover of *Born to Run*. He could
easily have been mistaken for a stagehand. I could picture him sitting
with Dylan in that truck stop outside Chicago a few years earlier, both
unnoticed. However dispirited the afternoon scene, Bruce appeared to
be a man reborn when he stepped on the stage that night. The crowd,
an even mix of young and old, cheered each of the songs, but the audience hushed as soon as Bruce started introducing "Youngstown," a
song about the steel town that the country had relied so heavily on in
its war efforts and had since abandoned: "This is about the men and
women who lived in this town and who built this country. It's about
the people who gave their sons and daughters to the wars that were
fought and who were later declared expendable."

The people of Youngstown knew the story of the song all too
well—the way the town's very heart had been torn from it when the
grand old mills began shutting down in the late 1970s, leaving more

than ten thousand workers unemployed. Many I later spoke with had either worked in the mills at one time or were related to someone who had. Some saw the song as a salute to the generations of workers who forged the steel for the tanks and planes that helped win the nation's wars. To others, the song was a painful reminder of the betrayal they'd felt when owners closed the mills rather than upgrading them to better compete with foreign rivals.

The roar was thunderous the first time he sang the word "Youngstown" in the lyrics. But the audience mostly listened in silence, and I watched tears on the faces of people around me. Every line rang true, and it reminded me of the power of honest, illuminating music to shape and frame our emotions. When the song ended, the crowd gave Bruce a standing ovation. Moments later, hundreds jammed the aisles in front of the stage. Bruce shook every outreached hand before he left.

I thought about how fickle pop music audiences are. When I started out as a critic, I was very idealistic. I thought that the more great albums people heard, the more great albums they would demand. But the sales charts are a constant reminder of how music buyers settle for mediocrity. The sales chart a year after John Lennon's marvelous *Imagine* was filled with the same—pick your label: garbage, soulless music, aural wallpaper, anonymous pop—as before. Similarly, *Born to Run* hadn't uplifted people's tastes forever. Neither had Bob Marley's best work, or Prince's or U2's. But it struck me as especially disheartening that the fans touched by *Born to Run* and *Born in the U.S.A.* would not have enough faith in Bruce to follow him wherever his artistic impulses led. Any Bruce fan that missed the *Tom Joad* shows missed some of the most stirring shows of his career.

He had been scheduled to leave town right after the show, but he stayed over for a day to visit historic sites in the area. I, too, went around the town to check how residents felt about Bruce and the song. Staughton Lynd, a lawyer who represented local unions in a 1979 lawsuit to prevent US Steel from shutting its Youngstown mills, frowned when I said some people thought Bruce's music had become irrelevant. "It's hard to name all the people who have just passed by while this town was bleeding and dying," he said. "But Springsteen walked across the street. He cared—and hopefully people in other cities will remember the song and learn from what happened here."

I told Bruce about Lynd's feelings later in the day and he was pleased. "If you look at the general arc of my career, I've had a very large cult audience from when I started," he said. "Then I hit *Born in the U.S.A.*—and suddenly a lot of people who weren't interested in my music before and who haven't been interested in me since bought that record. I always felt that whole 'the Boss' thing is fundamentally silly. I never for a second had the slightest idea or interest in going out and trying to [duplicate that success]. I knew what it was the minute it happened—it was an anomaly. I knew my audience would go back to its regular level. I didn't see that it might happen. I knew it would happen."

The mistake a lot of musicians make, he said, is they imagine an audience and then try to make a piece of music to fit it. "They get caught up in the race, and it can be dangerous to your creativity, and probably your sanity. What you have to do is start with a piece of music and then search out the audience for it, and if this is the audience for the new album, that's fine. That's where I should be right now." Bruce said he didn't have any plans to put the E Street Band together again, but he assumed at some point it could happen.

The parallel between Bruce in Youngstown and Dylan in Chicago was far from exact, but in both instances the artists were following their music, rather than following their audiences. Whatever the rest of the pop world might be saying, Springsteen and Dylan were following their hearts. I learned that it was just as engrossing to follow artists at the supposed low points in their careers as at the high points. In fact, it might be even more revealing because the artists are often at their most vulnerable.

The acoustic *Tom Joad* tour was an artistic triumph, but Bruce found it represented only one side of his musical and creative personality. He also loved to rock 'n' roll, and for all that he defended the band he had put together after E Street, he knew it just didn't work. There was no way to deny the sense of loss expressed by the fans, and even Bruce realized that something was missing without saxophonist Clarence Clemons, guitarist Miami Steve Van Zandt, and the gang by his side. I joined lots of other Americans who made the trip to Barcelona to see the official start of the reunion tour at the twenty-two-thousand-seat Palau Sant Jordi Arena. Hours before the first show in April of 1999, hundreds of fans sat on the grass outside the arena and listened to the sound check. Many used their cell phones to describe the scene to friends back home.

This was the most anticipated reunion tour in rock since Dylan and the Band in 1974, and Bruce and his band didn't waste time showing they could still make spirits soar. The most emotional moment came near the end, when Bruce redesigned one of his loveliest ballads, "If I Should Fall Behind," so that four band members—Miami Steve, Nils Lofgren, Clarence, and Patti—each took the microphone separately to deliver a few lines of the song about devotion. But even that wasn't enough. Bruce and the band left the crowd on an upbeat, idealistic note with a spiritually tinged new song, "Land of Hope and Dreams."

The second night's show was just as dramatic, but more relaxed and more fun. I attended a small party for Bruce and the band afterward at their hotel. The first person I saw was Miami Steve, who was his usual cordial self. We talked for a few minutes before Bruce came over.

"This tour is about rededication, rebirth," Bruce said. "The only way we wanted to do this was to make everything feel current . . . to put all the music into the present to make the emotion true to right now. It's not about when a song was written or when it was released. Roy Orbison, until the day he died, sang every one of those songs like he wrote it yesterday. That's how it felt to me tonight."

He said he had begun thinking in earnest about touring with the band again after the *Tom Joad* tour. "It was something about the time," he said, sitting down at a table to focus on his thoughts. "It's the turn of the century, and I started thinking where I want to be on that [December 31] night. The answer is, I want to be with the people I built my life around. I want to be with them on this stage doing this thing. It's one of the greatest things I can do."

It was past 2:00 a.m. when I left the hotel and there were no cabs on the street, so I just started walking toward lights at the other end of the harbor, where cabs were waiting. But I wouldn't have minded walking the three miles back to my hotel. It was a lovely night, one of those many nights when I truly felt I had the best job in the world.

There was troubling news, however, on the Dylan front. Bob, who was still touring regularly, suffered deep chest pains and entered a hospital in May of 1997, where it was discovered that he was suffering from a rare fungal heart infection. The word was that the problem was severe, but treatable. Bob only spent a few days in the hospital before he was out and talking about going back on the road. In a press release, he joked, "I'm just glad to be feeling better. I really thought I'd be seeing Elvis soon." The release also carried this second piece of welcome news: A new album was on the way.

Time Out of Mind was a major return to form, a series of reflections so thoughtful and urgent that I assumed he wrote them after his hospital scare. For much of the record's seventy-three minutes, Dylan sounded like a man nearing last rites. When Bob once spoke about traveling down the road, it was with the optimism and independence shared by a Kennedy-inspired generation in love with its own sense of destiny. Now, Bob was speaking from the point of view of a man who knew his generation was nearing the end of its journey— and was not sure what to do about it. "It's not dark yet, but it's getting there," he wrote.

When I interviewed Bob in December in Santa Monica, he spoke about regaining his sense of purpose after those hundreds of nights on the Never Ending Tour, and he spoke freely about the disillusionment he had felt for years. "I remember playing shows with Tom Petty and looking out thinking I didn't have that many fans coming to see me," he said. "They were coming to see Tom Petty and the Heartbreakers. I was going on my name for a long time, name and reputation, which was about all I had. I had sort of fallen into an amnesia spell. I didn't feel I knew who I was on stage."

He was in such good spirits that I asked if the word "happy" might apply to him. He laughed. "I think that it's hard to find happiness as a whole in anything. The days of tender youth are gone. I think you can be delirious in your youth, but as you get older, things happen." It was a marvelous answer, one that summarized in three sentences the essence of *Time Out of Mind*.

For all the acclaim it garnered, I got the feeling that Bob didn't really think as much of *Time Out of Mind* as critics and fans did. But he felt so strongly about his next album, *Love and Theft,* in 2001, that Larry Jenkins, his publicist, personally took it around to some critics to play it for them. I was on vacation, but he came to the house. There were still moments of struggle and confusion, but they were offset by disarming wit (including a goofy knock-knock joke) and a warm, jubilant spirit. The heart of the album was as much in the colorful, lilting arrangements as in the lyrics. In alternating gentle and wailing instrumentation, Bob and his band pulled us back to the start of rock 'n' roll and even earlier, reminding us of the innocence and energy of those times.

Bob was so pleased when I talked to him in September of that year that I felt it was a good opportunity to try to get him to talk more about his creative process. Now that he had answered the question about how long a musician could remain productive, I had a new goal. I had always valued songwriting more than anything in rock 'n' roll, and here was the greatest songwriter. I started to try to learn about his method by pointing to the humor in the collection.

"I try to make songs as three-dimensional as possible," he said. "A one- or two-dimensional song doesn't last very long. It's important to have humor where you can. Even the most severe rapper uses some humor." I also asked where he tends to do the most writing—on the road or at home. "Some things just come to me in dreams," he said, "but I can write a bunch of stuff down after you leave . . . about, say, the way you are dressed. I look at people as ideas. I don't look at them as people. I'm talking about general observation. Whoever I see, I look at them as an idea . . . what this person represents. That's the way I see life. I see life as a utilitarian thing. Then you strip things away until you get to the core of what's important."

I asked if the success or failure of a particular work has any influence on his writing process. He wasn't sure what I meant, so I asked how it felt to get booed, first at the 1965 Newport Folk Festival for going electric and then on the *Slow Train Coming* tour. "Miles Davis has been booed," he said. "Hank Williams was booed. Stravinsky was booed. You're nobody if you don't get booed sometime." So when it does happen, does it make you just as likely to dig in as ease up? Bob said it depends on what kind of artist you are, and that's when he set out the three kinds he sees: the superficial, the natural, and the supernatural.

Did he ever feel he was just a superficial artist?

Bob called the Band tour in 1974 superficial. "I had forgotten how to sing and play," he said. "I had been devoting myself to raising a family, and it took me a long time to recapture my purpose as a performer. You'd find it at times, then it would disappear for a while." About reconnecting with his sense of artistic purpose on stage in the mid-1990s, he said, "That's when I escaped the organized media. They let me be. They considered me irrelevant, which was the best thing that could have happened to me. I was waiting for that. No artist can develop for any length of time in the light of the media, no matter who it is. If the media was commenting on every article you wrote, imagine what it would do to you."

I had brought Bob's book of lyrics with me because I knew I was going to get to the hotel early and wanted to look over them while waiting to see him. At the end of the interview, Bob looked at the book on the table and assumed I had brought it along for him to sign. I would never have asked him to sign the book because I got the feeling he wasn't big on autographs. But he picked up a pen and signed it. I took it, thanked him, and headed into the hall. In the elevator, I peeked at what he had written: *To Mister Robert, The most supernatural of all the natural critics (but not in a superficial way), Bob Dylan.*

My first thought was "how sweet," but then I found myself more and more puzzled by his words. On the drive home, I tried to dissect them, just as I would one of his songs. What about the "Mister"? Was that a nod to Mister Jones—the journalist he mocked in "Ballad of a Thin Man"? And what did "the most supernatural of all the natural critics" mean—that I was at the top of the second level of critics, or that no critic really was beyond the natural level? Did he mean to leave me with those teasing questions? Or was he merely being nice? How perfect, I thought. I didn't just have Bob's autograph. I had a private sample of his artistry. I felt I was a step closer to the time I'd sit down with him to truly examine that creative process.

INTERLUDE
MY ROCK 'N' ROLL DINNER PARTY GUEST LIST

Of present and potential Rock and Roll Hall of Fame members, these are the ones I've most enjoyed being around.

BONO. When I asked Bono a few years ago if he worried about a backlash to all the attention he gets for his music and his humanitarian work, he smiled, leaned across the table, and whispered, "Look, I'm sick of Bono, and I *am* Bono."

JOHNNY CASH. I listened to "Folsom Prison Blues" for five decades before asking myself, *If the guy in the song shot a man in Reno, what's he doing in prison in California?* When I asked John about it, he burst out laughing. "I never did get good grades in geography."

ELVIS COSTELLO. Elvis must have been born with an extra supply of brainpower. Name a subject and he can give you a funny, provocative, and insightful thousand or so words on it. If he's in the right mood, there's a good chance you'll both laugh so hard tears will run down your cheeks.

CHUCK D. Nothing can undercut a journalist's credibility more than factual errors, and I was sometimes obsessive about fact-checking. At a Public Enemy concert, I noticed a man on stage with Chuck who looked like Professor Griff. If it had been him, it would have been significant because Griff had not been in a few shows after some of his remarks were branded anti-Semitic. When the record company couldn't help me before my 10:00 a.m. deadline, I phoned Chuck's hotel room and he answered in a sleepy voice. I tried to camouflage my real purpose by saying I wanted to congratulate him on a great show. Then, I casually asked if that was Griff on stage. When Chuck said yes, I again congratulated him on the show and apologized for waking him up. He's such a nice guy that he said in that still sleepy voice, "Call anytime."

BOB DYLAN. For all his enigmas, Bob can be disarmingly playful. He was in such an upbeat mood the day I interviewed him just before the release of his *Love and Theft* album that he greeted me at the hotel door with the words "Five stars."

I had no idea what he was talking about.

"That's what *Rolling Stone* gave the new album," he said. "How many artists have you interviewed in the last fifteen years that have gotten a five-star review?"

Thinking he was putting me on, I replied, "Well, you're not getting five stars in the *Times.*"

He looked puzzled. I quickly explained that the paper only has a four-star rating system, but he got all four.

After we both laughed, I asked if a five-star review really meant that much to the most acclaimed songwriter of the modern pop era.

But Bob trumped me.

"Wouldn't you get excited if you won a Pulitzer Prize?"

Of course I would, and it felt good to know Bob could still be so excited about the positive reception to his work.

AL GREEN. He isn't a trailblazer like the early Ray Charles was, but Al is probably the most consistently exciting soul singer ever. I've seen him arrive at a Hollywood recording studio, walk in and do a knockout duet with Lyle Lovett on "Funny How Time Slips Away," and be back in the limo and on the way to the airport within twenty minutes. And the ordained minister is at his vocal best when leading Sunday services at his church in Memphis. Shouldn't be hard to get him to say grace.

EMMYLOU HARRIS. Emmylou is a long shot to make the Rock and Roll Hall of Fame because even her mentor, Gram Parsons, hasn't been voted in yet, and that's the hall's loss. Emmylou came up through country music, but her vision is as bold as that of anyone in rock, which is why three of our dinner guests (Bob Dylan, Neil Young, and Conor Oberst) have asked her to sing on their records. Besides an angelic voice, she also has a warm, generous spirit. I've met her a dozen times over the years and always come away with a list of new artists to check out. Plus, I've had a crush on her for thirty years.

CHRISSIE HYNDE. Chrissie was often called moody and temperamental early in her career, and she pleaded guilty when I asked her about it during her first US tour with the Pretenders. Like others from the British punk and new wave movements, she wasn't out to please or impress anyone during interviews. "If someone asks me a really stupid question, I'm not always that polite and understanding," she said, puffing aggressively on a cigarette. "If someone is hanging around who has no business being there, I might tell him to fuck off. I'm easily distracted. My concern is my music, not being a nice guy." But, of course, she turned out to be a "nice guy" after all—funny, sharp, and socially committed.

ICE CUBE. Who could have imagined that this architect of gangsta rap would someday be the star of family movies? Then again, there aren't many people in the pop world who are as grounded, hardworking, and personable as Cube. He'll have a smile for you whether you bump into him at a concert or a Lakers game.

ELTON JOHN. I've never met a more enthusiastic music fan, so he can be in charge of picking records for the evening.

JANIS JOPLIN. You know how they talk about the best prizefighter pound for pound? Janis may have had more zest for life per pound than anyone in music. Even on a night when she would be surrounded by all of these remarkable people, she would do or say something that we'd all remember.

JOHN LENNON. Guess what we can serve with cream for dessert?

CURTIS MAYFIELD. If the Reverend Martin Luther King Jr. had been a singer-songwriter, he would have been Mayfield. There is in the best of his music a spiritual eloquence and unwavering faith. Thanks to his *Superfly* album, Curtis was at his commercial peak the first time I interviewed him in the early 1970s, but the thing I most remember about him was his gentle manner and seeming lack of ego. I never spent time with Curtis without coming away feeling inspired.

JONI MITCHELL. One of my biggest disappointments is not having been able to interview the press-shy Joni during the 1970s when she was turning out some of the most finely crafted albums ever made, but I have interviewed her numerous times since and she's a great subject—someone so filled with ideas and opinions that she's like an exercise coach for the mind. Just don't call her writing style "confessional." The last time I did, I could see fire in her eyes. "To be called a 'confessional writer' is repugnant to me," she snapped. "The term makes what I do seem cheap and gimmicky. 'Confession' to me is having a gun stuck to your head or going, 'Forgive me, Father, for I have sinned,' and that's not what I do." Look forward to sitting next to her, but don't say you weren't warned.

CONOR OBERST. When listening to his songs, I hear someone looking at the world through the eyes of a new generation. He's turning out songs as fast as Bob did in the 1960s and I haven't heard a throwaway yet. He's also unabashedly gracious.

SINÉAD O'CONNOR. Sinéad was in her early twenties when I first met her in England, where she was already on a fiercely combative mission against child abuse and what she saw as widespread hypocrisy. Shortly after her version of Prince's "Nothing Compares 2 U" earned her a Grammy nomination for single of the year, she asked me to do a story announcing that she was withdrawing to protest the "false and destructive materialistic values of the music industry and the world." Knowing how many fans thought she was already over the top, my first thought was "No, Sinéad. Why don't you just stop at the false and destructive values of the music industry? You don't need to take on the whole world." A fearless, marvelously gifted artist.

ELVIS PRESLEY. The guest of honor.

KEITH RICHARDS. B.Y.O.B.

PATTI SMITH. Patti Smith wasn't the first woman in rock 'n' roll, but she was the first to demand to be judged by rock 'n' roll rules. She came across in the mid-1970s like nothing before her—a renegade angel who celebrated rock's defiant outcast role. "But Patti ultimately proved to be the den mother to a generation of rock fans and musicians, male and female. Her spirit is as positive and uplifting as her music.

BRUCE SPRINGSTEEN. My copy of *The River* arrived so late that I had to listen to it on the plane to Cleveland, where I was going to interview Bruce. To help me remember the various songs, I wrote a brief description of each in my notebook along with a letter grade. We took a break during the interview in Bruce's hotel room, and I went to the bathroom. Upon returning, I saw him looking at my notebook, which I had accidentally left open to the page with the grades. "Well, what do we have here?" he said, chuckling. "What does this 'C' next to 'Jackson Cage' mean?" Luckily, there were only four Cs and I quickly pointed out that the rest were As and Bs. One of the first things he said to me after *Born in the U.S.A.* came out was, "Well, how many Cs this time?"

BERNIE TAUPIN. Bernie writes the words for Elton John and is almost as big a music fan, though his taste runs to vintage country and blues, whereas Elton thrives on contemporary music. It's always fun seeing Bernie, but especially so at his ranch in California's picturesque Santa Ynez Valley, far from the glitter and spotlight of Hollywood. The key to getting him talking is to mention any early blues figure.

JACK WHITE. I'll make sure not to serve hamburgers. Jack once drove me some thirty miles to a Dearborn, Michigan, bar, raving the whole time about its double cheeseburgers. After I mentioned the experience in a story, *Blender* magazine had fun with it in its irreverent feature "When Will Your Favorite Pop Star Croak?" The goofy column predicts a star's life expectancy, adding or subtracting years depending on the star's lifestyle. In Jack's case, his double-cheeseburger craving cost him four years. So for our next lunch he took me to a restaurant near the Vanderbilt University campus in Nashville, where he now lives. Passing on the high-cholesterol items, he ordered a health-conscious chicken-fettuccine salad. As we sat down, he leaned over with a smile and said, "This should give me back a couple of years."

STEVIE WONDER. If my track record with him is any indication, we shouldn't expect him to show up until long after dinner, but he'll be the center of attention once he arrives. Everyone respects him, and not just because of his musical prowess. There's something almost spiritual in Stevie's view of the world. When it's time to listen to some live music, we could gather around him at the piano.

NEIL YOUNG. Neil often seems to be deep into his own thoughts, but he has a teasing side. Before I could get out the first question in a 1999 interview, he said he'd thought about buying me a gold watch after my review of one of his early concerts in Los Angeles where I wanted to hear more of his *Tonight's the Night* album. "You thought the show was too short and I was going to send you a gold watch because if the length of a show is so important to you, I wanted to make sure you had a good watch." I laughed because it had been twenty-three years since the show.

"A performer should always be aware of his audience," he said, "but he can't let the audience dictate what he should do. That show was representative of me that night. I couldn't have done the *Tonight's the Night* album because it was a group of songs from a particular time . . . a certain character. You don't always feel that character. Look at the cover and you see that person. That wasn't the same person you saw on *After the Gold Rush* or *Harvest.* You change."

CHAPTER
TWENTY-EIGHT

had given up on seeing Johnny Cash again in concert, but Lou Robin, his devoted, longtime manager, told me in 2003 that John and June still played occasionally at a community barn dance in a quiet Virginia valley whcre they had a vacation home. John had invited me for years to visit them at the house where June grew up with her parents, Ezra and Maybelle Carter, and two sisters. It was in this valley at the base of Clinch Mountain, just across the border from Tennessee, that the Carter Family—A.P., Sara, and Maybelle—worked on the music that laid the foundation in the 1920s for modern country music. As a child in Arkansas, John heard the Carter Family on the radio and first dreamed of being a singer himself.

The Cashes bought the family home in 1980 and spent a few weeks each year there, heading down the road—health permitting—on Saturdays for a guest appearance at the barn dance sponsored by other Carter Family descendants. Admission for the informal, one-thousand-seat amphitheater was just four dollars for adults, and seating was first-come on the odd assortment of school bus seats, church pews, and movie theater rows. It was the only place John, who was seventy, performed anymore, and Janette Carter, June's cousin, didn't advertise his appearances because she didn't want to put pressure on him if he didn't feel up to performing. Besides bouts of pneumonia, glaucoma had robbed John of much of his eyesight, while asthma left him short of breath, requiring him to take rests during recording sessions.

There were no address markers identifying the Cashes' house on the two-lane country road, but I followed Lou's directions as far as I could. Then I just turned into the nearest driveway, figuring if it wasn't the Cash house, the residents would surely be able to help me. They pointed to a home on a slope at the base of the mountain. When I got there, I couldn't see the faces of the figures on the porch as I stepped from the car, but a baritone voice told me immediately I had found the right place.

"Hello, I'm Johnny Cash."

Well, he really only said hello; my mind filled in the rest of the line that John had used thousands of times to open his concerts or network TV show. He was standing on the porch. Instead of the solid shock of black hair and black shirt and pants, John's hair was now white and he was relaxing in a khaki shirt jacket and gray slacks. After we shook hands, John sat in a rocker and told me how much he loved the valley. "It comes down to solitude and peace of mind," he said. "That's something we cherish now. The phone rarely rings up here."

We went through a bit more small talk, but it was obvious that John was straining. He paused every couple of minutes to catch his breath. "It's the asthma," he said, reaching for a glass of water. June soon joined us on the porch, and after a breakfast of ham, scrambled eggs, and biscuits, John took a nap.

June, still wonderfully energetic at seventy-three, showed me her beloved valley. From behind the wheel of the couple's Lincoln sedan, she pointed out places where members of the Carter Family had gone to school or fished. She took me to the cemetery to show me the graves of A.P. and Sara. "I loved this place, but I also felt there was more outside of these mountains and I was going to see it," she said. "I went to New York to study acting, but I eventually went back to music. I remember first hearing Johnny Cash on the radio and he sounded so lonesome. It reminded me of something deep inside of me. It was like there was a piece missing in both of us, and God put us together and made us whole."

By the time we got back to the house, John was up and wanted to play me a tape of him singing some black gospel songs that he was thinking about including on his next album. When the tape ended, John picked up an acoustic guitar and sang some more songs in a similar style, and his voice was straight and true with no signs of his asthma.

At the barn dance that night, the room exploded with cheers when John took the stage, and for a moment the magic was back. Joined by a three-piece band, he opened with "Folsom Prison Blues," and his rich, deep voice was as strong as that day in 1968 at the prison. John's voice remained commanding during "Sunday Mornin' Comin' Down," but he had shortness of breath on "Suppertime," an obscure country song he recorded in the 1950s. Most of the fans were too excited to notice when he missed a word here and there, but June picked up on it and she took over the microphone at the end of the number, giving John a rest. He rejoined her at the end of the song and the crowd roared once more. After their set, the Cashes retreated backstage for a few minutes before leaving the building. As John headed down the steps to the car, several admirers stepped forward to help steady him.

I joined them at the house a few minutes later, and June was already in her robe, eating corn bread and milk. John sat in a chair opposite her, ignoring the tray of cookies and milk in front of him. He looked tired. He wasn't happy with his performance, and I sensed a vulnerability that I hadn't noticed earlier in the day when he spoke about the gospel album as if it were a foregone conclusion that he would make it. He admitted that he had feared his fourth album with producer Rick Rubin, which was about to be released, would be his last. He wasn't pleased with some of the vocals, and he suspected Rick was losing patience because of all the health problems.

"I finished my last vocal for the record, and I shook hands with Rick and I said, 'It's been fun.' I think it was my way of saying I understood if he wanted to call it quits. But he immediately asked what I wanted to do next. I mentioned the black gospel album and then I mentioned an album of songs that would show my musical roots, and Rick said, 'Let's do them both.' I was dumbfounded. It was just what I wanted to hear. I had thought I might finally be at the point where I would only be singing for myself."

With that, he stood up and struggled to hold his balance. June was quickly by his side and led him to the adjoining bedroom. She came back, and we talked for a few more minutes before I headed back to Nashville. By the time I got to the end of the long driveway, the house lights were out. It was 9:00 p.m. I drove past the barn dance on the way out of town and the party was still in full swing. There was something terribly sad about the juxtaposition of all the energy and good spirits of the crowd—and imagining the thousands of hours John and June had been on stages around the world—with the quiet, darkened house.

I spoke to John on the phone a few times after that, and he spent much of the time talking about June's failing health and how he couldn't imagine life without her. A few days after June's death on May 15, 2003, I spoke with John, and he tried to put on a brave face, but it was hard for him to get through even a brief conversation without talking about her.

Rubin and John's son, John Carter Cash, were so concerned about him that they kept encouraging John to work on a new album, but it wasn't to be. John died before the end of the year, on September 12. In our last phone conversation, he said, "I'm ready to go, Bob."

. . . .

John's death hit me differently than the others. This wasn't murder or self-destruction. John was only seven years older than I was, nine years older than Dylan. In the weeks after his death, I thought often about my own rock 'n' roll journey and how long musicians can stay relevant in rock, how long the music itself could remain a dominant cultural force. I had been looking all these years to Dylan to answer the question about how long a musician could remain vital, but I realized that John had given me the answer. He was a great artist until the day he died. The jury was still out on the second question, however, and the evidence wasn't looking good. We have seen golden ages come and go in all sorts of creative fields, so why not rock?

· ·

It was clear by this time that rock even among the young had become a minor piece in a music business that was dominated by hip-hop, *American Idol,* R&B divas, Disney teen stars, and crossover country acts. The new artists able to reach mass audiences came mostly from outside of rock, including Eminem, Garth Brooks, Alicia Keys, Norah Jones, and the audacious Kanye West.

This shift in tastes was accompanied—and, in part, hastened—by the virtual collapse of the record industry. As sales slipped alarmingly, anxious executives pointed a finger in various directions. They blamed piracy and downloading along with competition from video games and the Internet for young people's attention. The sales drop meant labels had to cut costs, which often led to slicing artist rosters.

Slow to realize how true the complaints were, I thought it was just an excuse. I believed the real reason for the sales slump was that millions of rock fans had lost faith in the music. If enough good bands hit the scene, I assumed sales would follow. I knew from the past that all it took was one great musician to turn things around—and I thought I'd found that voice the night I walked into the Troubadour, the same club where I had found Elton John, and first saw Jack White.

The singer and guitarist in a Detroit duo named the White Stripes, Jack scored high on every measurement of my private rock 'n' roll scorecard. He had charisma, songwriting skills, vocal command, musicianship, personal vision, and a defiance that told me you couldn't make him compromise his music even if you hit him with a two-by-four. At that first sighting, I thought he could be the most important figure in rock since Kurt Cobain.

"There was a time when I thought rock 'n' roll was dying or certainly being watered down, so I tried to sit down in my bedroom and write songs that I wanted to hear on the radio," Jack White told me the first time I met him. He was referring to the 1980s, when glam rock, hair rock, and metal bands dominated MTV. The more I was around Jack, the more I realized that our tastes in music overlapped, which intrigued me because of our age difference. He was in his mid-twenties, and I was almost old enough to be his grandfather. How did he ever discover the country and blues artists of the prerock era?

"I went back to the time Dylan and the other great figures in rock were growing up and listened to the music that influenced them and that's when I discovered the blues and country," he explained. "Most of the music they were playing on MTV was so simple and tame, whereas all this music I started hearing was just filled with energy and spirit."

Besides his own songs, that night at the Troubadour Jack sang an old country song, an old blues tune, and a Bob Dylan number with equal authority. And best of all: None of it sounded dated. He took the musical strains that gave rock its passion and power and wove them together in a new, inviting package. He played guitar with such flash and sang with such power that he could have taken over both roles in Led Zeppelin if Jimmy Page and Robert Plant had gotten sick. I thought Jack White was so remarkable that if he had walked into the Sun Records studio in Memphis before Elvis in 1954, he could have been the first King of Rock 'n' Roll. The question was whether Jack White could make lightning strike in the modern rock world.

· ·

I decided it was time to stop focusing on the day-to-day of my job as a critic and do something more ambitious—a series on songwriting that would be definitive in the spirit of my early hero, critic, and editor Ralph Gleason. I felt jaded. I found it hard to get interested in a new band unless I felt it had a chance to be truly great. In reviewing artists, I found myself trying to evaluate not just their new albums, but also what I could project for them three or four albums down the line. Besides the Stripes, a few other new bands lived up to that test, including the Arcade Fire and Bright Eyes, and I wrote extensively about them.

Meanwhile, I wanted to proceed with the series. The idea was to sit down with six or seven of the best writers from different genres and write a comprehensive portrait of each writer's creative process. I'd devote each article in the series to a specific writer, tracing his or her craft from early influences through actual writing methods and thematic viewpoints. Unlike most interviews, I'd need several hours, hopefully spread over a couple of days, to make sure I covered every aspect of the process. The editors at the *Times* were wonderfully supportive and I put together a list of artists from country to rap. The hardest part was picking just two classic singer-songwriters from a group of favorites that included Joni Mitchell, Bruce Springsteen, Neil Young, Paul Simon, and Elvis Costello.

For input on the final list, I turned to people I respected in the record business, including Jimmy Iovine, the head of Interscope Records. The first thing Jimmy asked when he saw my wish list was "Where's Dylan?" I told him I didn't know if Bob would have the time to participate and I didn't want to raise the editors' hopes only to have Dylan say no. Jimmy held his ground. "How can you do a series on songwriters without having Dylan?" I knew he was right.

I phoned Larry Jenkins at Columbia Records and explained the concept. He said Bob wasn't doing any interviews at the time, but that he'd run it past him. Less than twenty-four hours later, Larry was back on the phone. "Bob's in."

CHAPTER
TWENTY-NINE

We all agreed we should start the series with Dylan. The others would include Merle Haggard, Lucinda Williams, Ice Cube, and U2. I wanted to put Bruce Springsteen and Paul Simon on the list, but I felt that Joni Mitchell offered the best contrast to Dylan among the traditional singer-songwriters. For the final spot on the seven-piece series, I wanted someone in his twenties to represent the new generation of songwriters. I went back and forth between Jack White of the White Stripes and Conor Oberst of Bright Eyes, and finally decided to focus on both of them. For one thing, I thought it would put too much pressure on them if I selected just one to be in the company of Dylan, Mitchell, et al. Plus, they represent such different manifestations of the rock songwriting experience.

The interview with Bob was set for an off date on his 2003 tour, which meant he should have had lots of free time to talk to me. But when I arrived in Amsterdam, I started getting nervous. Did Bob understand that I would need a lot of time? Would he open up? The first two times I phoned his tour road manager, there was no answer in the hotel room so I left messages. Finally, I reached him and he told me to be at the hotel lobby by 6:00 p.m. I started to ask how long Bob had set aside for the interview, but he hung up.

I met the road manager in the lobby and raised the issue of time, but he didn't seem to know. He led me to the room, where Bob was sitting in a chair next to a table with a cookie platter and a pot of coffee. He was strumming an acoustic guitar. "Welcome to Amsterdam," he said with a smile. I tried to read his mood, but he gave no clue. He motioned me to a chair opposite him and waited until the road manager left the room. To my relief—almost exactly as he had done in San Francisco during the "born again" interview—Bob started talking about songwriting. He had obviously been thinking about the subject and he got right to it.

While growing up in Hibbing, Minnesota, he'd listened at night to country, blues, and early rock 'n' roll, including Elvis, on a Louisiana station whose signal came in strong and clear. "When I got into rock 'n' roll, I didn't even think I had any other option or alternative," he said. "It showed me where my future was, just like some people know they are going to be doctors or lawyers or shortstop for the New York Yankees." He told me about how he started leaning toward folk music during his teens and eventually discovered his greatest influence, Woody Guthrie.

"To me, Woody was the be-all and end-all," he said, his curly hair framing his face as it had on album covers decades ago. "Woody's songs were about everything at the same time. They were about rich and poor, black and white, the highs and lows of life, the contradictions between what they were teaching in school and what was really happening. He was saying everything in his songs that I felt but didn't know how to."

This was great stuff, but it didn't tell me about Bob's songwriting process, and my heart started racing when I heard a knock on the door. I knew from doing hundreds of interviews that a road manager's knock could mean the end of the interview. Either he was reminding the artist that he had another appointment or giving the artist a diplomatic way to end the interview if things weren't going well. I pictured my series hanging in the balance as I waited for Bob to respond to the knock. I wanted to hug him when he waved the road manager off: "Give us another hour."

Bob went back to Guthrie. He had spent so much time playing Woody's songs in his early club and coffeehouse days that he was called a Guthrie jukebox. He said he had no plans to be a writer until a guy came up to him after one of his sets to say he liked what he heard but that there was another singer doing the same thing down the street. Bob saw Ramblin' Jack Elliott for the first time and was "shocked" to hear Elliott singing Guthrie tunes and singing them well. It was a pivotal moment in his life, he said. "It's like being a doctor who has spent all these years discovering penicillin and suddenly finding out someone else had already done it."

If Bob had had less ambition, he could have just kept on doing Guthrie songs. There's certainly enough room in the music world for two singers who admire Guthrie. But Bob wanted something that was his own, and that proved to be songwriting. He had toyed with writing earlier, but didn't feel he had enough vocabulary or life experience. This was a key point for me—the issue of how you teach yourself to be a songwriter. I mentioned how thousands of aspiring songwriters have used his albums as textbooks.

"No, no, no," Bob said sharply at the thought. "It's only natural to pattern yourself after someone. If I wanted to be a painter, I might think about trying to be like Van Gogh, or if I was an actor, act like Laurence Olivier. If I was an architect, there's Frank Gehry. But you can't just copy somebody. If you like someone's work, the important thing is to be exposed to everything that person has been exposed to. Anyone who wants to be a songwriter should listen to as much folk music as they can, study the form and the structure of the stuff that has been around for a hundred years. I go back to Stephen Foster."

As he sat in the quiet of this elegant hotel overlooking one of the city's canals, Bob painted a picture of his evolution as a songwriter that was very different from the one I had expected from an artist who had arrived in the 1960s with his visions and skills fully intact. His lyrics for "Blowin' in the Wind" were printed in *Broadside,* the folk music magazine, in May of 1962. He was twenty-one. The story he told was one of trial and error, false starts and hard work.

When I started writing about music, I thought of rock 'n' roll as an inevitable chain of events—each artist or sound was like one in a series of thousands of dominoes that neatly fell one after another once

Elvis and Chuck Berry helped kick things off. But I eventually realized that that concept was naive. If you took away as few as two dozen artists from that endless row of dominoes, rock would have collapsed as an art form. Imagine your record collection without Bob Dylan, the Beatles, or U2.

More than anything else, the interview with Dylan underscored how rock 'n' roll hadn't evolved through a series of falling dominoes. If Bob's focus had only been on Elvis and Little Richard, there would have been no motivation to lift the music's aspirations. He kept stressing that he didn't set out to change pop songwriting or society, but it's clear that he was filled with the high purpose he saw in Guthrie's work. Unlike those before him, his chief goal wasn't just making the charts.

"I always admired true artists who were dedicated, so I learned from them," he said. "Popular culture usually comes to an end very quickly. It gets thrown into the grave. I wanted to do something that stood alongside Rembrandt's paintings."

There was another knock at the door; the hour had passed, but before the road manager even opened the door, Bob said, "We're okay. Give us some more time—and some more coffee." He was on a roll. I checked my tape recorder to make sure the red light was on. Dylan seemed to be at a point in his life where he welcomed the opportunity to talk about his craft, possibly because he saw his story as part of that of a brotherhood of writers, from contemporaries like Cash back to Guthrie and the Carter Family and further back to scores of Scottish and English balladeers. He said he put songs together using everything from Beat poetry to daily newspapers.

After the Elliott experience, Bob said he pursued songwriting relentlessly in New York, reading a lot of poetry, going back and rereading Edgar Allan Poe, and diving headlong into John Donne and John Keats and Lord Byron. Bob once told me that he wrote songs so fast in the 1960s that he didn't want to go to sleep at night because he was afraid he might miss one. As he talked now about poets, I could picture him soaking up influences so rapidly during those early years in New York that it would be hard to turn off the light at night, too. Why not read more?

He came across a book of François Villon's poetry and he recalled the excitement of tapping into the inspiration from fifteenth-century France. "He was writing about hard-core street stuff and making it rhyme. It was pretty staggering, and it made you wonder why you couldn't do the same thing in a song. I'd see Villon talking about visiting a prostitute and I would turn it around. I won't visit a prostitute, I'll talk about rescuing a prostitute. Again, it's turning stuff on its head, like 'vice is salvation and virtue will lead to ruin.'"

He went on, quoting such lines as Shakespeare's "fair is foul and foul is fair," and I could see why he peppered his own songs with phrases that made us scratch our heads and, more important, question our assumptions—including the classic lines from 1965's "Love Minus Zero/No Limit" that juxtapose success and failure.

There is a danger in taking the mystery out of songwriting, but Bob's explanation of his method only gave me a greater appreciation. Chuck Berry was an early rock master of rhyme, using images from the everyday world, but Bob expanded the vocabulary of rock by drawing from the world of poets and novelists and journalists. He extended the themes of rock 'n' roll in the same way, beyond the parameters of teenage fun and rebellion. His music was also about adult issues, from social observation to personal relationships. In following Guthrie's lead, Bob turned rock 'n' roll on its ear. He turned the rebel without a cause into a rebel with a cause and committed the best rock 'n' roll to progressive ideals—a tradition followed by hundreds of other artists, most notably Springsteen and U2.

Themes, he said, were never a problem. When he started out, the Korean War had just ended. "That was a heavy cloud over everyone's head," he said. "The communist thing was still big, and the civil rights movement was coming on. So there was lots to write about. But I never set out to write politics. I didn't want to be a political moralist. There were people who just did that. Phil Ochs focused on political things, but there were many sides to us, and I wanted to follow them all. We can feel very generous one day and very selfish the next hour."

He said newspapers were a good source of stories, pointing to "The Lonesome Death of Hattie Carroll," the story of a wealthy Baltimore man who was given only a six-month sentence for killing a maid with a cane. "Who wouldn't be offended by some guy beating an old woman to death and just getting a slap on the wrist?"

We got together again the next night after the show and I asked Bob about the actual mechanics of writing.

He leaned over and picked up the acoustic guitar.

"Well, you have to understand that I'm not a melodist," he said. "My songs are either based on old Protestant hymns or Carter Family songs or variations of the blues forms.

"What happens is, I'll take a song I know and simply start playing it in my head. That's the way I meditate. A lot of people will look at a crack on the wall and meditate, or count sheep or angels or money or something, and it's a proven fact that it'll help them relax. I don't meditate on any of that stuff. I meditate on a song. I'll be playing Bob Nolan's 'Tumbling Tumbleweeds,' for instance, in my head constantly— while I'm driving a car or talking to a person or sitting around or whatever. People will think they are talking to me and I'm talking back, but I'm not. I'm listening to the song in my head. At a certain point, some of the words will change and I'll start writing a song."

All this time, Bob had been strumming the guitar, and the melody seemed vaguely familiar.

He wrote "Blowin' in the Wind" in ten minutes, just putting the words to an old spiritual, probably something he learned from Carter Family recordings. "That's the folk music tradition. You use what's been handed down." He told me "The Times They Are a-Changin'" came from an old Scottish folk song.

I tried to think of one of Bob's more radical moments—and "Subterranean Homesick Blues" came to mind. The 1965 number blended folk and blues in a way that made everyone who heard it listen over and over, trying to unravel it. Lennon once said the song was so captivating on every level that it made him wonder how he would ever compete with it. The lyrics were about a society in revolution and the music reflected the paranoia of the time and came at you with cannonball force. I asked Bob what song he was playing in his mind when he started that song. Without pause, he said the inspiration dated to his teens. It was from Chuck Berry, a bit of "Too Much Monkey Business," and some scat songs of the 1940s.

As we talked, the music from his guitar got louder until I finally realized he was playing one of the most famous songs of the twentieth century: Irving Berlin's "Blue Skies."

Was he working on a new song?

Had he been writing it the whole time we had been talking?

No, he said with a smile as he set down the guitar. He was just showing me how he writes a song.

∙ ∙

The Dylan songwriting story attracted e-mails from readers around the world, including two Ivy League English professors. *Mojo,* the British rock magazine, called the interview "legendary." It was a perfect kickoff for the series. The project helped me win my second *Times* award for the year's best work and my third Pulitzer Prize nomination. I was left wanting more ambitious projects. I thought of a dozen topics, more than I could ever do given the demands of daily journalism. For the first time in years, I thought it might be time to say good-bye to the *Times.*

I'd thought about leaving the paper only once before, when the head of a major record label had asked if I'd be interested in becoming vice president of artists and repertoire, the clumsy title for the person who signs the artists and works with them on their albums. I think the main reason I was tempted was that I was promised freedom in signing acts. The label chief felt the company had enough hit artists, but not very prestigious ones. He wanted me to bring high-quality artists to the company. That sounded like fun. I thought immediately about John Prine and Al Green, two artists who I thought were underperforming at other labels and might be available.

When I mentioned all this to friends at record companies, they laughed. Sooner or later, they said, the label would want those "prestige" acts to sell or they'd drop the acts and me.

Ultimately, I was glad that the offer was never finalized. Besides, I still loved what I did at the *Times.* But it was different this time. I was getting tired of covering Rolling Stones reunions and I sure didn't want to start treating *American Idol* and the Simpson sisters seriously.

CHAPTER
THIRTY

B y the spring of 2005, Springsteen was back with another album in the acoustic, underdog tradition of *Tom Joad* and *Nebraska,* and I much preferred it to 2002's *The Rising.* The new work, *Devils and Dust,* wasn't so much trying to comfort the nation as encourage it to deal with issues growing out of the Iraq War and outdated immigration policies. Bruce had met so many emotionally scarred Vietnam vets over the years that he knew how war can make even the most honorable men do dark, inhuman deeds when their lives are on the line. In the album's title track, he assumed the role of a soldier on patrol, unable to find comfort in even the friendliest foreign face and knowing that self-preservation can be all-consuming—relating how fear can turn a good heart bad. The same passion was poured into several moving portraits of migrant workers in the Southwest, where devils and dust of a different kind can be equally threatening.

The tour opened in Detroit at the 5,100-seat Fox Theatre and Bruce was at his evocative best. He devoted most of the two and a half hours to material from the new album, and he didn't just sing the songs, he assumed different voices—a cowboy twang, a gruff rebel snarl, a tender sigh—to bring out the individual qualities of the tunes. I sat in the fourth row and remembered all the inspiring nights Bruce had stood on stage and declared that anything is possible in this world and made us believe it. I felt equally privileged to be listening to these songs—songs not as much about dreams as about the real world, as Bruce liked to say. I came to a surprising conclusion: I would rather see Bruce at this stage of his career in this solo, acoustic format than with the E Street Band. I would always prize the old shows, but I didn't need to see him racing around the stage, trying to recall for us all the glory days of our youth. I preferred that he move forward in this more intimate, challenging direction.

Backstage, I shared those thoughts with Bruce, half expecting him to say that he, too, preferred the solo shows. But he wouldn't bite. "It's just two sides of what I do and what I've always done," he said, smiling at my enthusiasm for the new material. "It's not like one's my day job and the other's my night job. Some of the songs can work equally well in either style with a few changes of arrangement. I love being a front man. I always wanted to write songs that connected with the construction workers and the firemen and the policemen, the guys and girls on the street. The E Street Band reached that audience. It's fun to be riding down the street and some firemen go by and they say, 'Hey, Bruce!' I enjoy that." He paused, picked up his acoustic guitar, and added, "But I also feel there are some times when I just want to go out on stage and connect with audiences on a different level."

U2 had replaced the E Street Band as the rock 'n' roll outfit that best captured the idealistic spirit of the times, but Bruce's dual role as stadium rock star and solo troubadour was a remarkable accomplishment, one that could serve as a model for future rock musicians.

For all the influence of Woody Guthrie on Dylan, Springsteen may, in fact, be the one who came closest to fulfilling Guthrie's political spokesman ideals. He was such a powerful voice of American hope that it was only natural to see him stand alongside Barack Obama at a key campaign rally in 2008. The economy was in crisis and American troops were still in Iraq, but it was hard not to feel hopeful watching that thrilling scene: two men who, in the best spirit of America, believed in the Promised Land.

. . . .

Just months after Bruce's *Devils and Dust* tour, I had lunch with Bono at the Chateau Marmont hotel in Hollywood. It was the day after the first Southern California stop on the group's *How to Dismantle an Atomic Bomb* tour and the first time we had talked since the album's release the previous November. Bono often spoke privately about feeling too self-conscious to be deeply personal in his songs, but the lyrics on the new album touched increasingly on personal matters. The album was a thoughtful look at family, faith, and rejuvenation. In "City of Blinding Lights," he spoke about maintaining youthful innocence and faith—a song that brought him full circle to U2's debut album.

> *Time . . . time*
> *Won't leave me as I am.*
> *But time won't take the boy out of this man.*

Elsewhere, he looked back at the innocence and aspirations of youth. "Sometimes You Can't Make It on Your Own" was about Bono's efforts to mend bruised feelings with his dying father. Between shows on a 2001 concert tour in Europe, he'd flown home to be by his father's hospital bedside. In the final days, he had sat with his father and read to him.

At the San Diego concert a few nights before our lunch, he even surprised me by talking about the background of the song—something he might not have done years earlier. This time, however, he told me about discovering during those last weeks how dependent he was on his father despite the distance between them. Recalling John Lennon's outcry for his parents in *Plastic Ono Band,* Bono reached out for his father at the end of the song.

The songs worked spectacularly in concert, where the band aimed for intimacy in the arenas by employing only a modest screen above the stage, forcing the audience to watch the band members rather than the larger-than-life video images. I again thought of Springsteen, the only other artist of the last thirty years with mass appeal to approach each show with U2's unwavering dedication and passion. Bruce tried to give his best each night, he said, because someone in the audience might be seeing him for the first time and he always wanted that new-comer to see the band at its best. In San Diego, I felt that U2 was taking the mission even further—as if they imagined people in the audience who had been to every show and wanted to make sure those fans were touched more deeply each time.

Though U2 continued to pick up acclaim and awards, Bono was getting equal attention for his humanitarian efforts to combat poverty and disease in Africa. He was continuing to meet with world leaders, writing essays for various publications, and even going on news and interview shows to spread the message. Whereas only young rock fans would once have recognized him in a restaurant, he seemed to be recognized by everyone as he made his way to my table at the Chateau. Some were people in the industry paying their respects, but others were complete strangers who wanted to thank him for his charitable deeds.

"I'm not sure if it's Catholic guilt or what, but I genuinely believe that second only to personal redemption, the most important things in the Scriptures—2,103 passages in all—refer to taking care of the world's poor. Each generation has to ask itself what it wants to be remembered for. Previous generations have ushered in civil rights in America, gotten rid of apartheid in South Africa, and brought down the Iron Curtain. I think this generation can bring that kind of energy and conviction to the problems in Africa. There are six thousand people a day dying there just because we can't get them drugs that are available in the West. If we don't do something to change that, we are going to look in history like barbarians."

Bono was forty-four, and I tried to picture Lennon sitting next to us. John was skeptical of a lot of show-biz do-gooders, and he might have thought Bono was full of hot air—until he met him. But he would have recognized in Bono's words his own sense of idealism. Time and again, he and Yoko had talked about how "love" and "peace" weren't just hippie dreams, but genuine possibilities if only people committed themselves to change. And here was Bono, nearly twenty-five years later, carrying on that tradition.

As Bono and I continued our conversation, I imagined how, after talking for hours about world affairs, he and John could have gone back to Bono's room and played Elvis records. I knew Bono also loved the Beatles, so I finally mentioned how much John would have been impressed by what Bono was achieving—and how he was now taking it much further than John could ever have done because John was too much the rebel to have felt comfortable with world leaders, at least in the age of Richard Nixon. Maybe today he would have been more likely to stand by Bono's side in demanding justice.

Just as we ended lunch, an aide rushed up to Bono with some messages. One was about the tour, but the others were all about DATA (Debts, AIDS, Trade in Africa), the nonprofit organization he cofounded to combat poverty and disease. (It has since combined with another antipoverty group, the ONE Campaign.) The DATA messages may have been much more urgent than the tour message, but still I wondered if it didn't say something about Bono's priorities when he said he'd call the DATA person right back and he'd deal with the tour issue later. I asked him what it was like to have, in effect, two jobs.

"I don't think of it as two jobs anymore," he said. "When we started getting behind social causes, Paul [McGuinness, the band's manager] warned us there might be a backlash of sorts. He said, 'Musicians are supposed to describe the problems of the world, not fix them.' And he's right. But we have a unique power in this ridiculous thing called celebrity, and our job isn't finished when we write the songs that grow out of concerns."

Before we left the table, Bono added one other thing. "And never think that John Lennon didn't do enough. His music was enough for millions of people. When I talk with people like Tony Blair and President Clinton, we talk about rock 'n' roll sometimes and they say how they got a lot of their social values and dreams from rock 'n' roll. And I am right with them. I was thirteen, I suppose, and I heard 'Imagine' and I became enthralled with John's dream, too."

CHAPTER
THIRTY-ONE

The music scene appeared increasingly fragile in the second half of the decade. Not only was rock 'n' roll continuing to drift, but the music business itself was on life support. I was surprised by how much pessimism I found in late 2008 when I spoke to executives in the music business. The industry's fatal mistake, they agreed, was embracing a technology that was initially hailed as a savior—the compact disc. The move to digital in the 1980s resulted in windfall profits because consumers who had grown up with vinyl albums bought the same music all over again on CD, allowing the record companies to make millions of dollars from music that was stored in their vaults. Ultimately, however, music fans found they could make their own copies of CDs without any loss of sound quality. This led to easy piracy, free downloading via Napster and other Web sites, and, ultimately, a massive decline in sales.

After seeing annual industry sales nearly double from $7.5 billion in 1990 to $14.6 billion in 1999, sales sank by $4 billion over the next eight years, and there were no signs of a turnaround. Gone was the hope of selling ten and twenty million copies of a runaway best-seller. Now, best-selling acts were lucky to reach one million in sales, though piracy and downloading might mean five to ten million copies of that album were in circulation. On top of this, the iPod was king, and young fans started turning more and more to downloading one single songs rather than a whole album, a practice that raised doubts about the viability of albums.

To compensate for all this lost revenue, record companies began requiring bands to share revenue from areas of the business that were still profitable—publishing, touring, merchandise, ring tones—before they would sign them. Said one industry insider glumly, "Music is very disposable right now. It's like someone took the home run out of baseball." Another complained that most young rock bands in the growing indie world didn't even try to compete with hip-hop or other genres for sales. "Ever since Cobain, there has been a disconnect," he said. "They think they have more credibility if they don't aim for a hit." A third contact felt there were scores of fine bands around the country, but they were handicapped by the lack of a filtering system. "Consumers are overwhelmed," he said. "If you sign onto the Internet, you can read thousands of opinions about thousands of bands and the result is a blur. Say what you want about the 'evil' big record companies and radio stations, but it was a partnership that found and championed everyone from Elvis to Nirvana. Today, that system has broken down and there's chaos."

Several executives complained about the *American Idol* factor. "There's only room in the business for three or four acts to break a year and anyone who has twenty million people seeing them every week has a big advantage," one said. "You may have a record that is five times better, but radio is going to play the *American Idol* act or another TV-based act every time."

Despite the pessimism, everyone held out hope that someone will come along to excite young people the way Elvis and the Beatles did. One executive thought it might be a female because of the increasing role women are playing in politics and business. Another observer felt the conditions were right for a "black Elvis," someone who speaks "to the people on the street, not all that different than a Memphis truck driver in the 1950s." Noting all the emerging nations around the world, one said, "Why not someone from China?"

After days of talking to executives, I thought I should speak to some musicians. U2 was the last group to achieve this cultural dominance, so I thought Bono's take on the state of rock would be valuable. And what about Jack White, the musician I thought was most able to jump-start the music again?

• •

Bono was in town to address the Women's Conference 2008, and we talked over breakfast about why U2 has remained such a compelling force for so long. He stressed the importance of keeping your sights set on artistry, something they learned from Dylan and Lennon, among others. To illustrate his point, he told me about running into Bruce Springsteen years before. Bruce was coming back from the laundry with a big bag of clothes one day in London. What struck Bono was that Bruce was already huge, and Bono asked him about it. "I'll always remember his answer because he said, 'I always do stuff like that. I'm not going to be the rock star that it has been written for me to be.' And I've always admired him for that. And now he's living in New Jersey. He's found a real life, a community, and fate seems to protect him. He's as earthbound as he possibly could be.

"Bruce is probably one of the only people in the world who understands how to survive in this kind of a life, how to get through all this without dying or walking with a limp or with one eye—the way so many of these great people we've known and met did, these musical geniuses who didn't make it through the fire. The fire consumed them. They gave us beautiful music and they were left exhausted, empty. It's heartbreaking. You've got to be tough and you've got to avoid being self-conscious.

"I certainly went through a self-conscious phase and it makes you ugly. You can take the most beautiful faces and if you point a camera at them, it can change them because they know they are being photographed and suddenly they aren't so beautiful because they become self-conscious and it distorts everything. The problem is they begin to look at themselves through the same lens as the media. And it can change the way you walk and think because you don't want to let people down. You are always striving to live up to something. People think you are something special, so you'd better act special.

"I am much more recognized now than I ever was, but I don't notice it anymore. People come up to me all the time and I don't care if I've washed or if I'm crawling on my hands and knees out of a night-club. The artist's journey is away from self-consciousness. That's where you've got to have tenacity. Bruce certainly has that. Lennon had it. I had that. We are, in the end, if not pugilists, certainly scrappers, street fighters, and people who will not be bullied, including by our own ambitions. It's like we are locked into something and we will not let go of it. If your drug of choice is that song that's never been heard before but feels like it's always existed, then you'll do anything to protect it."

Despite the struggle he outlines, Bono doesn't feel rock is at the end of the line. "Rock brought together rhythm, harmony, and top-line melody: rhythm for the body, top-line melody for the mind, and harmony for the spirit. That's a very powerful concoction. Classical music has harmony and top-line melody, but it didn't have rhythm. That's why rock 'n' roll surpassed it. It's still the most powerful art form."

So why do young bands seem to be afraid of massive stardom or contemptuous of it? "I think one thing is they are suspicious of fame because fame is now associated with 'celebrity' and that has become oppressive in our society. The bands don't want to become part of this thing which is crawling all over us. But when they pull down the shutters and block out the light, they lose their curiosity. I've never seen art improved by someone who has double-locked the door, turned off the light, and found a little cupboard in the back of the house where no one is going to find them. There is something about the spotlight that keeps you sharp."

· ·

Jack White was in town on business and we met at his hotel. One of ten children of working-class parents in Detroit, he told a story of being inspired by rock 'n' roll that was similar to those I had been hearing from musicians for years. Music was, he said, the only thing that made sense to him, and it left him with a desire to use that music to touch others in the same way he had been touched.

"The area of Detroit I came from wasn't the golden age of Detroit in the 1930s and 1940s," he said. "It was the 1980s and nothing seemed to work. The potholes wouldn't get fixed and the garbage wouldn't get picked up. If you went to the store to get something, they'd be out of it or they wouldn't have enough change. It wasn't like a real city anymore. It was dysfunctional and there was this general attitude in town that made you feel it was never going to get any better and that you couldn't succeed, either. So, like a lot of artists do, you go to your room and you shut it all out. You look for something that makes sense to you and makes you feel good, and I don't think you really pick it. It picks you. It's like you don't get to pick who you fall in love with, it just happens. For me it was the drums. As soon as I started playing, it meant something to me immediately, just the pleasure of playing. But I had been told that you can't succeed for so long that it wasn't until the White Stripes got to England that I finally thought, 'Wow, you can do this.'"

Though the Stripes moved to Warner Bros. Records after four albums on minor labels, I wondered if he still clung to the widespread indie notion of fearing too much success.

"I never said 'I don't want to be famous' or 'I don't want to be the best I can be at what I'm doing' or 'I don't want to share my music with millions of people instead of a roomful.' I was willing to do whatever I had to do to reach an audience. But it was a fight all the time because it was the music scene around me in Detroit who would go, 'Oh, I don't know if you should be on the cover of *Rolling Stone*' or 'I don't know if it's a good idea to sell your records in Starbucks' or whatever. That's the reason I finally had to leave Detroit and move to Nashville, where you don't run into that thinking. I appreciated it when Edge and I did this film together [the 2008 documentary *It Might Get Loud*] and he said, 'Thanks for having ambition.'"

Though Jack said he could never picture himself in Bono's or Springsteen's "spokesman" role, he does share some of their values. "There was a period when I thought I was just making music for myself, but I sometimes feel it's bigger than that," he said. "I feel like I'm an antenna and I'm being used—by God or by whatever—and I want to be that antenna. I'm not going to stop it. I've never thought, I'd better slow this down because there's too much ambition or too much passion coming out of me."

Jack, thirty-three, wasn't so fast to answer when I asked if young rock audiences were as passionate about music as they were in earlier decades.

"I'm not a negative person, but I'm very realistic and it doesn't look good right now," he said. "I hope it gets better. I hope that children of the next generation are going to be shown there is more beauty and romance in tangible, mechanical things than in invisible, digital things. The artists of the past all had their rebellion. Elvis was rebelling against sexual repression and Dylan was rebelling against immorality and I feel like I'm rebelling against technology and the death of romance. I would pick this as the absolute worst time to connect with people through music. Today's generation takes a lot for granted when it comes to music. It's like, 'I'm going to play video games and when I come back to rock 'n' roll it's going to be there waiting for me.' They don't buy the CD, but they'll download it and give it to their friends."

As Jack spoke, it occurred to me that a common strand ran through the voices of John, Bruce, Bob, Bono, and him: a trace of idealism and commitment—or, as Bruce's aunt said, a touch of preacher.

• •

On the way home, I passed the Sunset Strip—the section of Los Angeles that was immortalized in the Buffalo Springfield youth anthem "For What It's Worth." Stephen Stills wrote the song after seeing hundreds of young people protesting the closing of Pandora's Box, a music club. I had driven down the stretch of Sunset Boulevard hundreds of times, especially at night when lines of fans stood outside the Roxy, where Springsteen played on his *Born to Run* tour, and outside the Whisky A Go-Go, where I first saw Elvis Costello and Tom Petty. I also passed Tower Records, where I'd spent hours looking through the bins for some hidden album or import single. The Roxy and Whisky were still there, but they no longer represented the pulse of the city's music scene, and Tower was boarded up. The whole street felt alien.

As I moved further along Sunset, past the turnoff to Phil Spector's old house, I wondered again about whether rock's golden age was ending. If it was in danger, it wouldn't be critics, musicians, record companies, or radio stations that would save it. The future belonged to young music fans—as it always has.

Even with the charisma of Elvis and the ringing guitar of Chuck Berry in the 1950s and the idealism of the Beatles and Dylan in the 1960s, the rock 'n' roll revolution would never have triumphed unless it filled an urgent need in teenagers. Rock 'n' roll was never just about a sound; it was about an ideal. In trying to explain that magical alchemy a half-century ago, historians speak about a convergence of forces rising up against such issues as sexual repression, social injustice, growing conformity, and the threat of nuclear annihilation. Even more than all that, the music was an article of faith—which helps explain why some of the most enduring anthems spoke about a better world, whether it was in Bob Dylan's "Blowin' in the Wind" or John Lennon's "Imagine" or Bruce Springsteen's "The Promised Land" or U2's "Where the Streets Have No Name."

One of the strengths of music is that it speaks to each of us in such a personal and affecting way. Many of my favorite artists over the past thirty-five years have been described as cult figures because they only reached a tiny fraction of the mass pop audience. Still, they helped me celebrate treasured moments and cushioned disappointments in my life. But my greatest joy was in finding artists who could speak to millions with the same intimacy and grace. I believe there is something about that massive, communal celebration that helps lift our spirits and aspirations. For old times' sake, I'd love to see rock 'n' roll continue to be the force that inspires new generations. If the young, including my two grandsons and two granddaughters, turn to another art form or a different style of music, I only hope it serves them as profoundly. May they always stay forever young.

ACKNOWLEDGMENTS

First, there's my book family to thank—Luke Janklow, an agent with a true rock 'n' roll heart; Shannon Welch, my editor at Rodale, who is blessed with a gentle touch and superb instincts; Leigh Haber, the former Rodale editor who first suggested the memoir approach. Also thanks to Nancy N. Bailey, senior project editor at Rodale; copy editor Nancy E. Elgin; and Claire Dippell at Janklow & Nesbit Associates for continuous encouragement and good cheer.

Then, I want to thank my long-standing journalism family at the *Los Angeles Times,* a group far too large to mention them all, but whose friendship and support was evident every day for 37 years—whether it came from the generous, dedicated pros on the copy desk or photographers, designers, and the cheerful tour guide who brought groups of visiting students by my desk so we could talk about their latest musical favorites.

But I want to single out a few *Times* coworkers, starting with Charles Champlin and Jim Bellows, who hired me in 1970, and on through Jean Sharley Taylor, Irv Letofsky, Shelby Coffey, John Lindsey, Oscar Garza, Kelly Scott, Sherry Stern, Alice Scott, Richard Nordwind, and John Montorio, each of whom trusted me when I'd come up with new favorites to rave about.

Special mention should go to John Carroll and Dean Baquet, the editors-in-chief in this decade who ushered in a new sense of respect for and commitment to Calendar, the paper's arts and entertainment section. John gallantly lifted the staff's spirits and sights during one of its darkest periods.

Dean and Calendar editor Bret Israel, a true renaissance man, championed the singer-songwriter series that led to some of my most rewarding days at the *Times*—and Donna Frazier edited the pieces with indefatigable care. Dean also showed me how to write a reminiscence of my *Times* years without seeming overly self-serving—and Betsy Sharkey's editing brought the piece alive.

I am grateful, too, for the team of pop writers, staff and freelance, who contributed so much to the paper's coverage over the years—especially Richard Cromelin, Chuck Philips, Geoff Boucher, Patrick Goldstein, Randy Lewis, Dennis Hunt, Kristine McKenna, Paul Grein, and Steve Hochman. Finally, Sean Reily, Cindy Hively, and Robin Mayper made available *Times* resources that helped greatly in putting this book together.

There is also my extended family in the musical community. Not only do I thank every artist and executive whose name appears in the book, but also the scores of other musicians who aimed courageously for artistry rather than mere fame. Special thanks, also, to those who allowed me to pick their brains while I was writing the book—especially Bono, Jack White, Jimmy Iovine, Elliot Mintz, Larry Jenkins, Paul Tollett, and Brian Murphy—as well as those who helped open doors in other ways, notably Yoko Ono, Kris Kristofferson, Bernie Taupin, Paul McGuinness, Jon Landau, Al Bunetta, and Donald Passman.

Most of all, I want to thank my personal family—starting with my wife, Kathi, who time and again read the manuscript to help me isolate the best thoughts. Also, Ruthann Snijders, my first wife, who assumed the lion's share of raising our two children while I was often out looking for the next rock 'n' roll hero. I'm also grateful for Kathy Morris and Rob Hilburn, my daughter and son who have lovely families of their own and who express their own views on music and life rather than feel any need to simply follow my sometimes dogmatic opinions. Thanks, too, to Ronald Morris and Sarah Coley-Hilburn and my four grandchildren, Christopher Morris, Lindsey Morris, Genevieve Hilburn, and Grant Hilburn, for their joyful spirits. And thanks to my parents, Alice Marie and John, who never made me turn the volume down.

INDEX